なるたる

shadow star

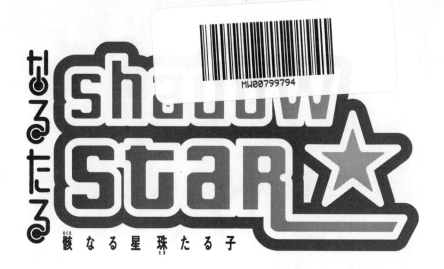

骸なる星珠たる子

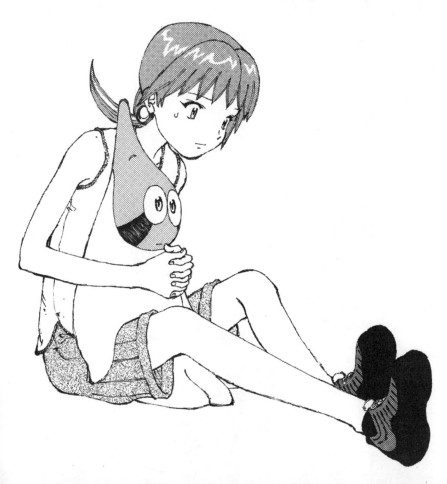

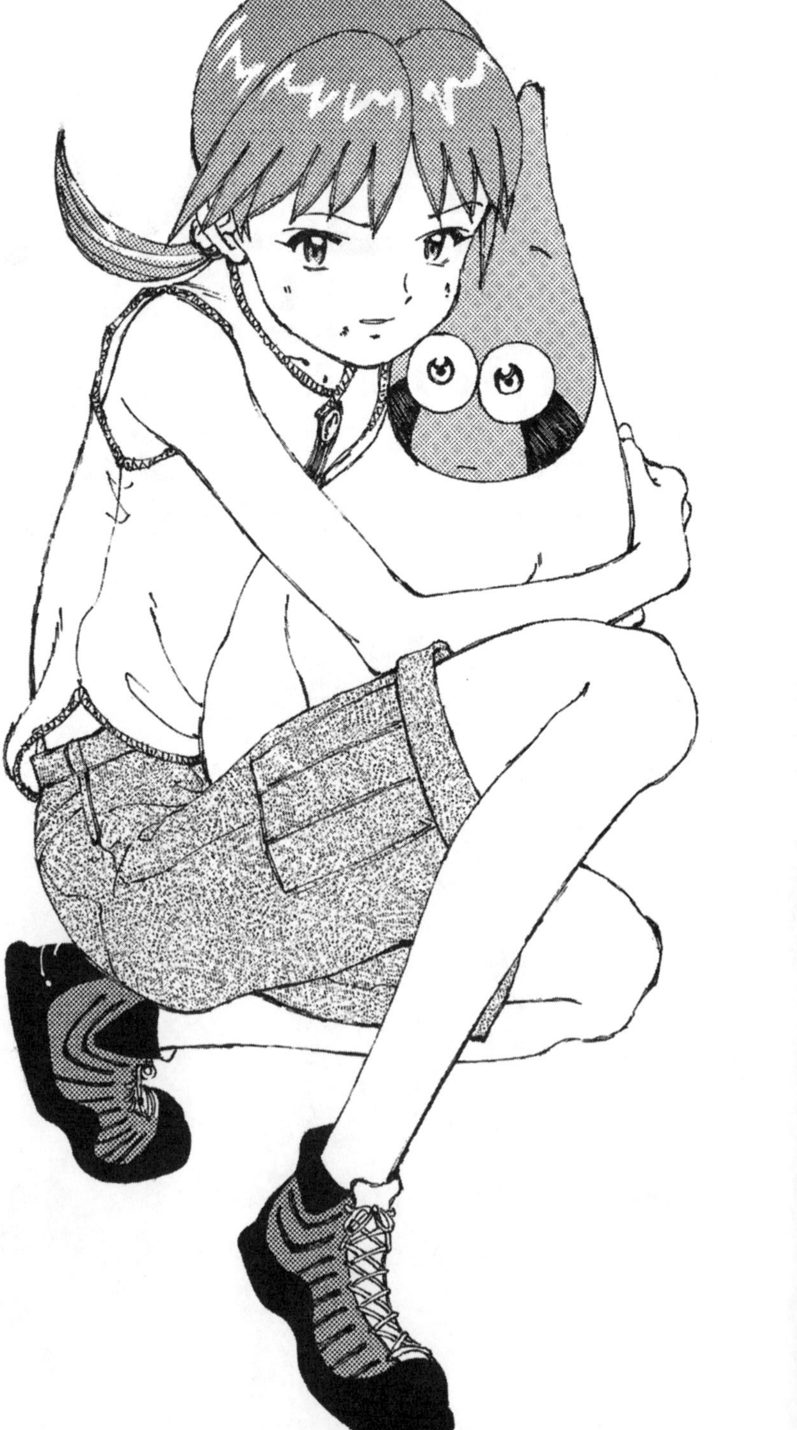

shadow star ☆

骸 なる 星 珠 たる 子

DARKNESS VISIBLE

story and art

MOHIRO KITOH

translation

DANA LEWIS, CHRISTOPHER LEWIS,

TOREN SMITH

lettering and touch-up

DIGITAL CHAMELEON,

AMADOR CISNEROS

DARK HORSE COMICS®

publisher
MIKE RICHARDSON

series editor
MIKE HANSEN

series executive editor
TOREN SMITH for **STUDIO PROTEUS**

collection editor
CHRIS WARNER

collection designer
DARIN FABRICK

art director
MARK COX

English-language version produced by Studio Proteus
and Dark Horse Comics, Inc.

SHADOW STAR Vol. 2: DARKNESS VISIBLE

This volume collects **Shadow Star** stories from issues seven through twelve of the Dark Horse comic-book series **Super Manga Blast!**

Published by
Dark Horse Comics, Inc.
10956 SE Main Street
Milwaukie, OR 97222

www.darkhorse.com

To find a comics shop in your area, call the Comic Shop Locator Service toll-free at 1-888-266-4226

First edition: April 2002
ISBN: 1-56971-740-0

10 9 8 7 6 5 4 3 2 1

Printed in Canada

DARKNESS VISIBLE

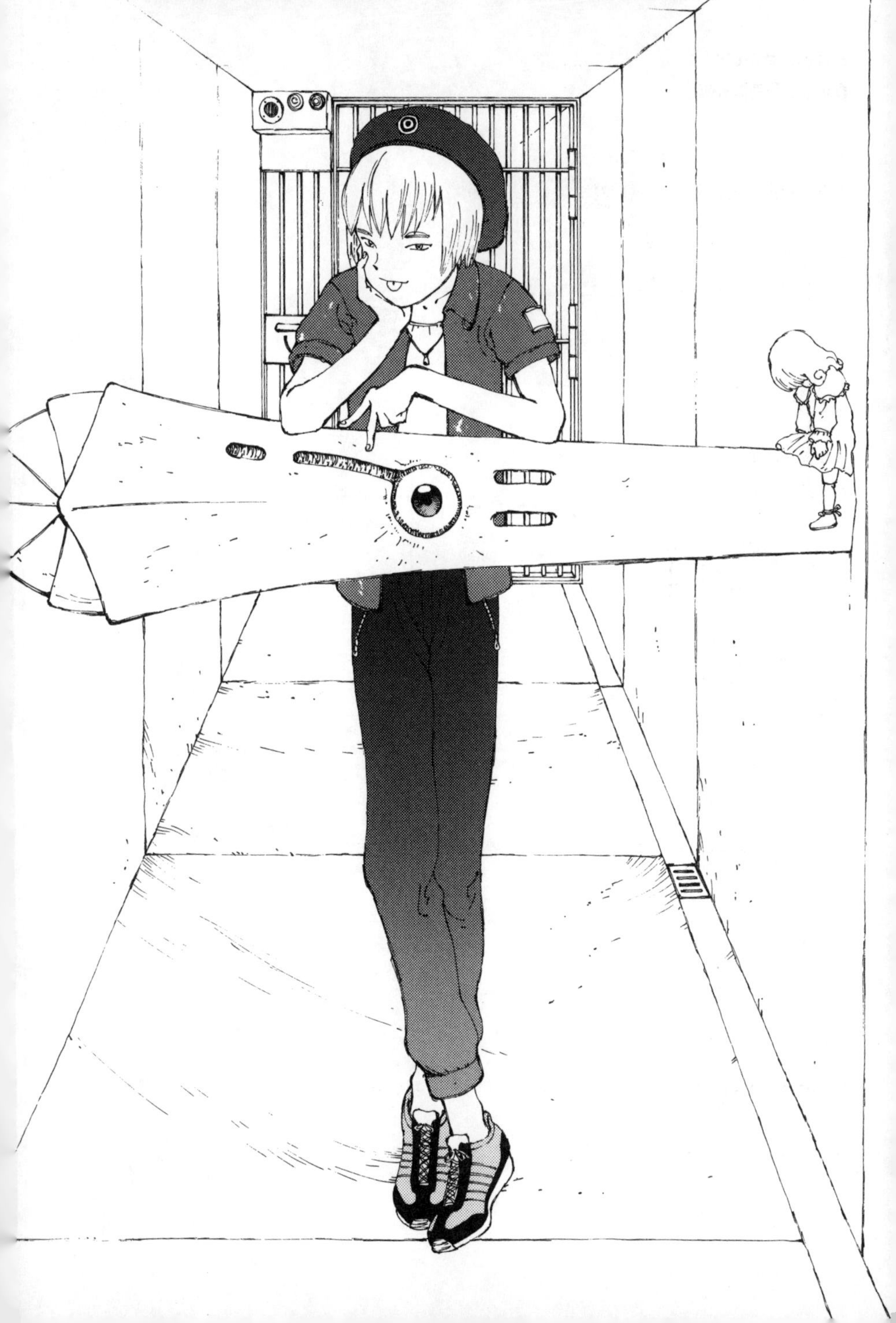

SAY... DID YOU GIVE YOURS A NAME?

Y... YES.

EN... EN-SOF.

"ENSOF"...?

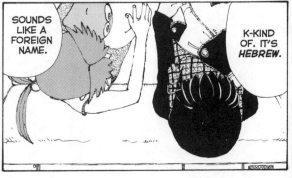

SOUNDS LIKE A FOREIGN NAME.

K-KIND OF. IT'S *HEBREW.*

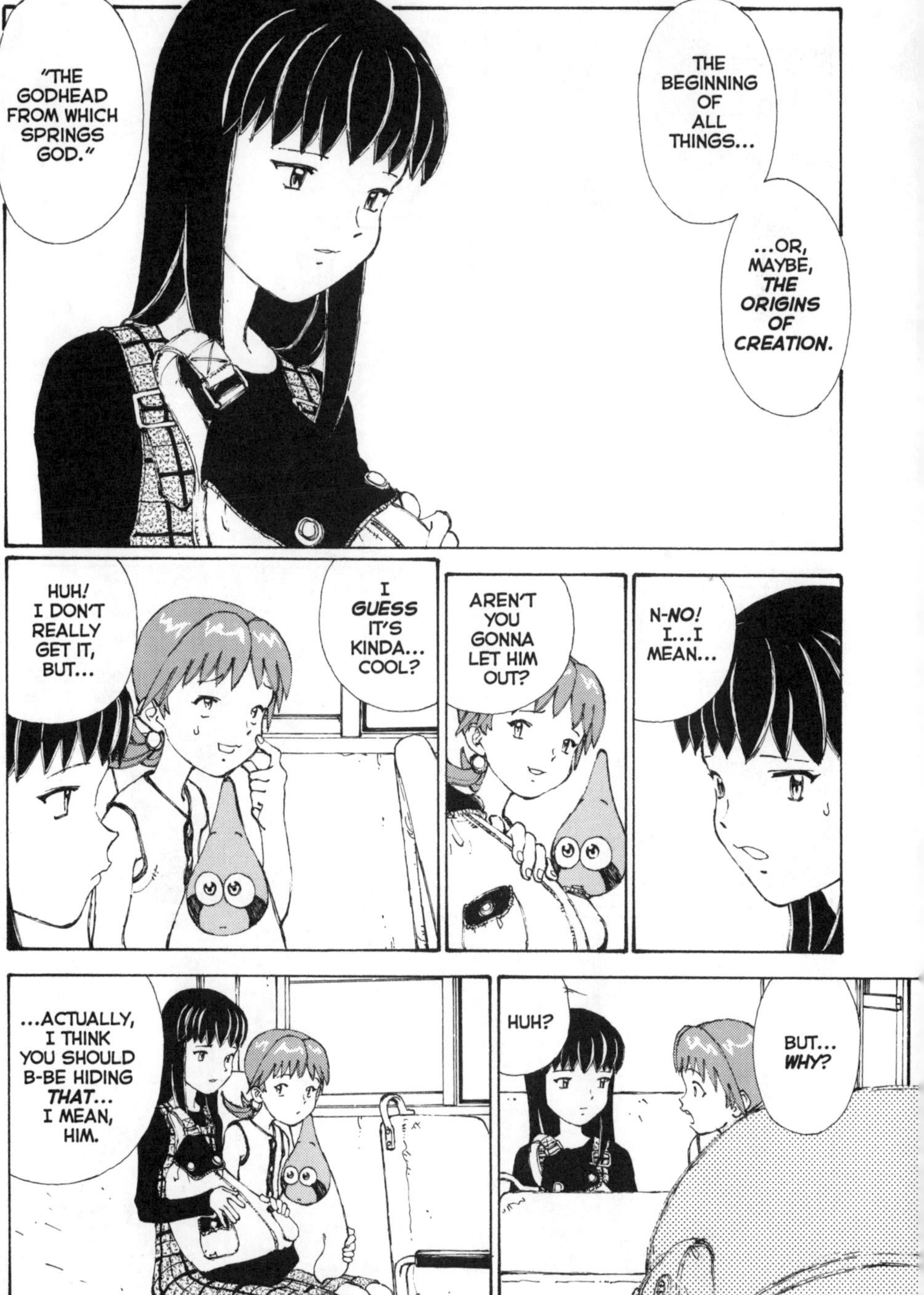
"THE GODHEAD FROM WHICH SPRINGS GOD."
THE BEGINNING OF ALL THINGS...
...OR, MAYBE, *THE ORIGINS OF CREATION.*
HUH! I DON'T REALLY GET IT, BUT...
I *GUESS* IT'S KINDA... COOL?
AREN'T YOU GONNA LET HIM OUT?
N-*NO!* I...I MEAN...
...ACTUALLY, I THINK YOU SHOULD B-BE HIDING *THAT*... I MEAN, HIM.
HUH?
BUT... *WHY?*

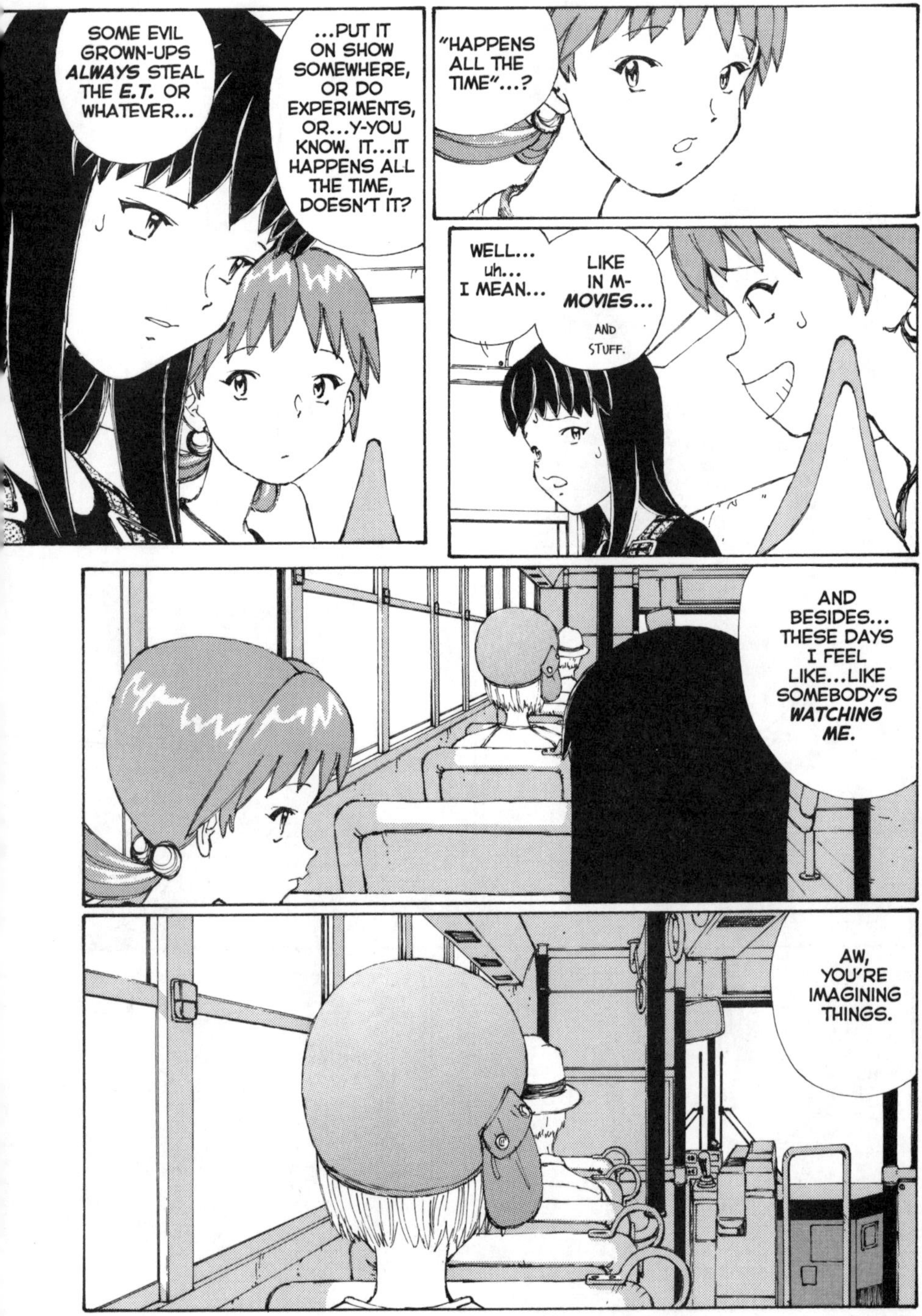
SOME EVIL GROWN-UPS ALWAYS STEAL THE E.T. OR WHATEVER...
...PUT IT ON SHOW SOMEWHERE, OR DO EXPERIMENTS, OR...Y-YOU KNOW. IT...IT HAPPENS ALL THE TIME, DOESN'T IT?
"HAPPENS ALL THE TIME"...?
WELL... uh... I MEAN...
LIKE IN M-MOVIES... AND STUFF.
AND BESIDES... THESE DAYS I FEEL LIKE...LIKE SOMEBODY'S WATCHING ME.
AW, YOU'RE IMAGINING THINGS.

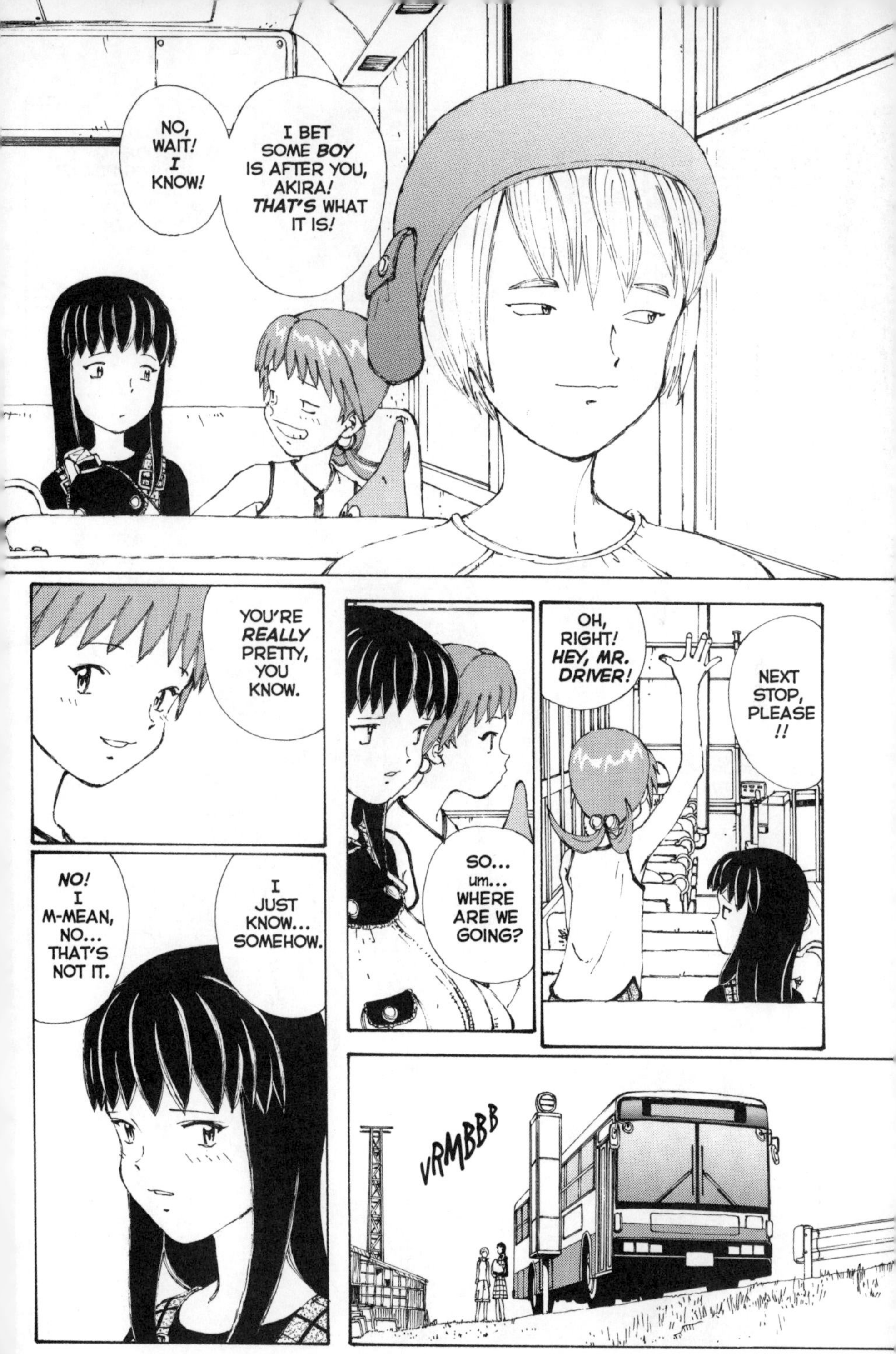
NO, WAIT! I KNOW!
I BET SOME BOY IS AFTER YOU, AKIRA! THAT'S WHAT IT IS!
YOU'RE REALLY PRETTY, YOU KNOW.
NO! I M-MEAN, NO... THAT'S NOT IT.
I JUST KNOW... SOMEHOW.
SO... um... WHERE ARE WE GOING?
OH, RIGHT! HEY, MR. DRIVER!
NEXT STOP, PLEASE!!
VRMBBB

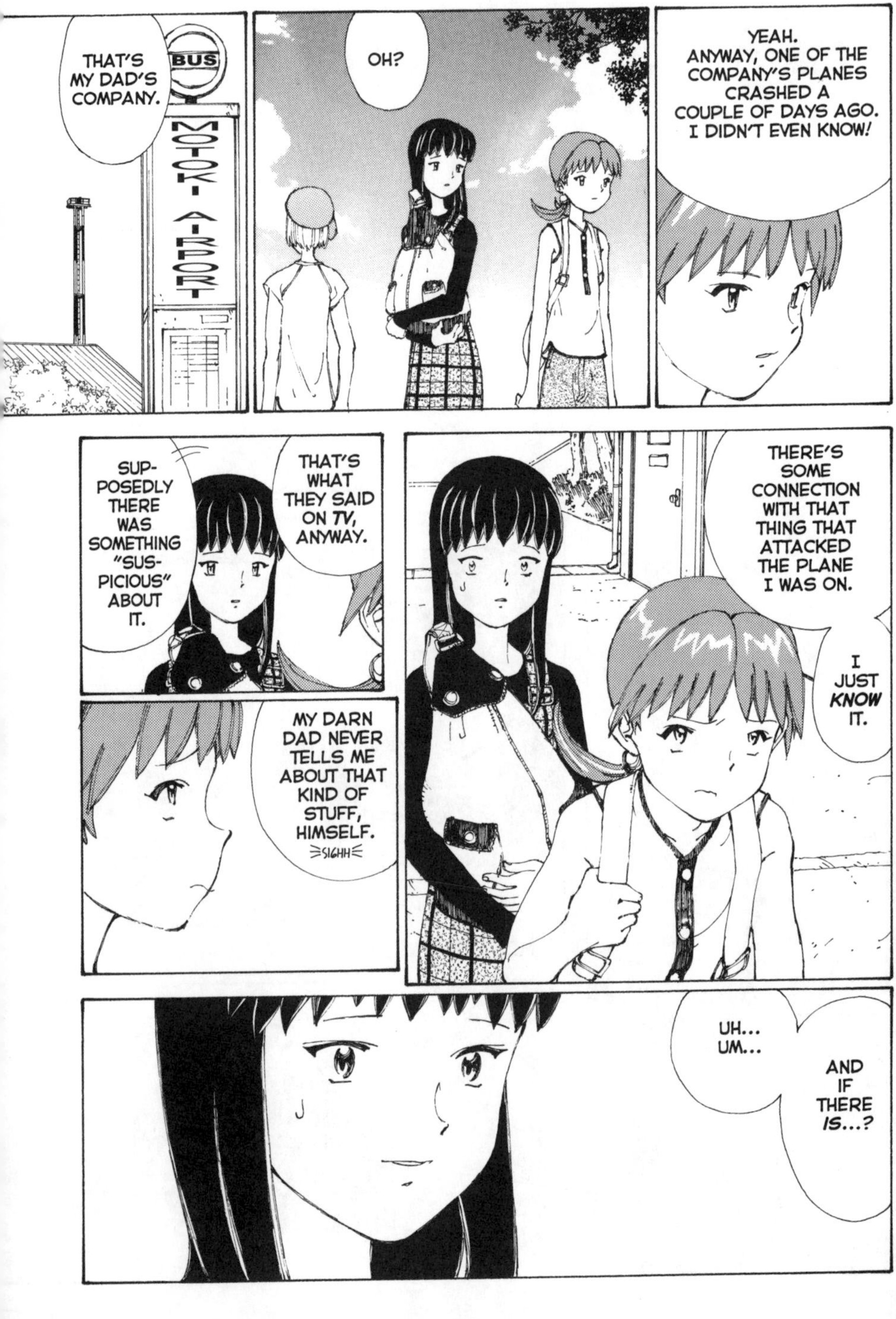
THAT'S MY DAD'S COMPANY.
BUS
MOTOKI AIRPORT
OH?
YEAH. ANYWAY, ONE OF THE COMPANY'S PLANES CRASHED A COUPLE OF DAYS AGO. I DIDN'T EVEN KNOW!
SUP-POSEDLY THERE WAS SOMETHING "SUS-PICIOUS" ABOUT IT.
THAT'S WHAT THEY SAID ON *TV*, ANYWAY.
MY DARN DAD NEVER TELLS ME ABOUT THAT KIND OF STUFF, HIMSELF.
SIGHH
THERE'S SOME CONNECTION WITH THAT THING THAT ATTACKED THE PLANE I WAS ON.
I JUST *KNOW* IT.
UH... UM...
AND IF THERE *IS*...?

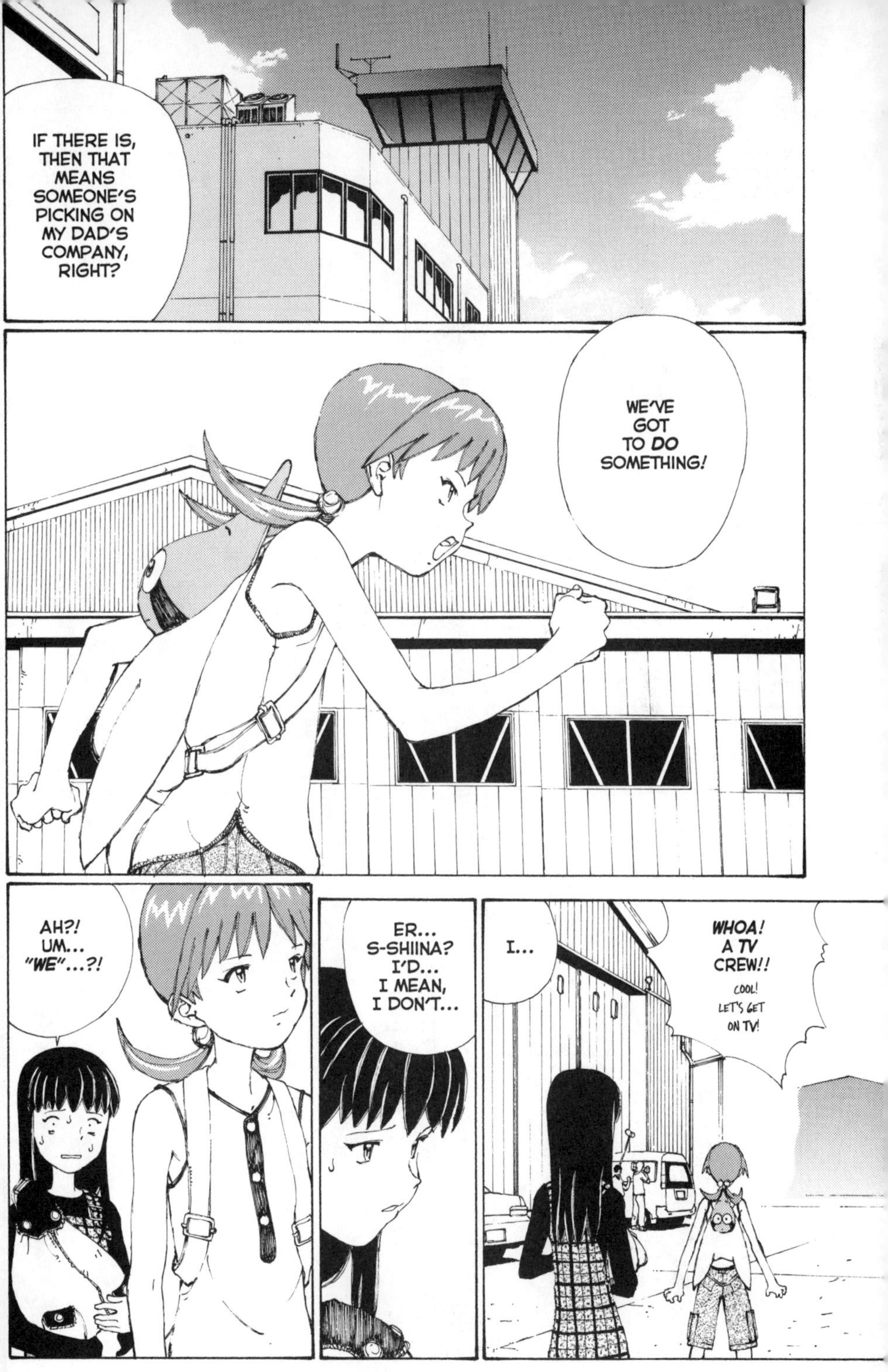
IF THERE IS, THEN THAT MEANS SOMEONE'S PICKING ON MY DAD'S COMPANY, RIGHT?
WE'VE GOT TO *DO* SOMETHING!
AH?! UM... "*WE*"...?!
ER... S-SHIINA? I'D... I MEAN, I DON'T...
I...
WHOA! A TV CREW!!
COOL! LET'S GET ON TV!

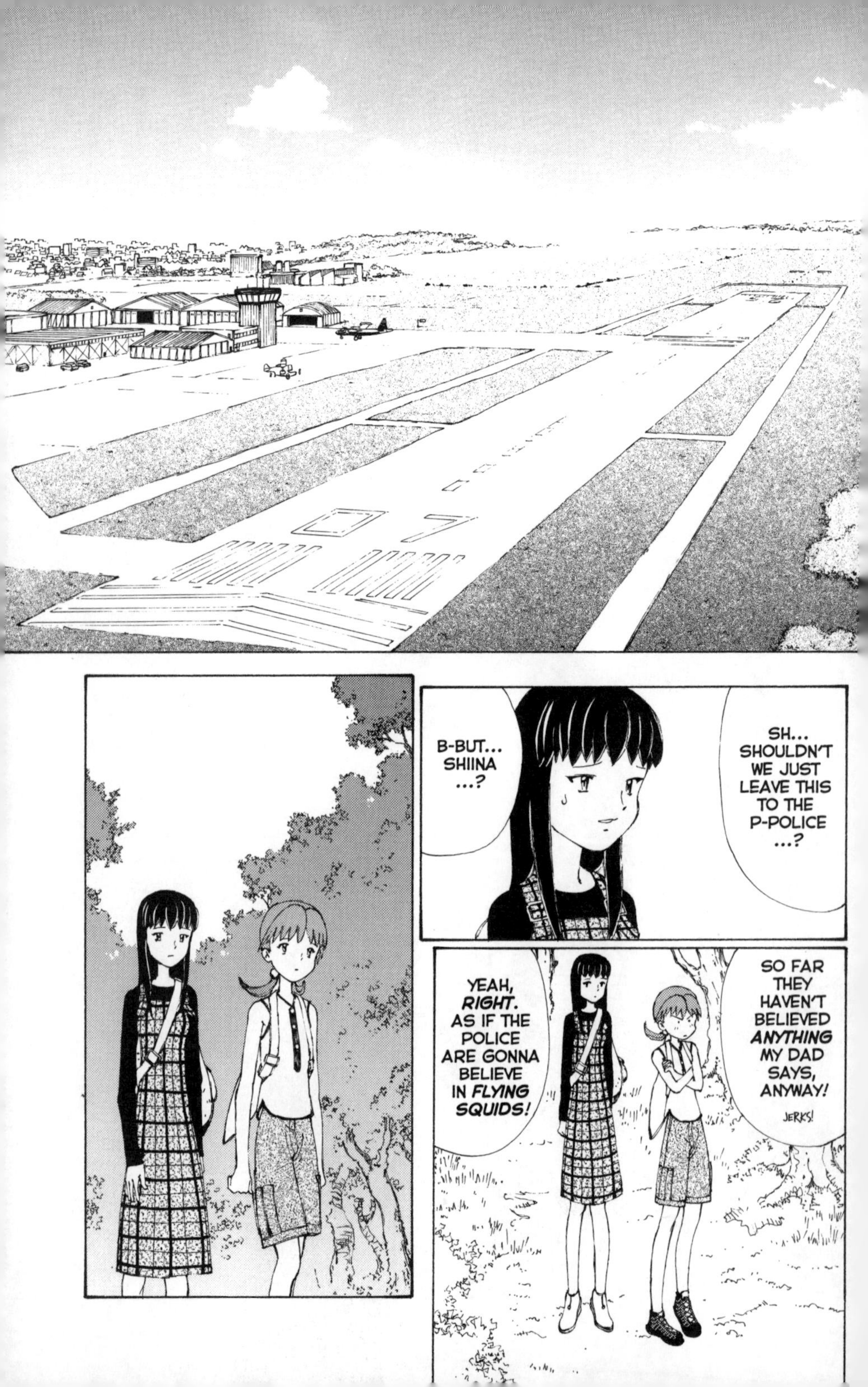
SH... SHOULDN'T WE JUST LEAVE THIS TO THE P-POLICE ...?
B-BUT... SHIINA ...?
SO FAR THEY HAVEN'T BELIEVED *ANYTHING* MY DAD SAYS, ANYWAY!
JERKS!
YEAH, *RIGHT*. AS IF THE POLICE ARE GONNA BELIEVE IN *FLYING SQUIDS!*

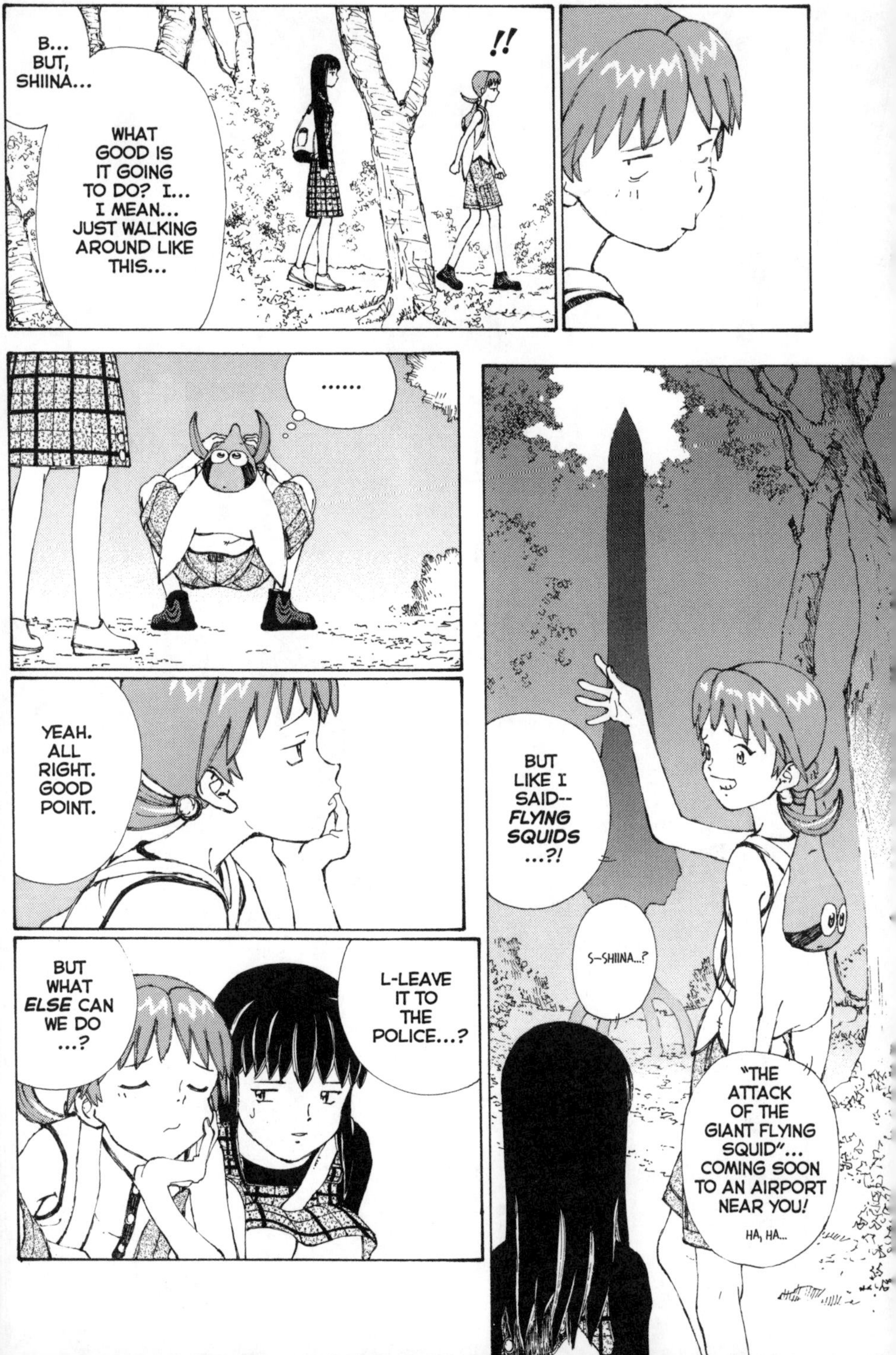
B... BUT, SHIINA...
WHAT GOOD IS IT GOING TO DO? I... I MEAN... JUST WALKING AROUND LIKE THIS...
!!
......
YEAH. ALL RIGHT. GOOD POINT.
BUT WHAT *ELSE* CAN WE DO ...?
L-LEAVE IT TO THE POLICE...?
BUT LIKE I SAID-- *FLYING SQUIDS* ...?!
S-SHIINA...?
"THE ATTACK OF THE GIANT FLYING SQUID"... COMING SOON TO AN AIRPORT NEAR YOU!
HA, HA...

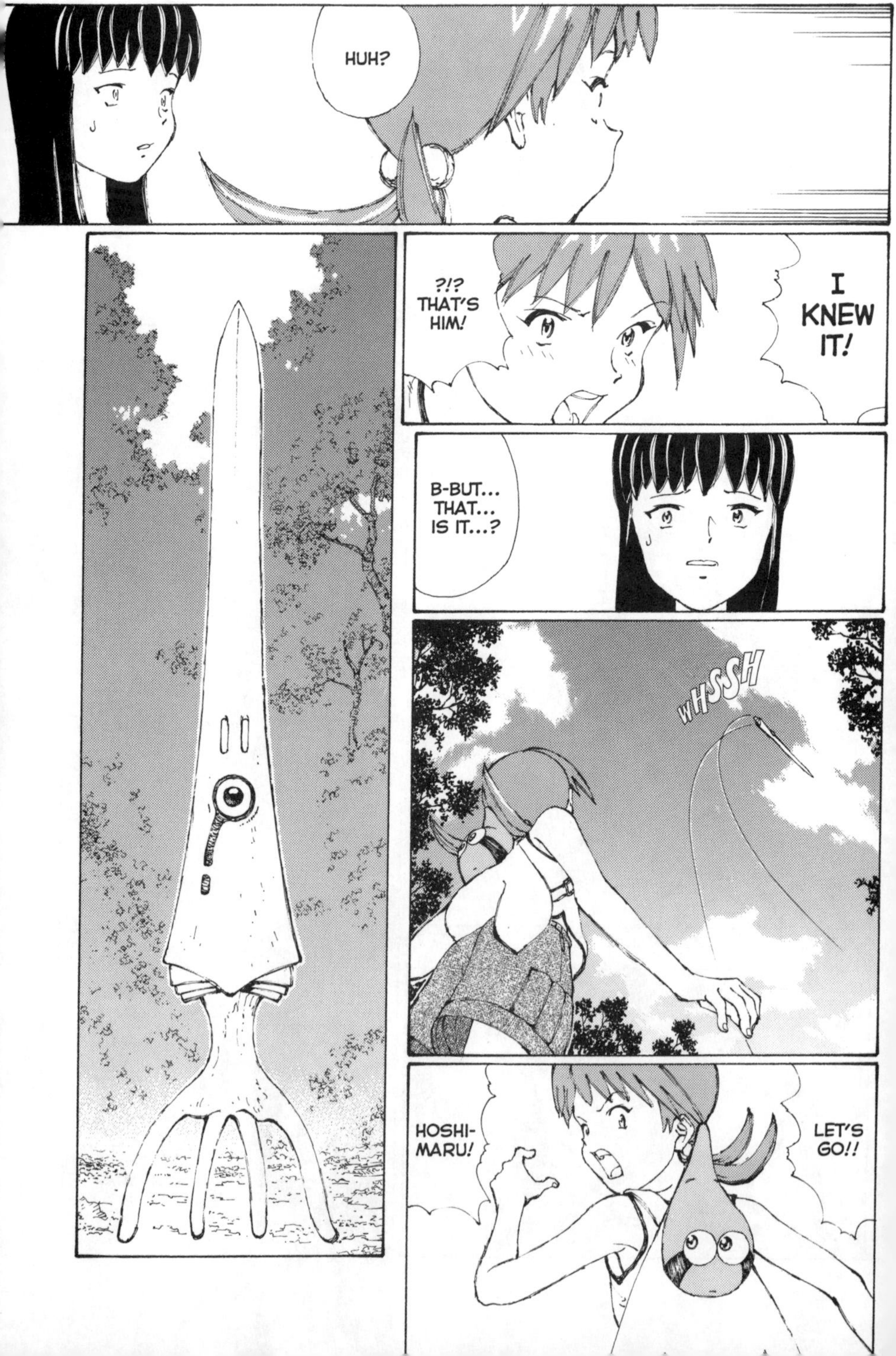
HUH?
?!? THAT'S HIM!
I KNEW IT!
B-BUT... THAT... IS IT...?
WHSSH
HOSHI-MARU!
LET'S GO!!

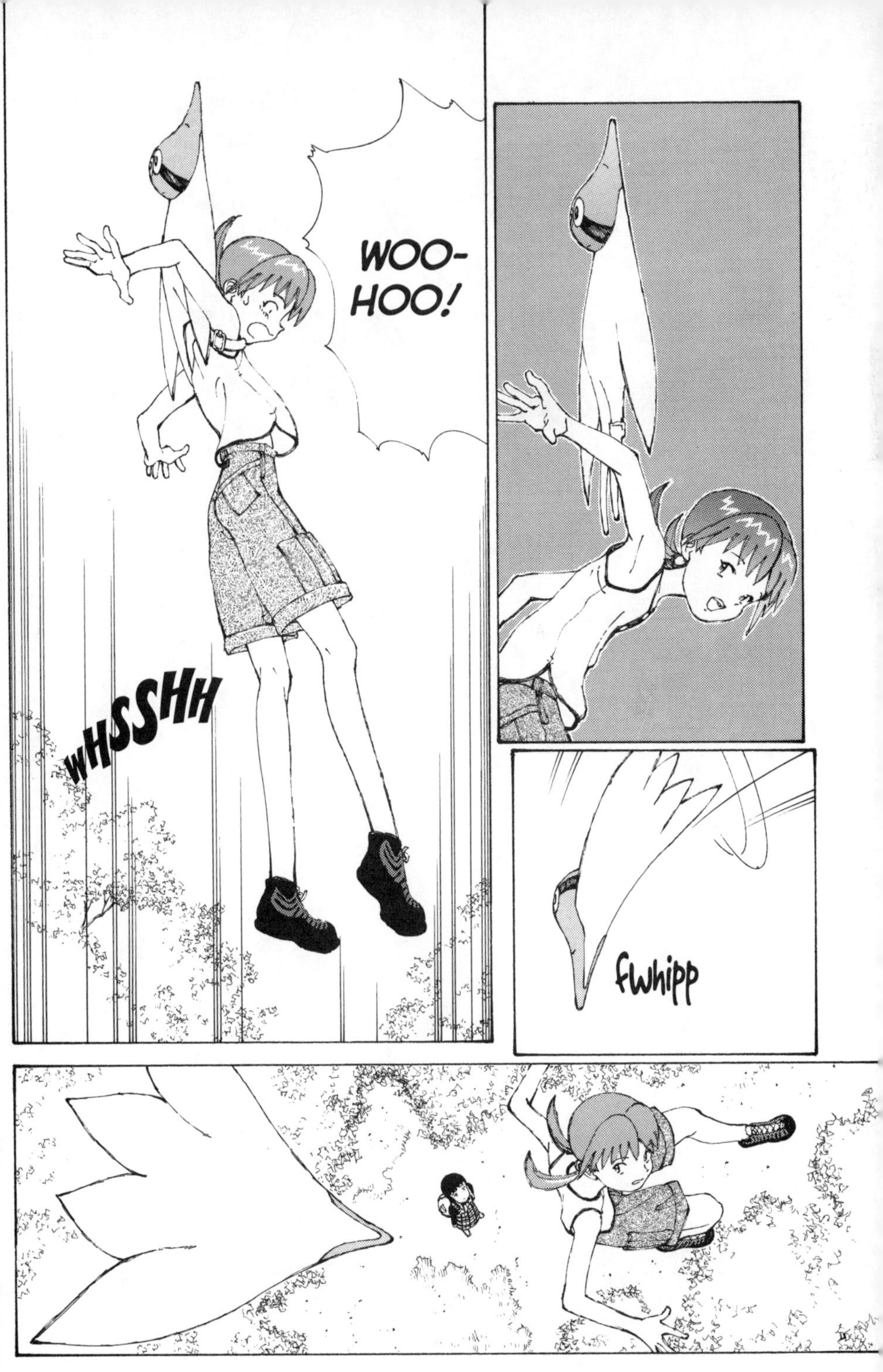
fwhipp
WOO-HOO!
wHSSHH

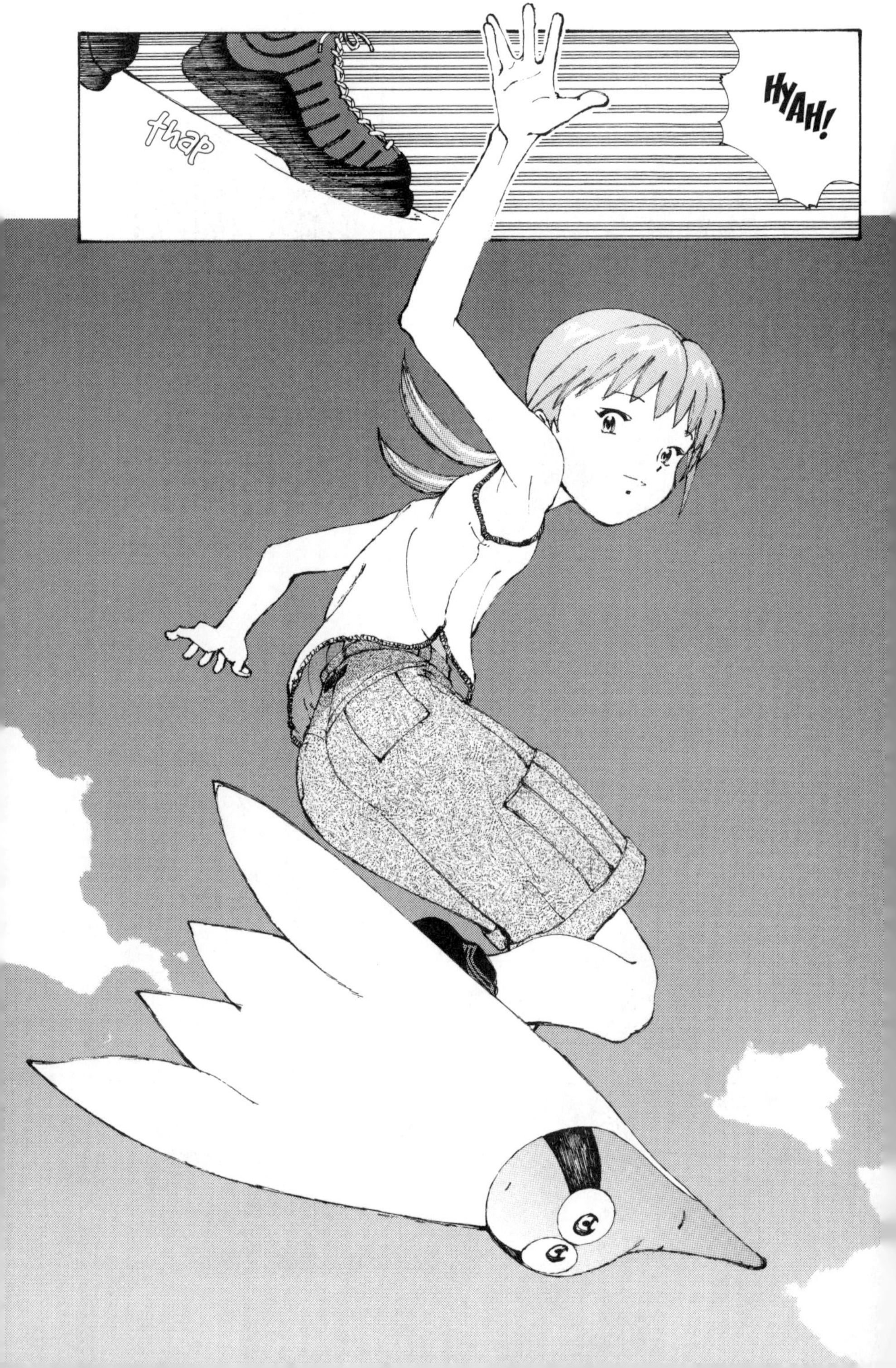
HYAH!
thap

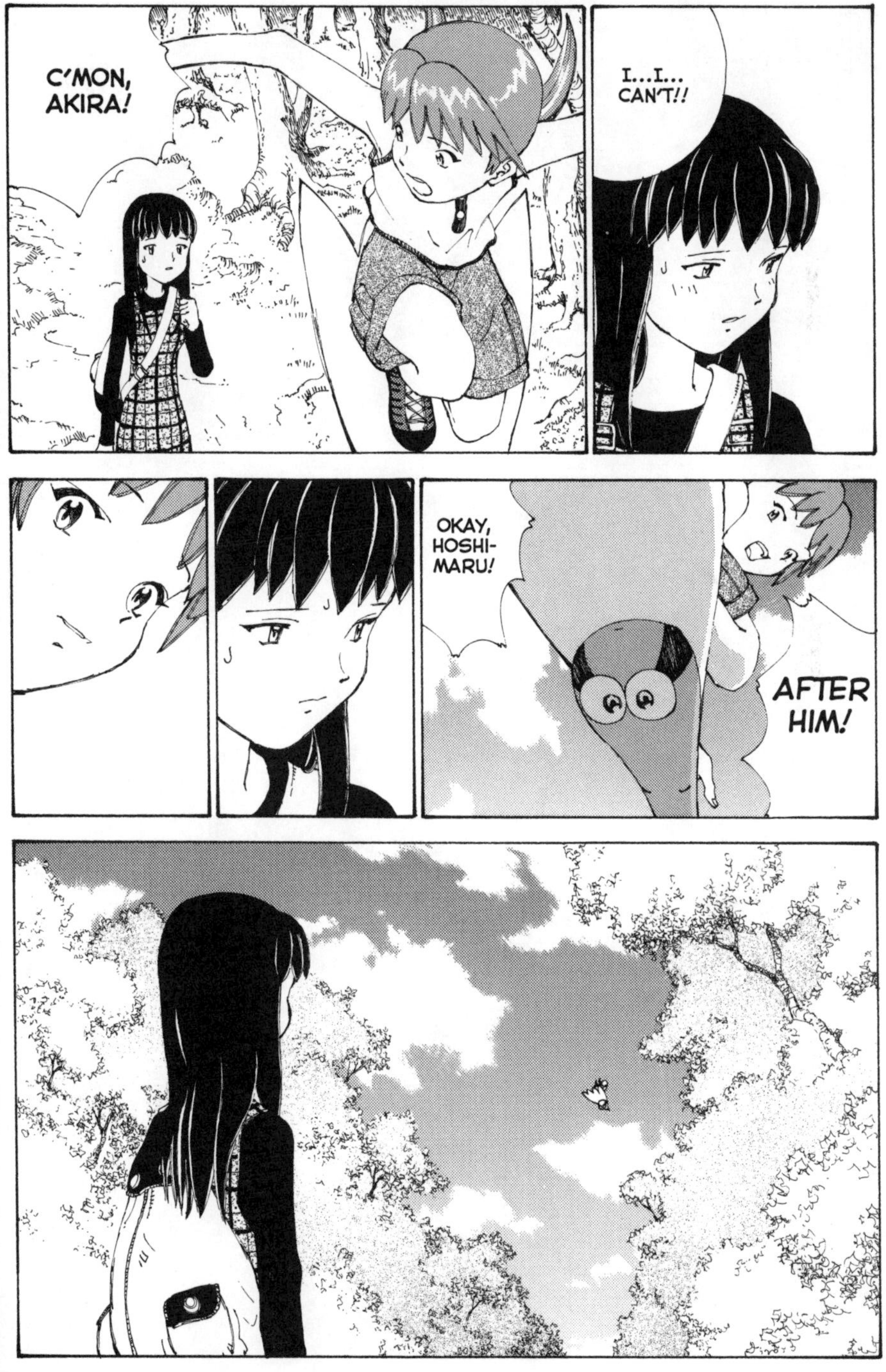
C'MON, AKIRA!
I...I... CAN'T!!
OKAY, HOSHI-MARU!
AFTER HIM!

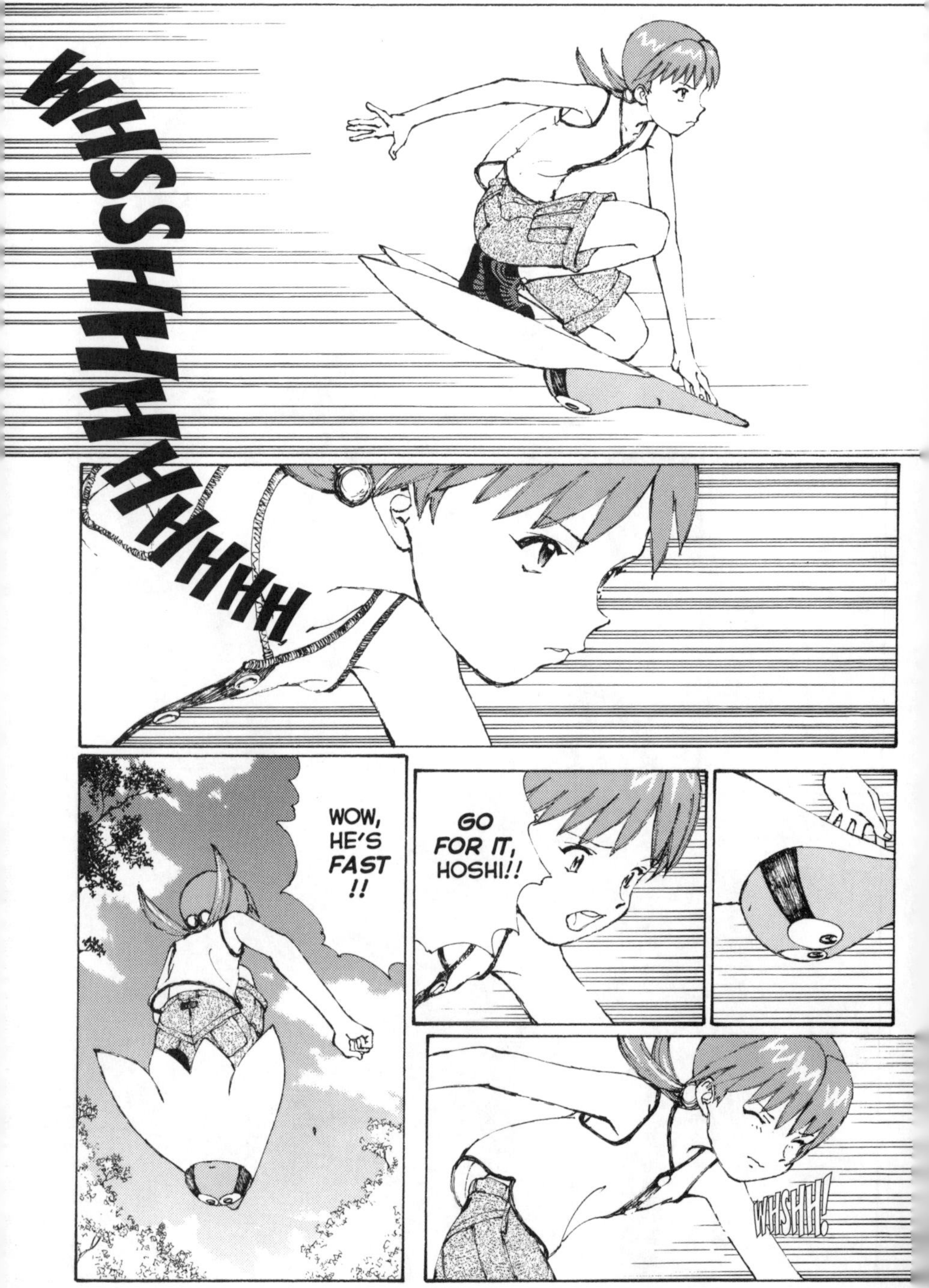
WHSSHHHHHHHHHHH
GO FOR IT, HOSHI!!
WHSHH!
WOW, HE'S FAST!!

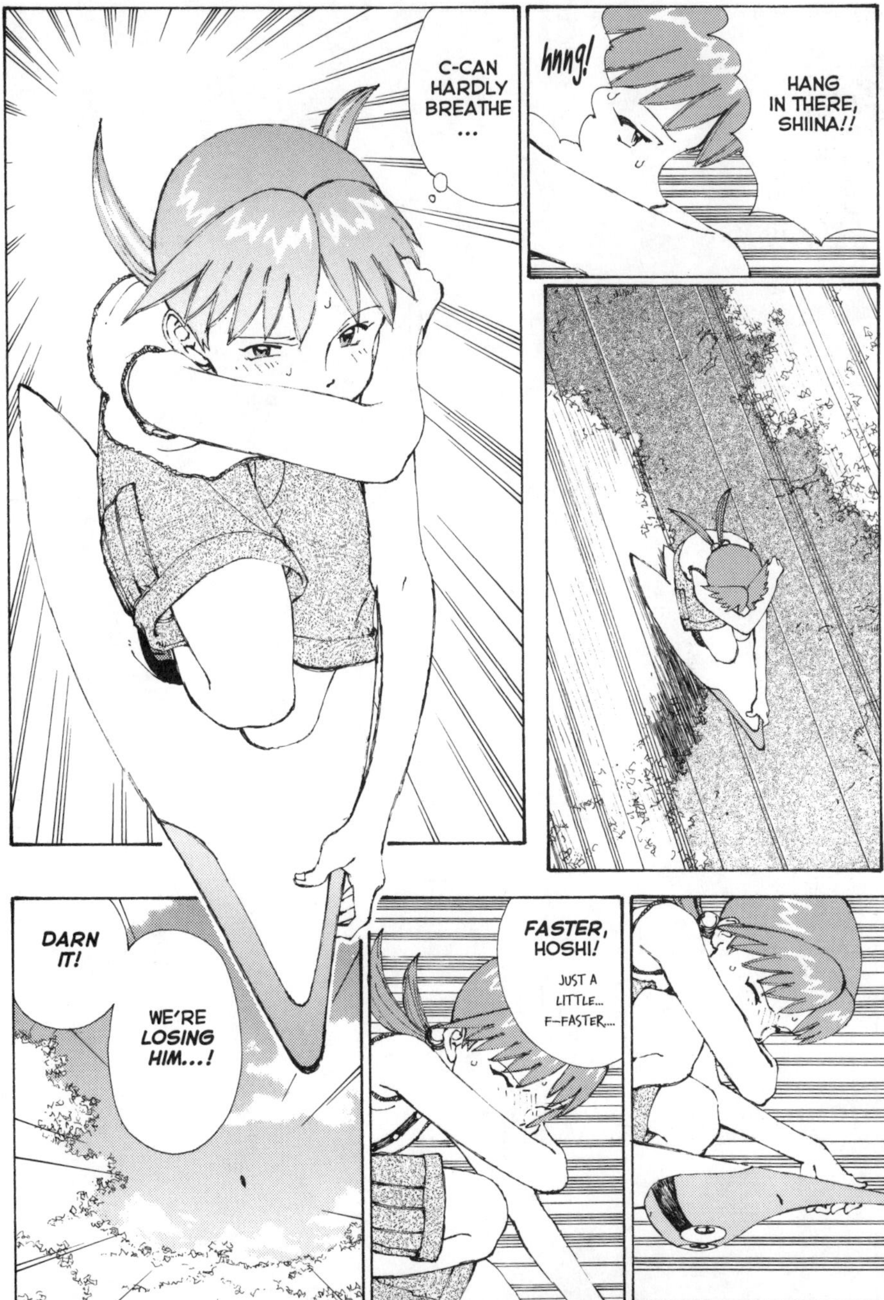
hnng!
HANG IN THERE, SHIINA!!
C-CAN HARDLY BREATHE ...
FASTER, HOSHI!
JUST A LITTLE... F-FASTER...
DARN IT!
WE'RE LOSING HIM...!

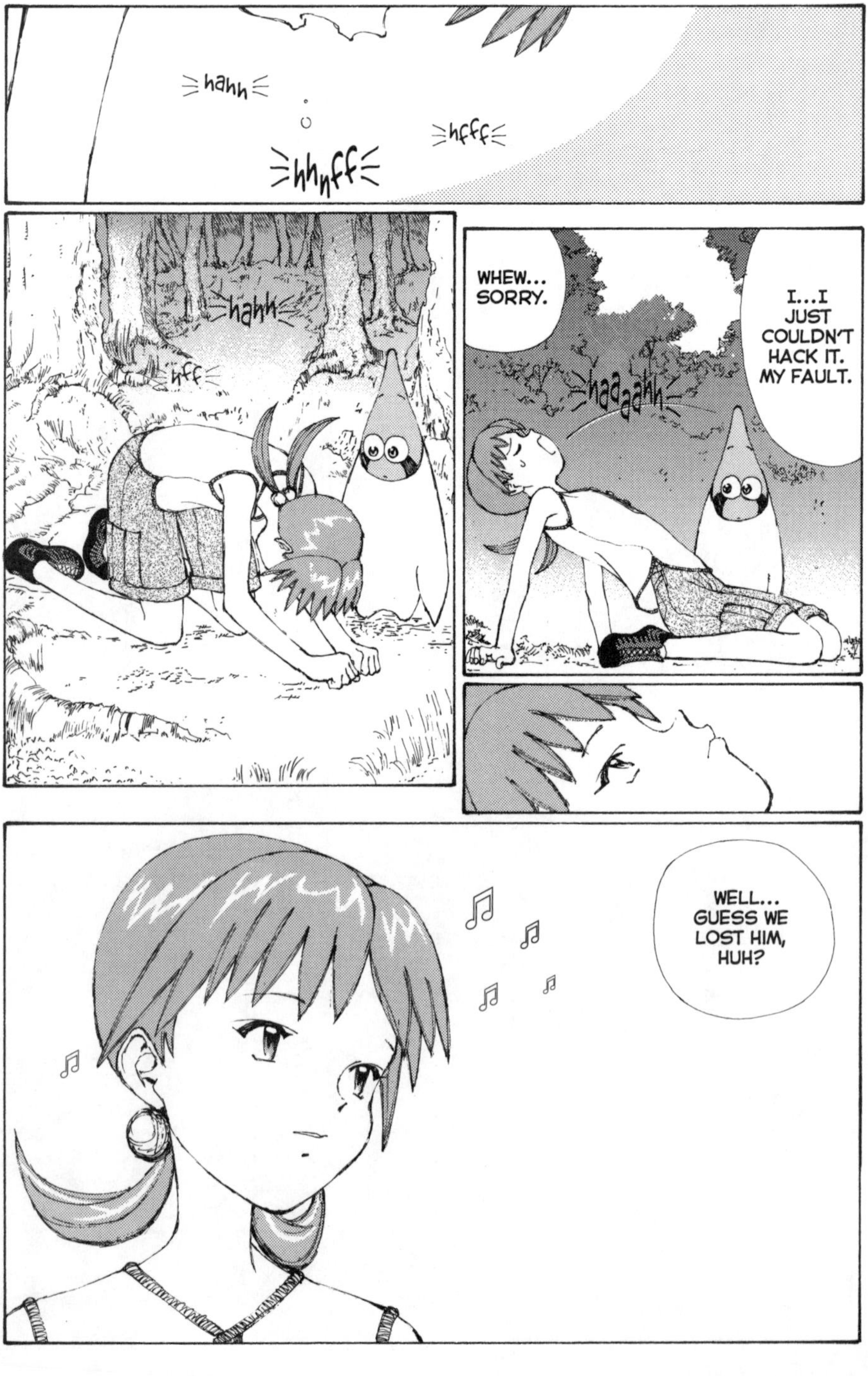
hahh
hfff
hhnff
WHEW... SORRY.
I...I JUST COULDN'T HACK IT. MY FAULT.
haaaahh
hahh
hff
WELL... GUESS WE LOST HIM, HUH?

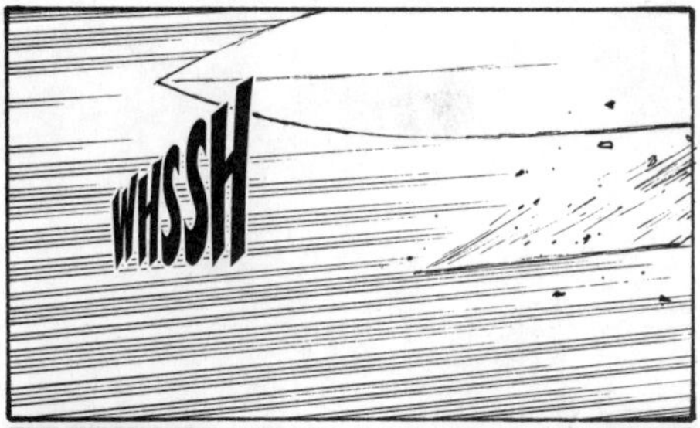
WHSSH
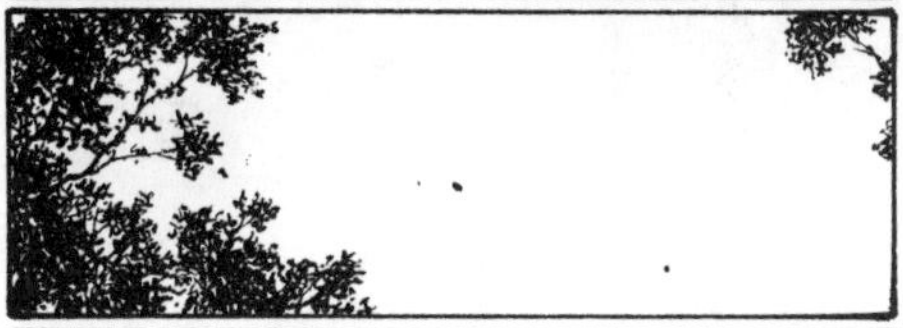
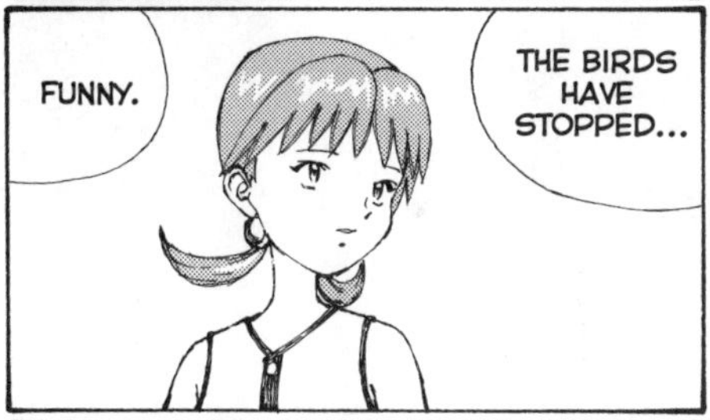
THE BIRDS HAVE STOPPED...
FUNNY.
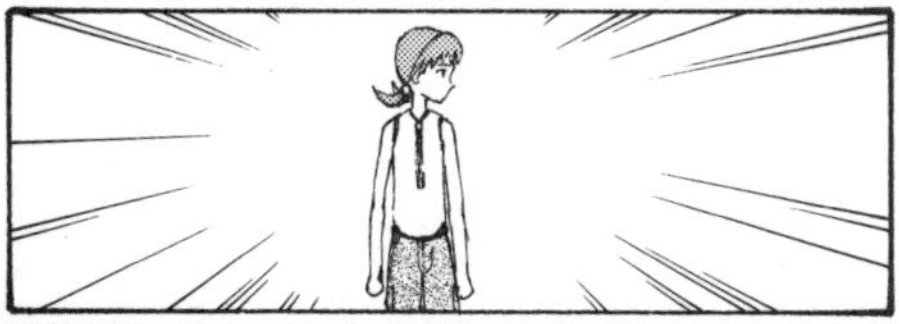
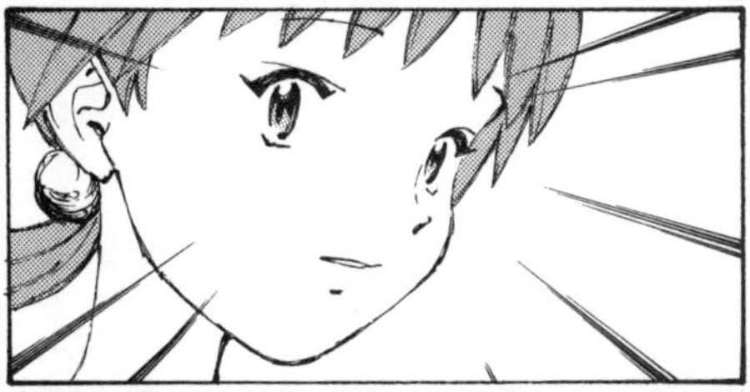
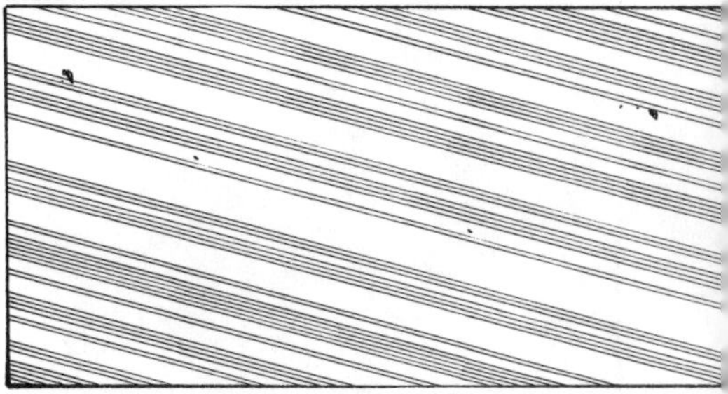
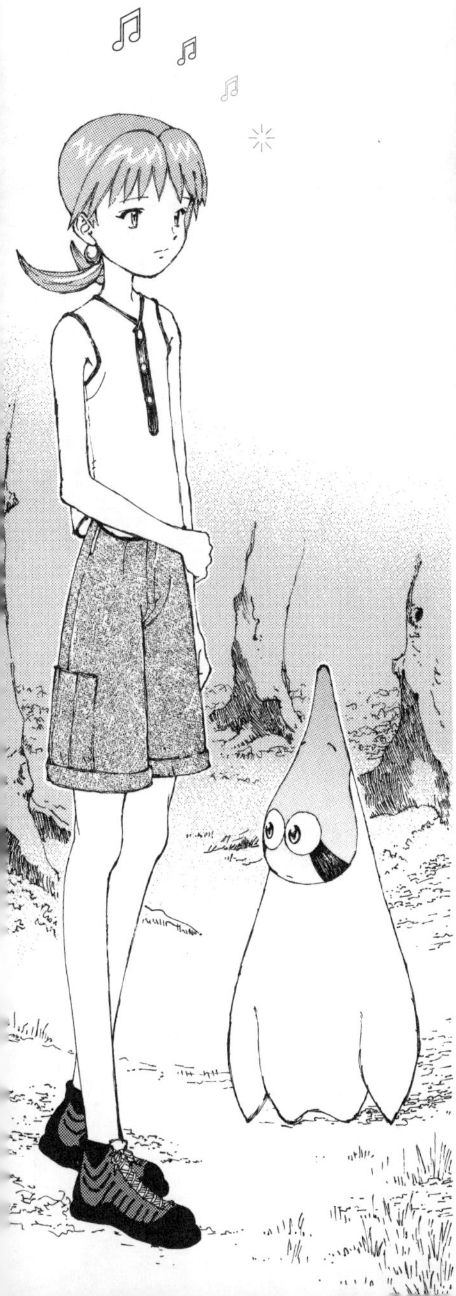

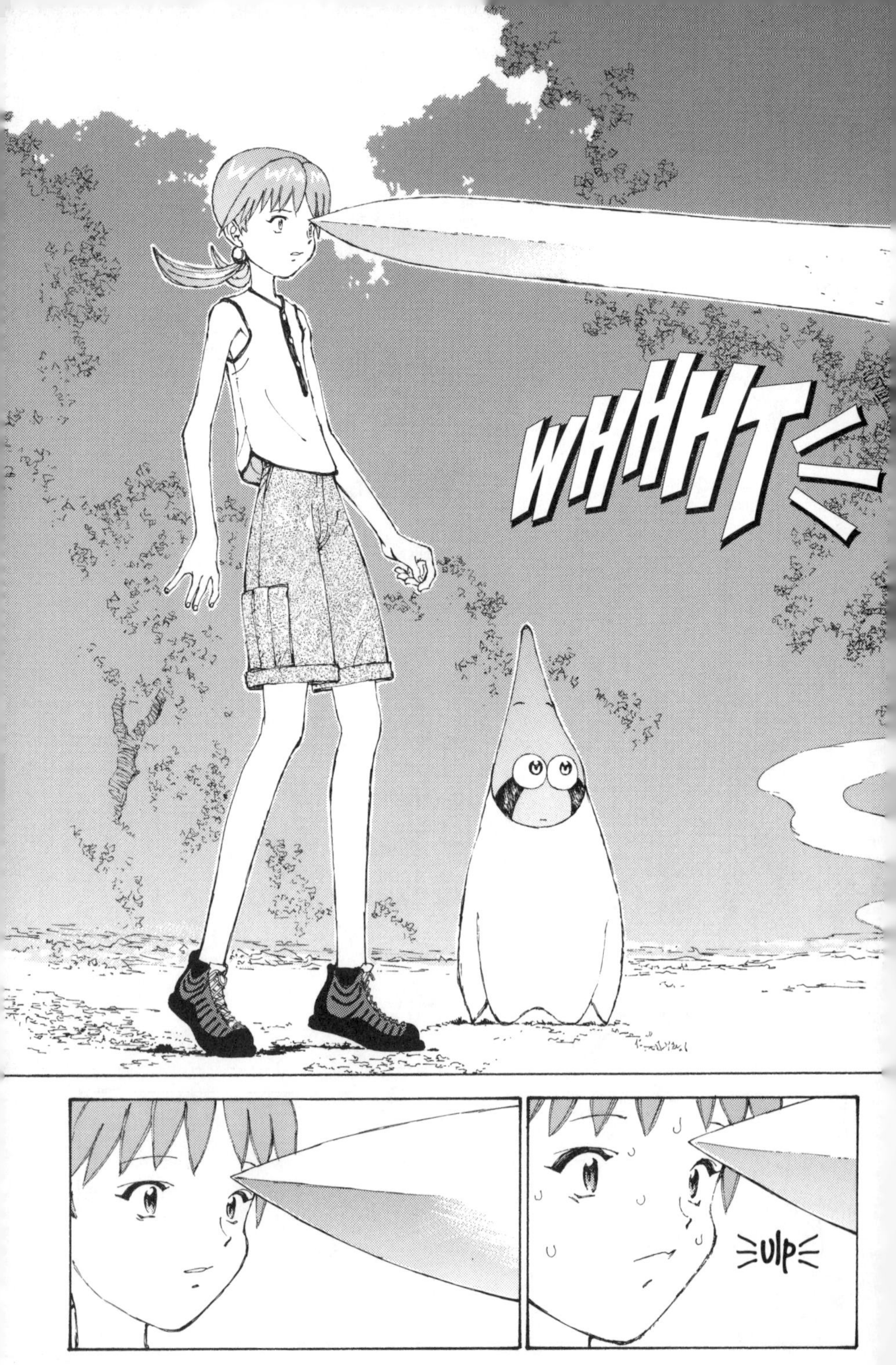
WHHHT
ULP

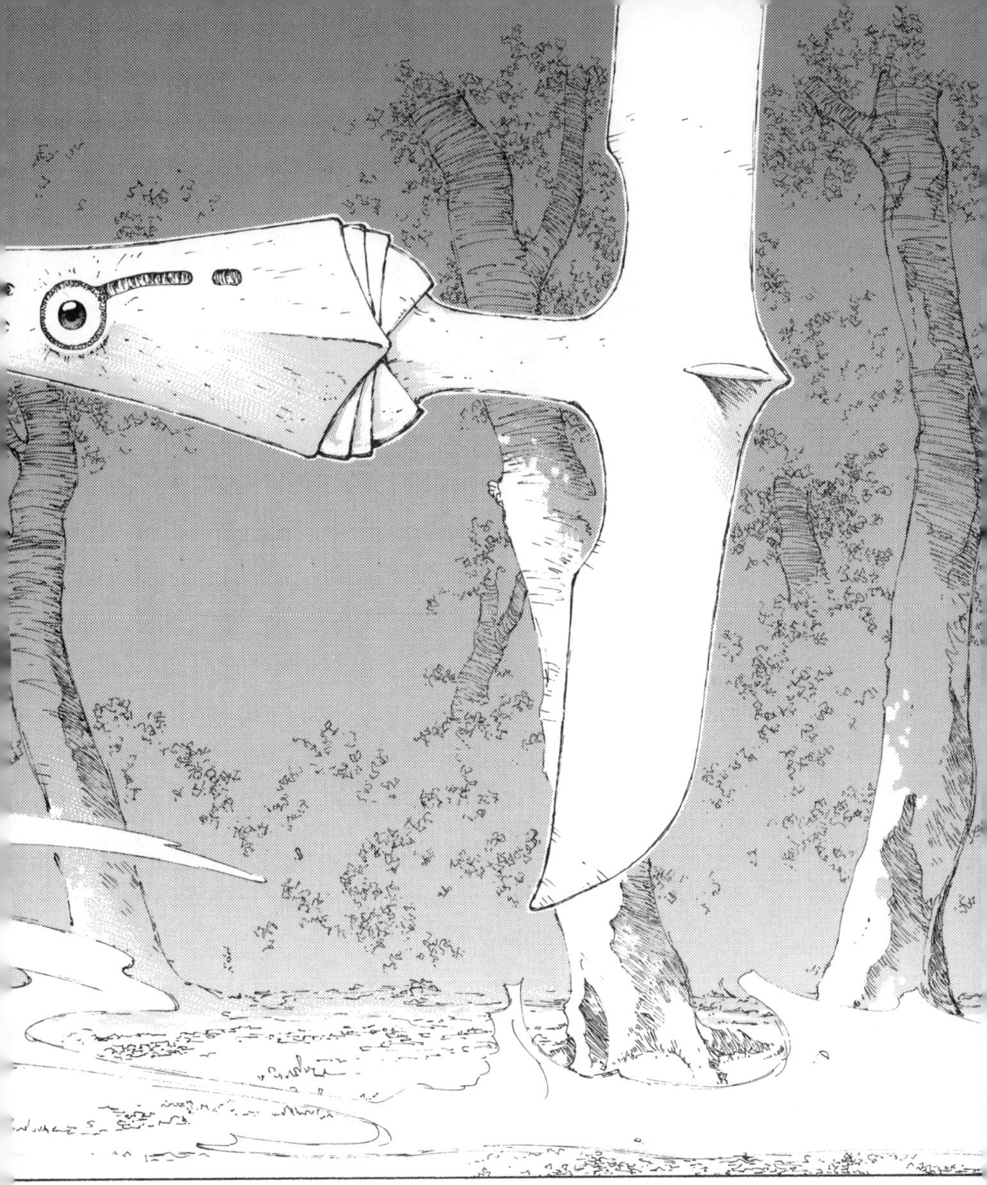

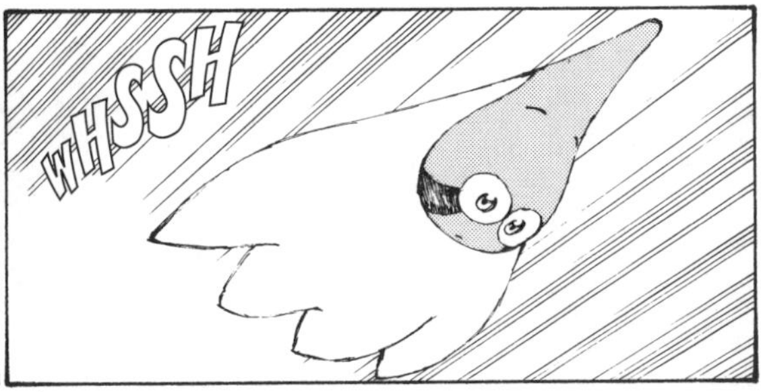
WHSSH

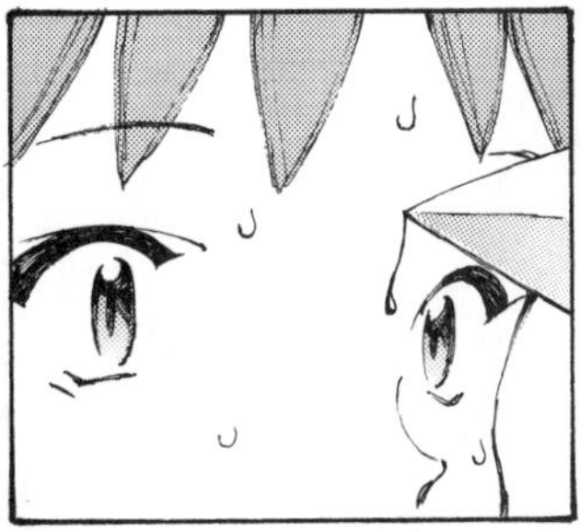

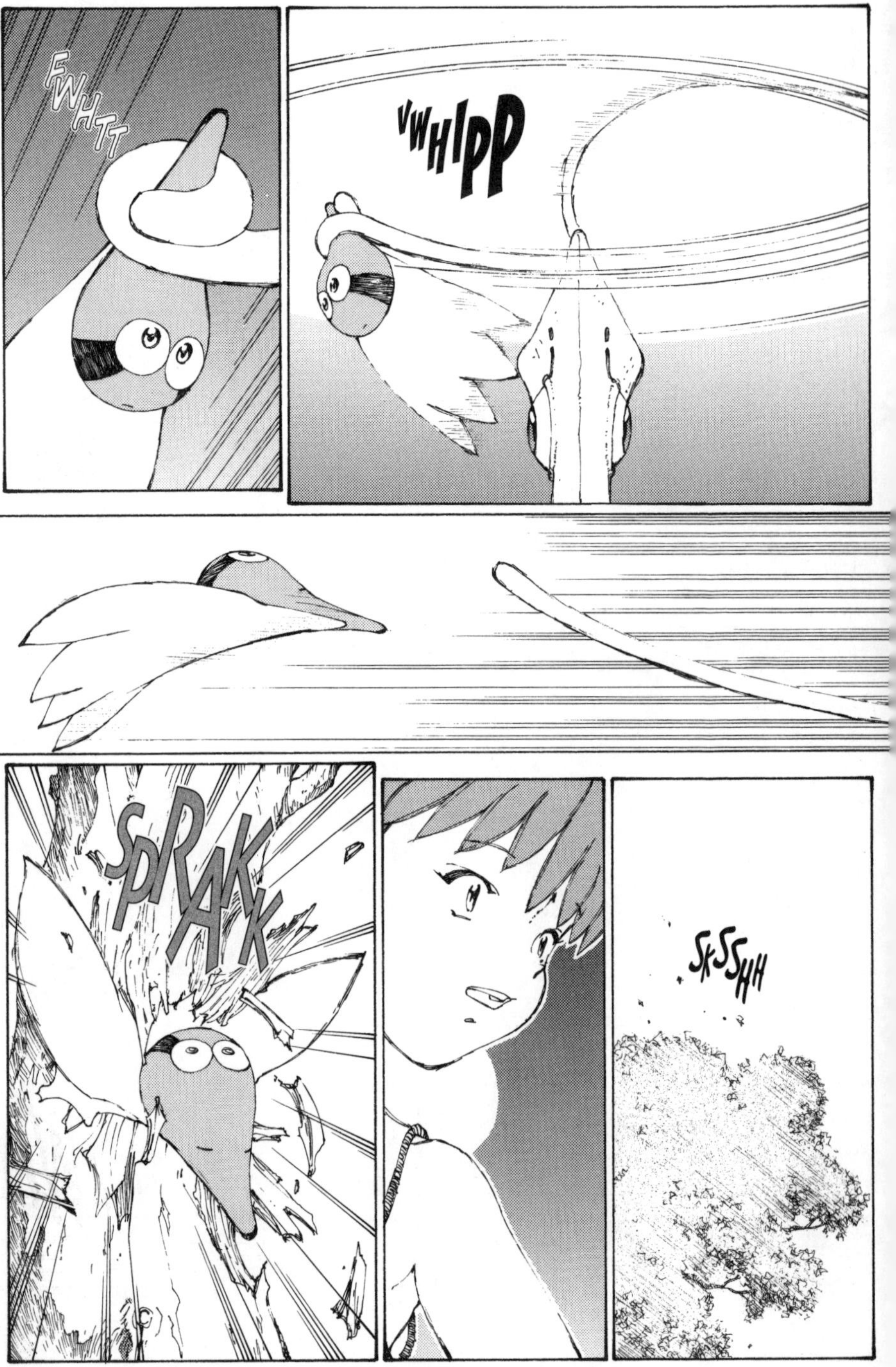
VWHIPP
FWHTT
SKSSHH
SPRAKK

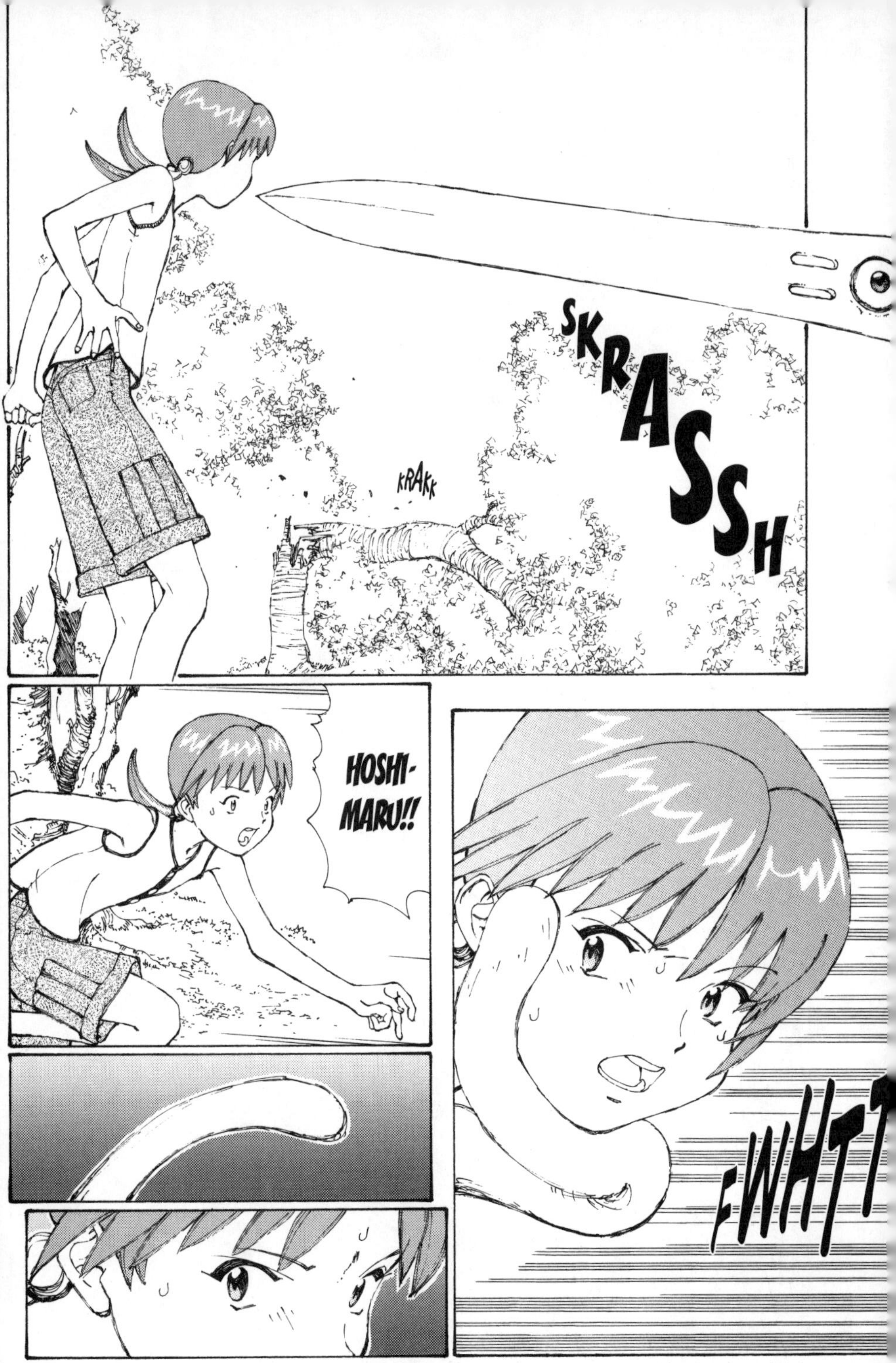
SKRASSH
KRAKK
FWHTT
HOSHI-MARU!!

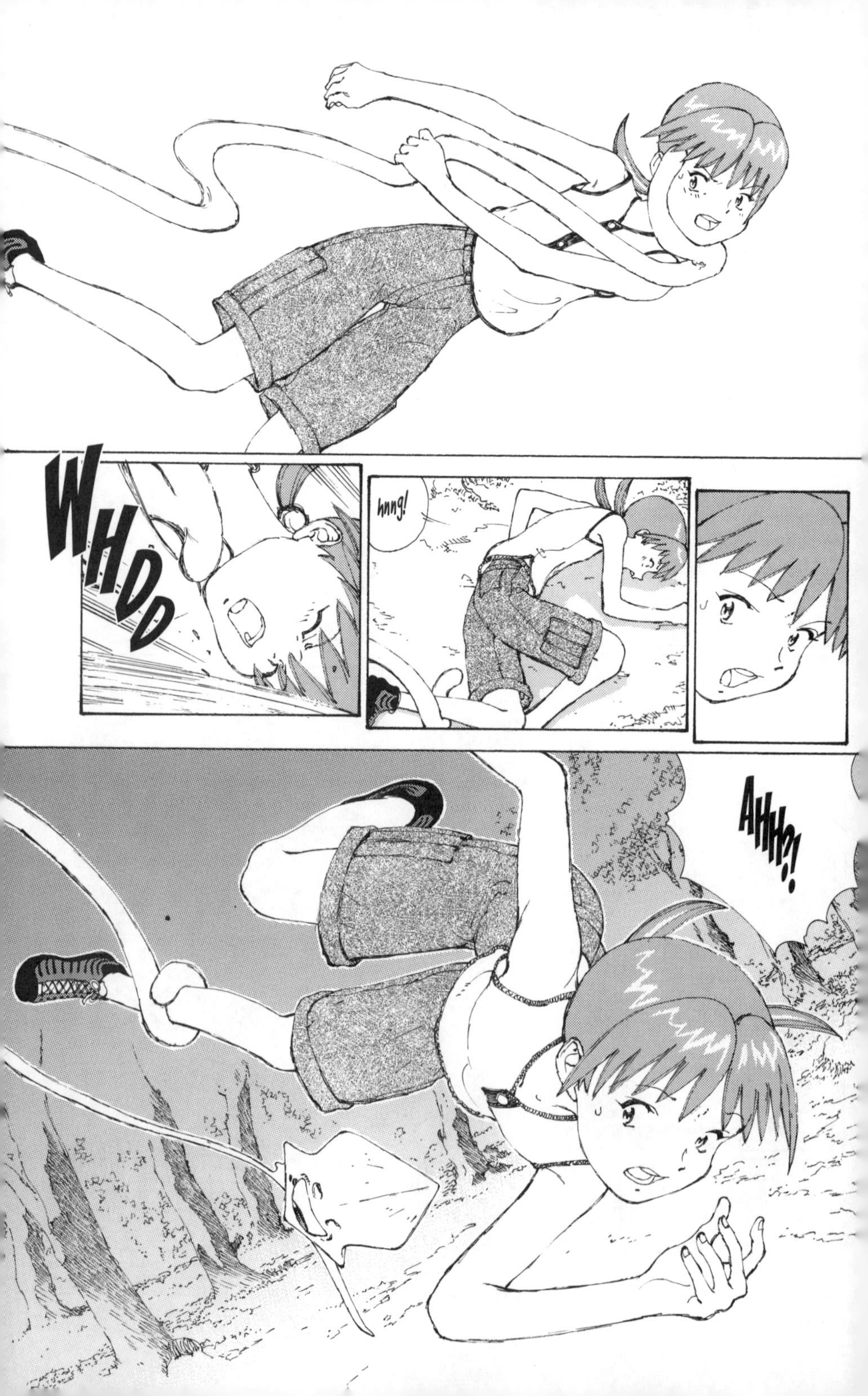
hnng!
WHDD
AHHH?!

I...I HOPE NOBODY S-SAW HER. THAT WOULD BE...BAD.

GO HELP SHIINA...?

B-BUT...IF THAT'S THE SAME KIND OF THING AS YOU...

...THERE'S *NO WAY*... WE CAN DO *ANYTHING* TO IT, RIGHT?

I MEAN... I... I T-TRIED...

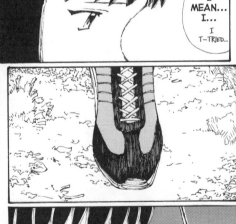

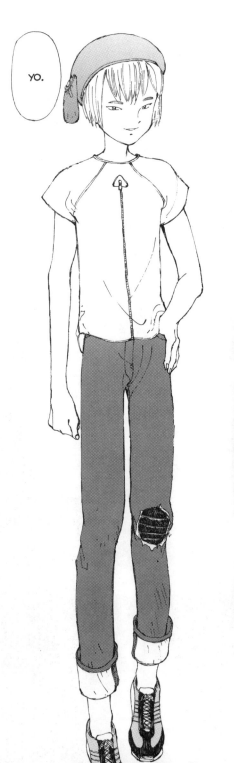

YO.

OH?!

WHO... AH!

HEY ...?

YOU'RE LINKED WITH A DRAGON-CHILD, TOO?

GREAT. THAT'LL MAKE THINGS EASIER.

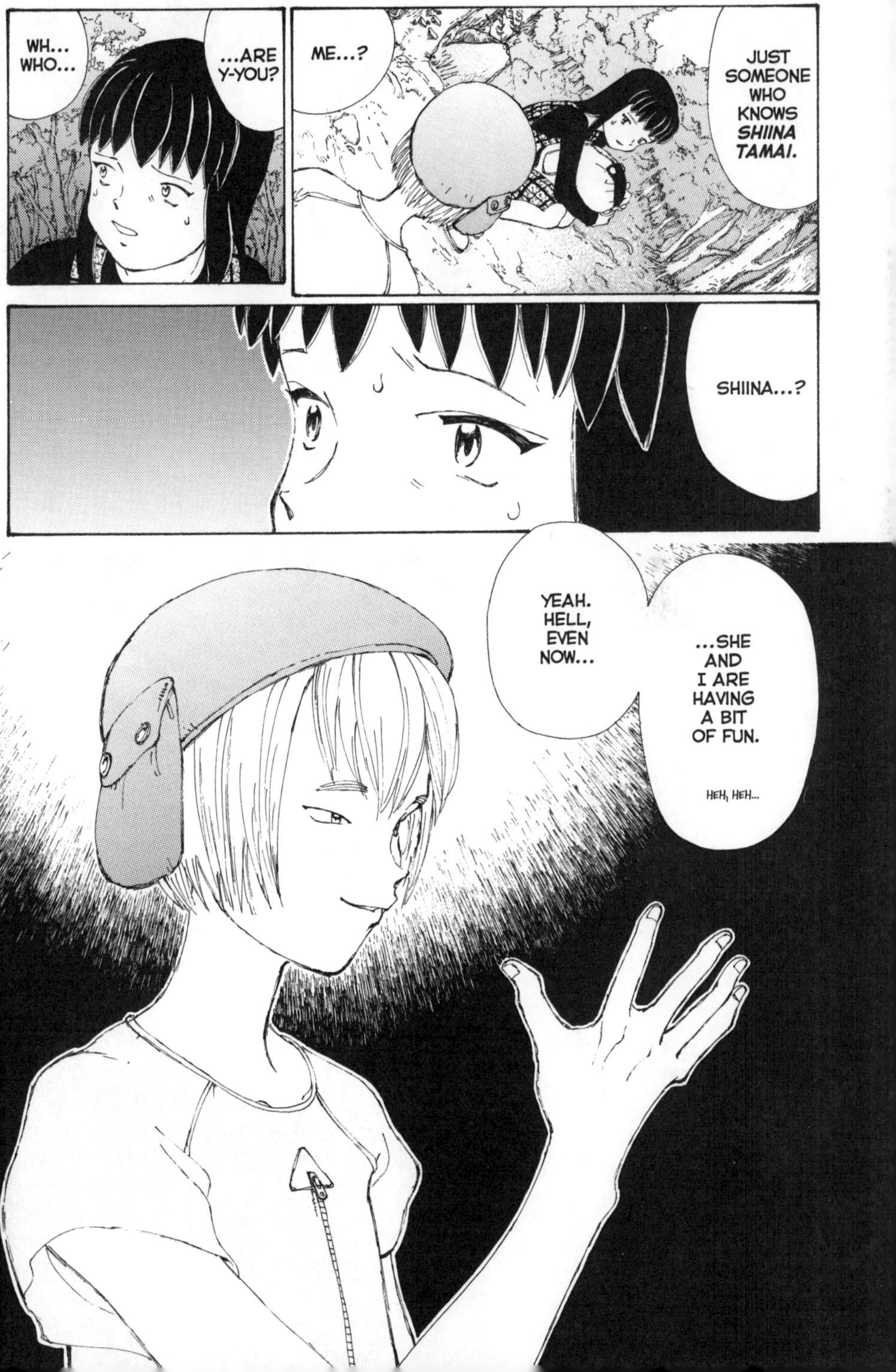
WH... WHO...
...ARE Y-YOU?
ME...?
JUST SOMEONE WHO KNOWS *SHIINA TAMAI.*
SHIINA...?
YEAH. HELL, EVEN NOW...
...SHE AND I ARE HAVING A BIT OF FUN.
HEH, HEH...

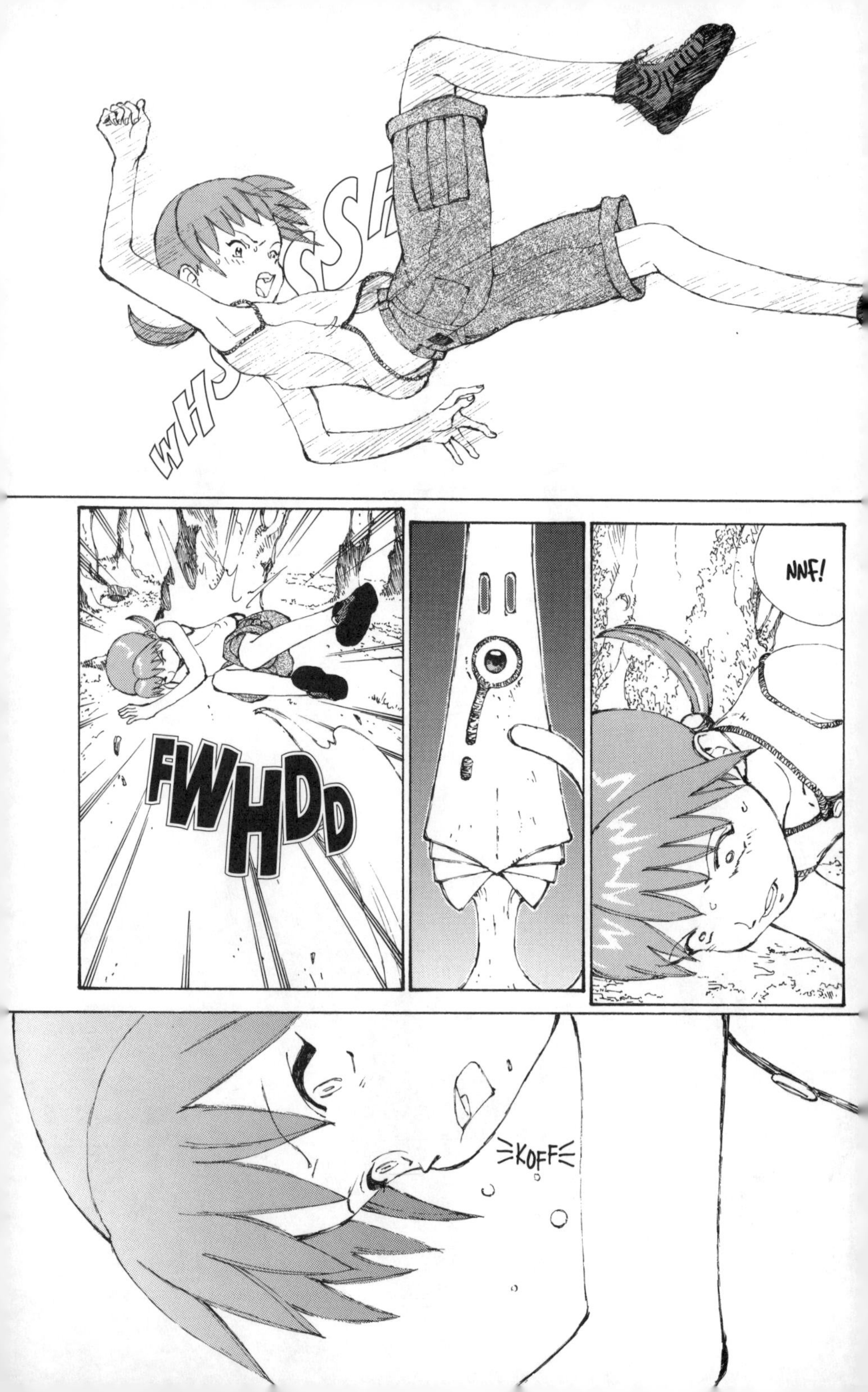
NNF!
FWHDD
KOFF

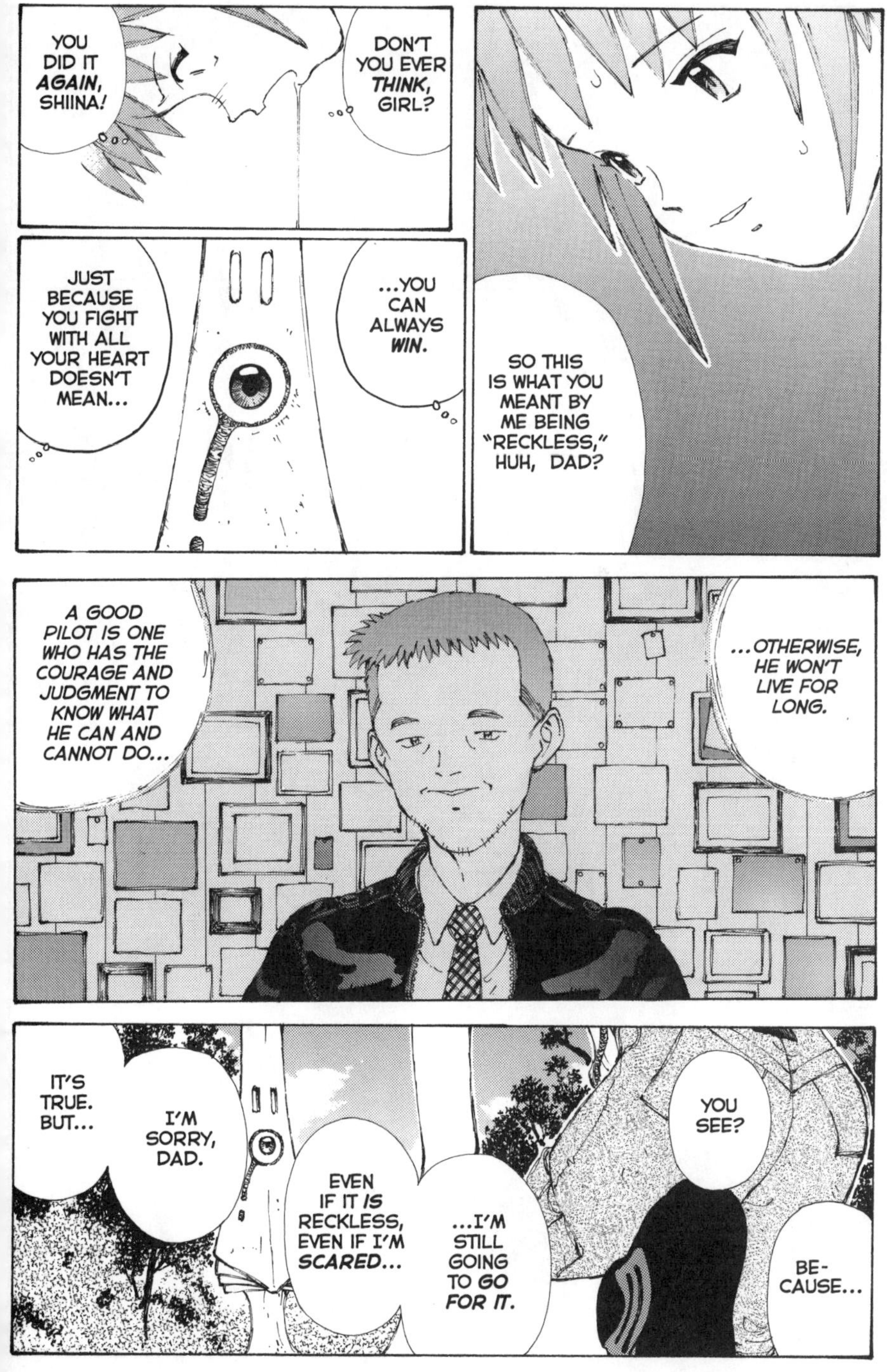
YOU DID IT *AGAIN*, SHIINA!
DON'T YOU EVER *THINK*, GIRL?
JUST BECAUSE YOU FIGHT WITH ALL YOUR HEART DOESN'T MEAN...
...YOU CAN ALWAYS *WIN*.
SO THIS IS WHAT YOU MEANT BY ME BEING "RECKLESS," HUH, DAD?
A GOOD PILOT IS ONE WHO HAS THE COURAGE AND JUDGMENT TO KNOW WHAT HE CAN AND CANNOT DO...
...OTHERWISE, HE WON'T LIVE FOR LONG.
IT'S TRUE. BUT...
I'M SORRY, DAD.
EVEN IF IT *IS* RECKLESS, EVEN IF I'M *SCARED*...
...I'M STILL GOING TO *GO FOR IT*.
YOU SEE?
BE-CAUSE...

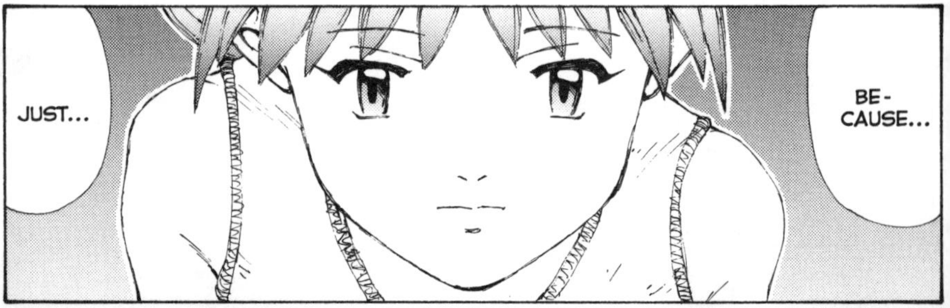
JUST...
BE-CAUSE...
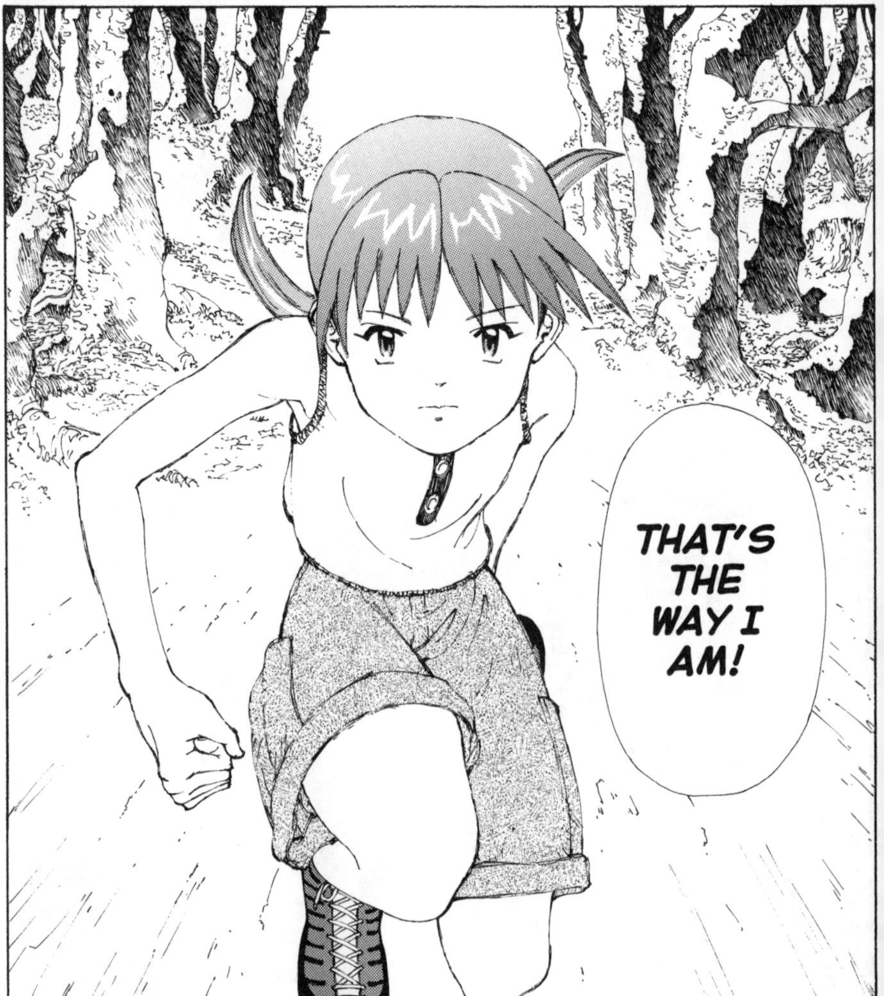
THAT'S THE WAY I AM!

KNIFE-EDGE

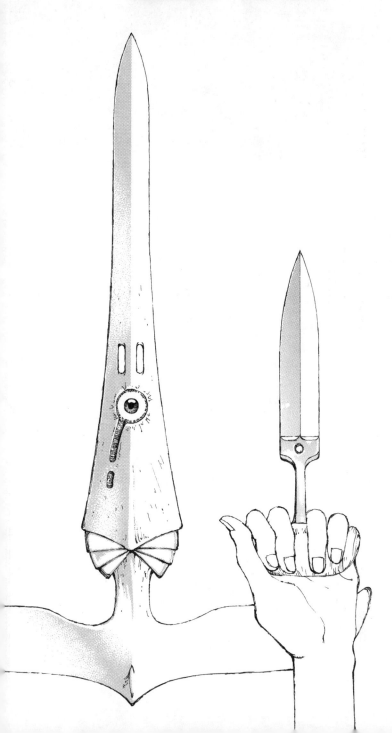

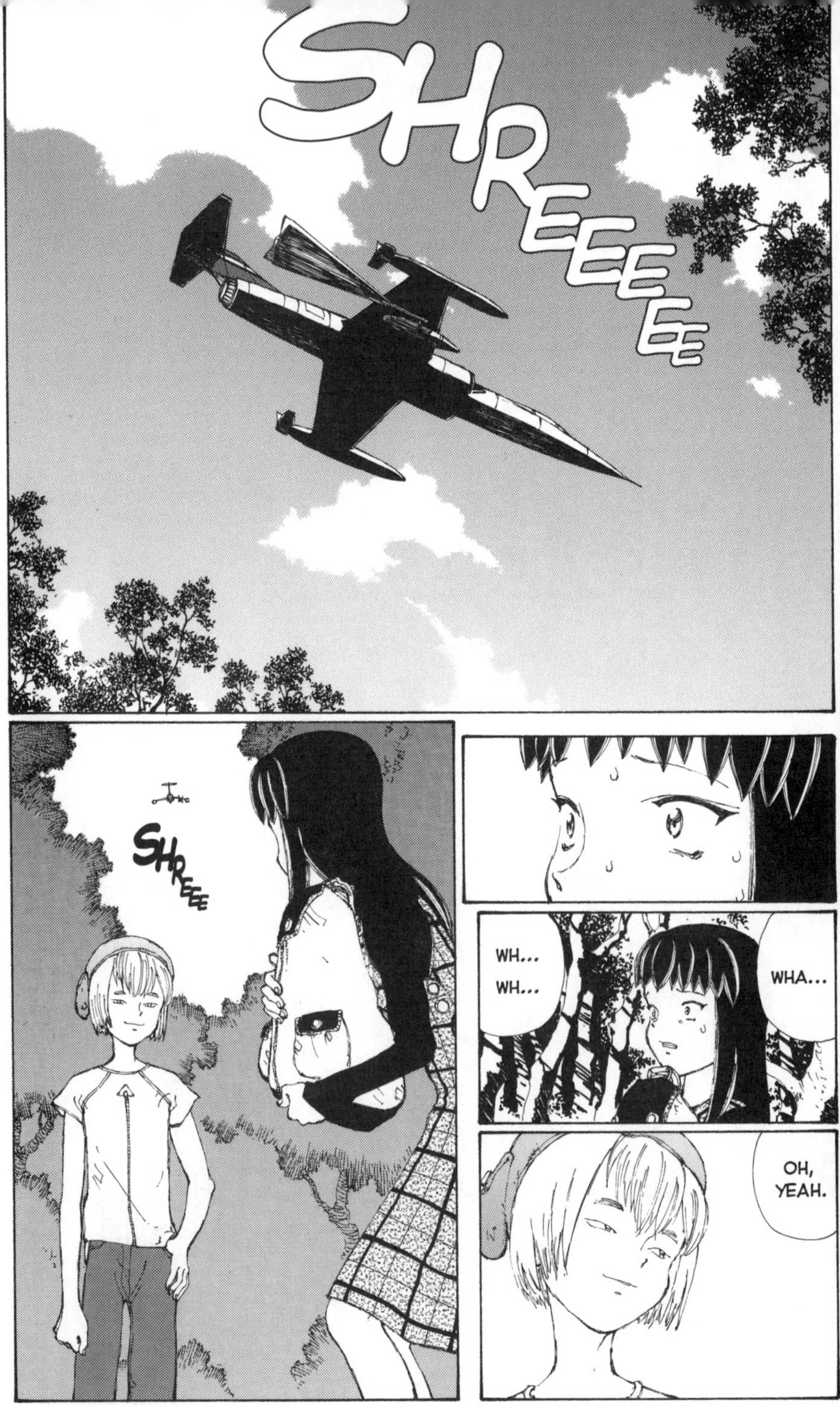
SHREEEEEE
WHA...
WH...
WH...
OH, YEAH.
SHREEE

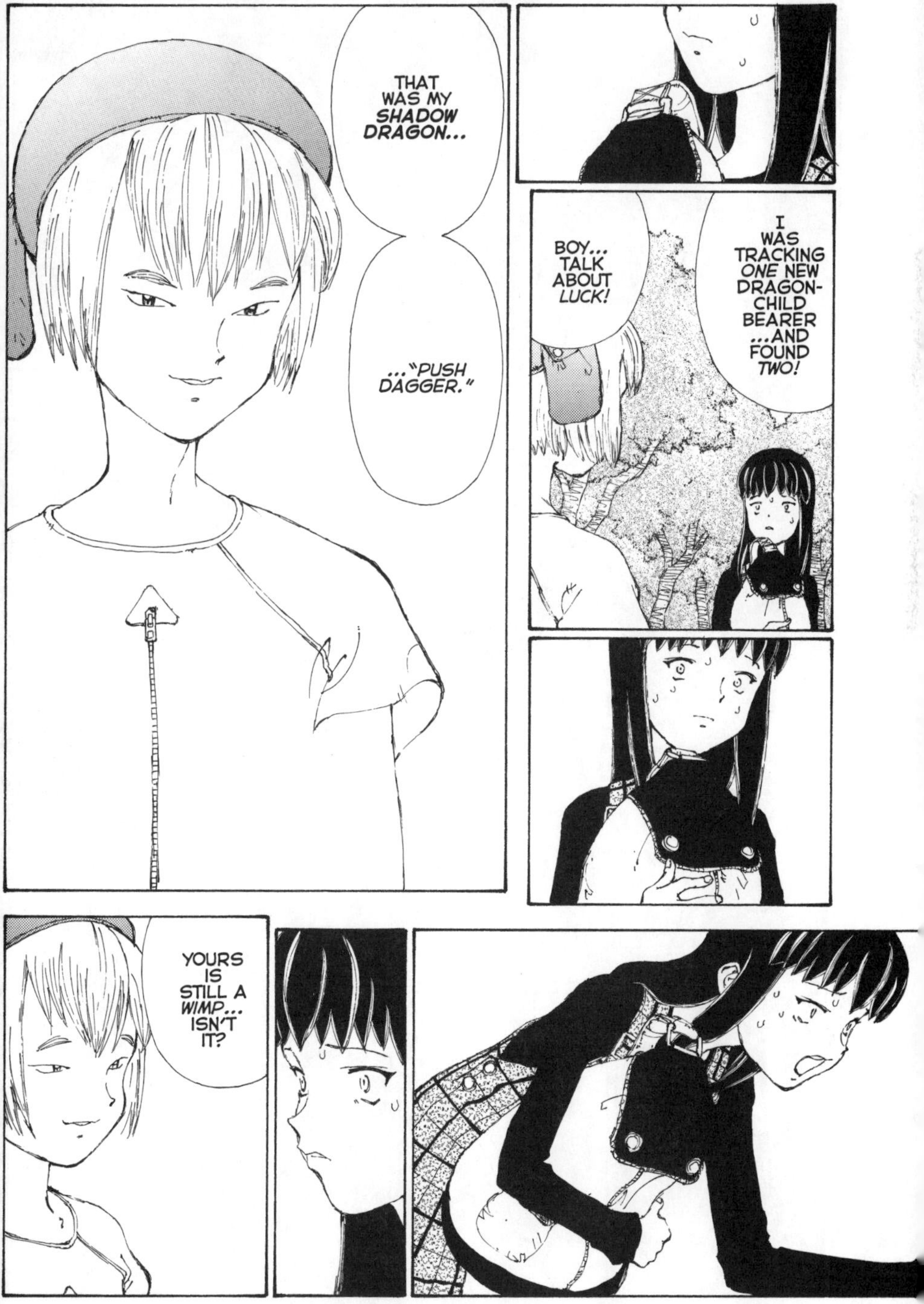
I WAS TRACKING ONE NEW DRAGON-CHILD BEARER ...AND FOUND TWO!
BOY... TALK ABOUT LUCK!
THAT WAS MY SHADOW DRAGON...
..."PUSH DAGGER."
YOURS IS STILL A WIMP... ISN'T IT?

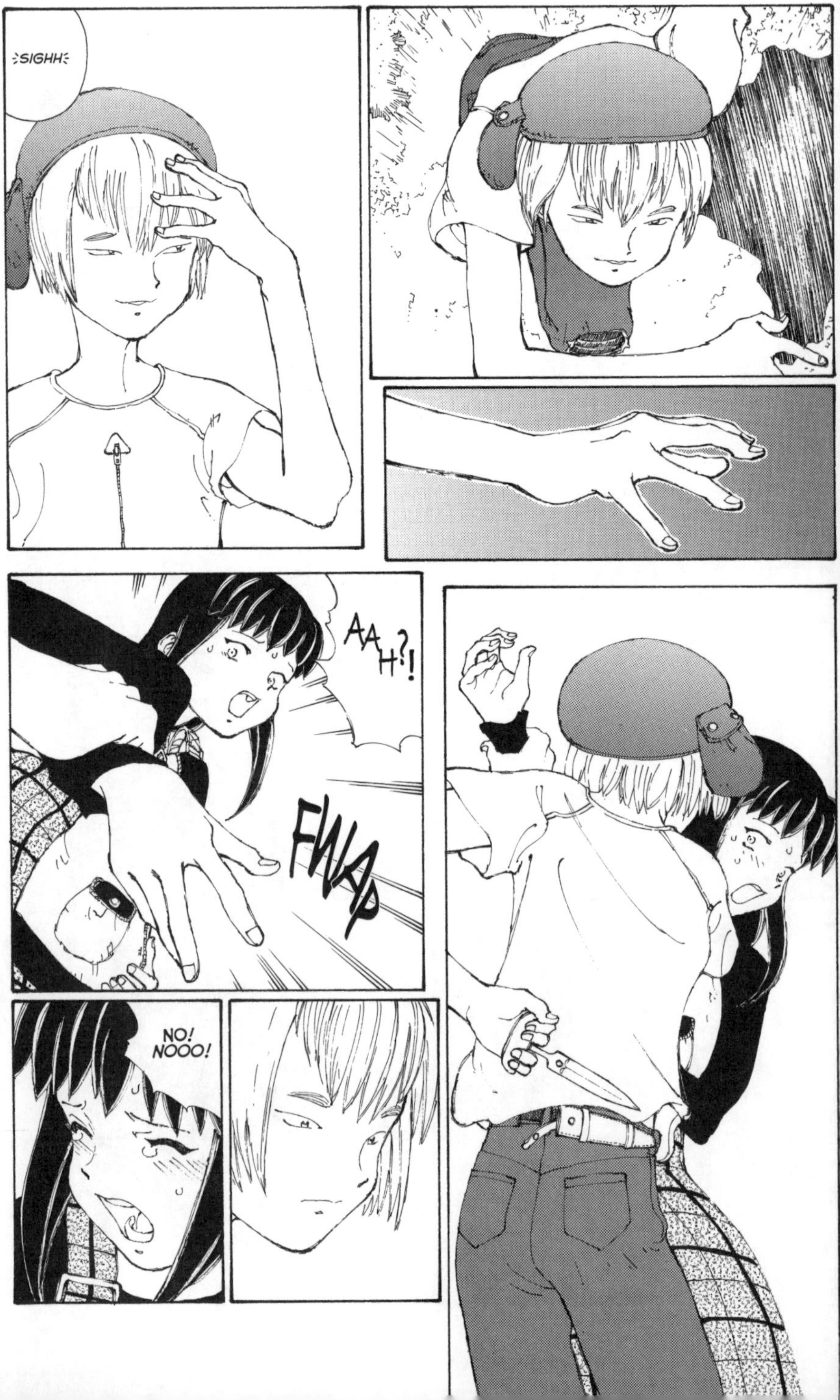

SIGHH
AAH?!
FWAP
NO! NOOO!

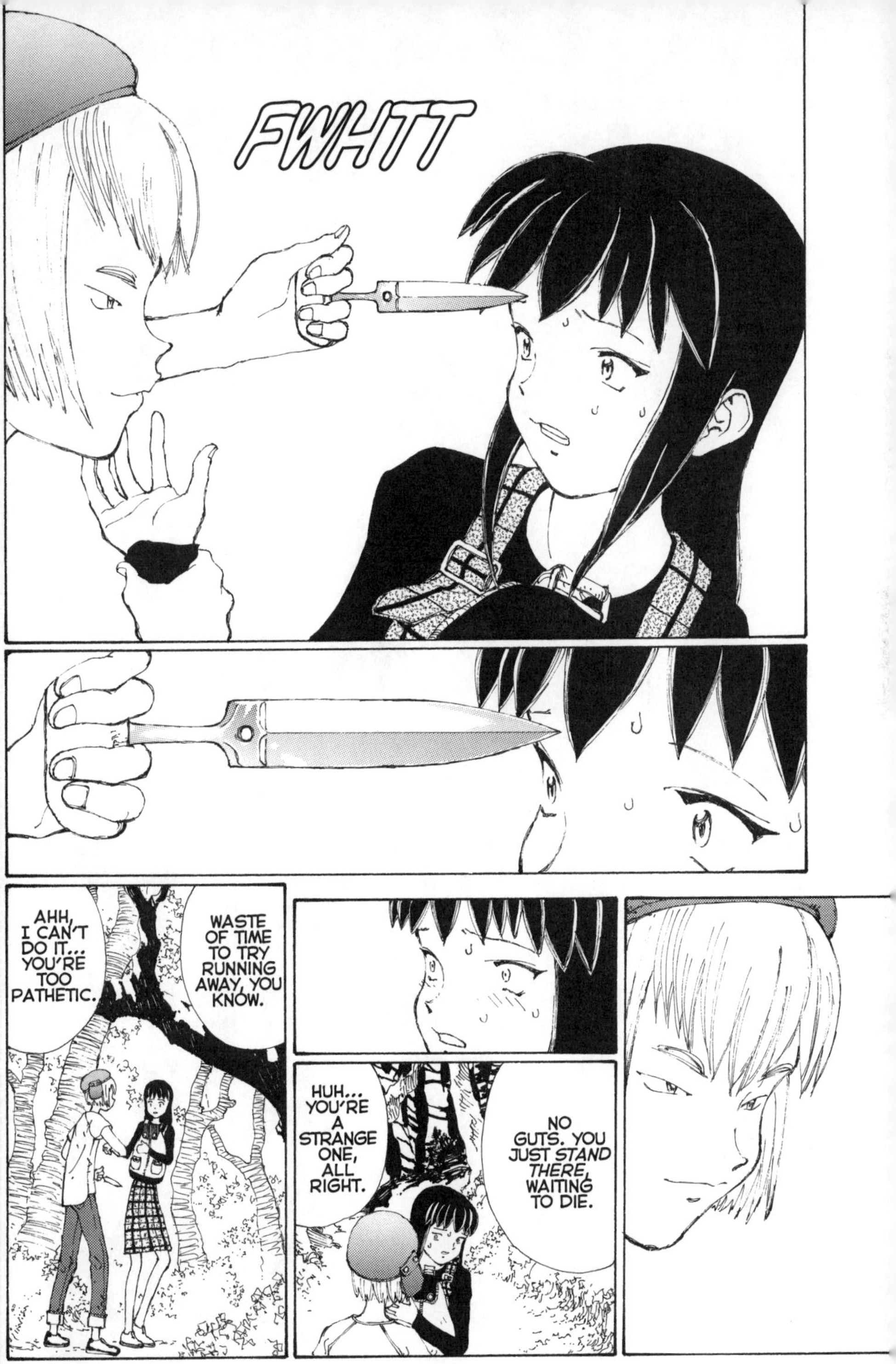
FWHTT
NO GUTS. YOU JUST *STAND THERE*, WAITING TO DIE.
HUH... YOU'RE A STRANGE ONE, ALL RIGHT.
WASTE OF TIME TO TRY RUNNING AWAY, YOU KNOW.
AHH, I CAN'T DO IT... YOU'RE TOO PATHETIC.

FUNNY TYPE FOR A DRAGONCHILD TO LIKE...

OWW!!

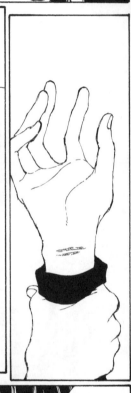

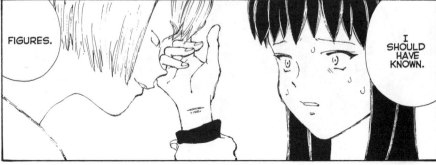

FIGURES.

I SHOULD HAVE KNOWN.

YOU'RE A COWARD.

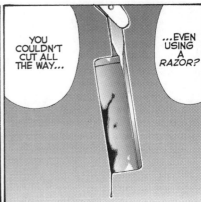

YOU COULDN'T CUT ALL THE WAY...

...EVEN USING A RAZOR?

HURTS, DOESN'T IT? CUTTING YOUR WRISTS...

...!

MOST PEOPLE BEND THEIR HANDS BACK. THAT MAKES THE VEINS SLIP BEHIND THE MUSCLE AND TENDONS AND STUFF, SO THEN YOU GOTTA CUT REALLY DEEP.

BUT IT HURTS. SO YOU WIMP OUT-- RIGHT?

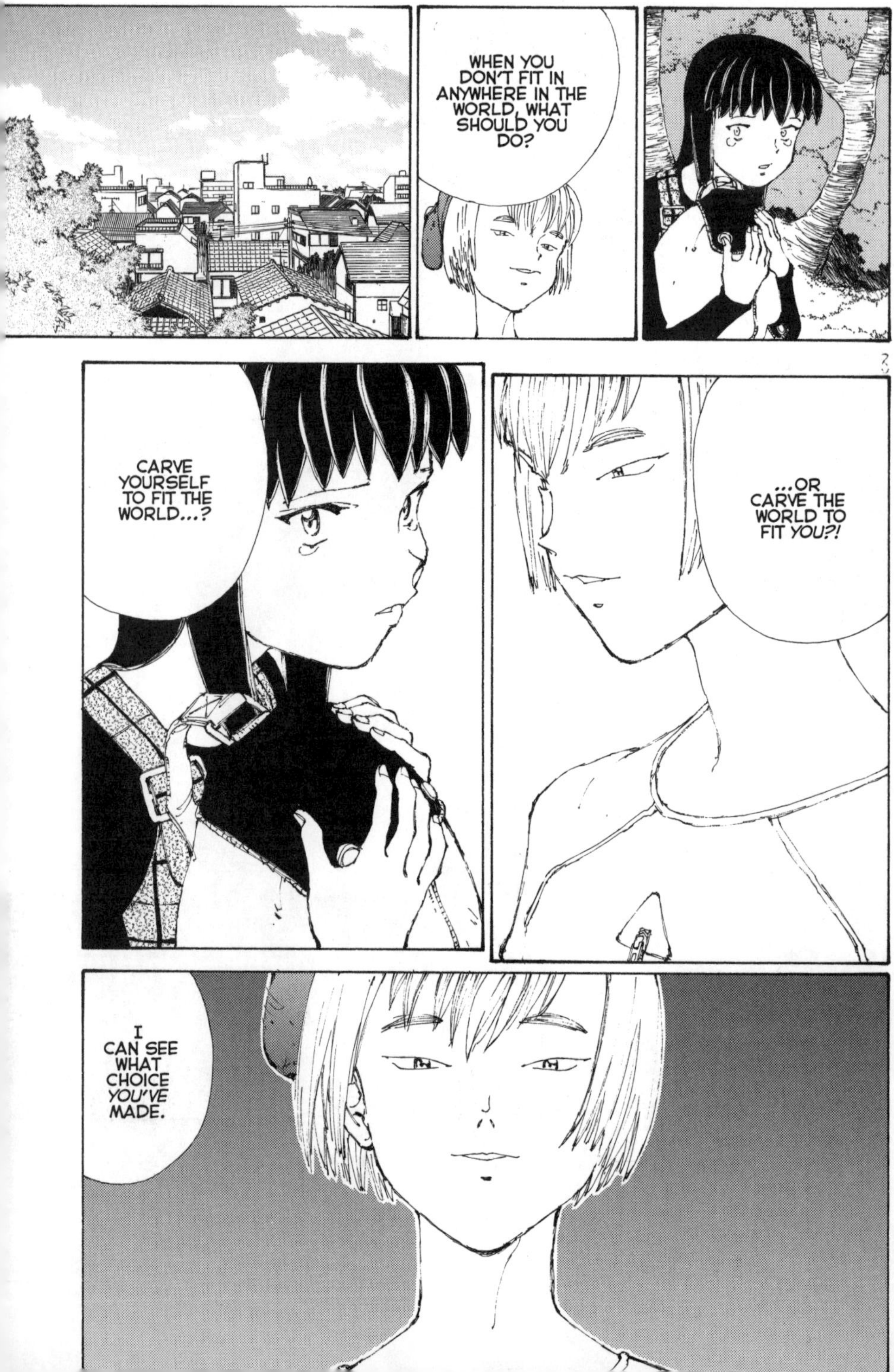
WHEN YOU DON'T FIT IN ANYWHERE IN THE WORLD, WHAT SHOULD YOU DO?
CARVE YOURSELF TO FIT THE WORLD...?
...OR CARVE THE WORLD TO FIT *YOU?!*
I CAN SEE WHAT CHOICE *YOU'VE* MADE.

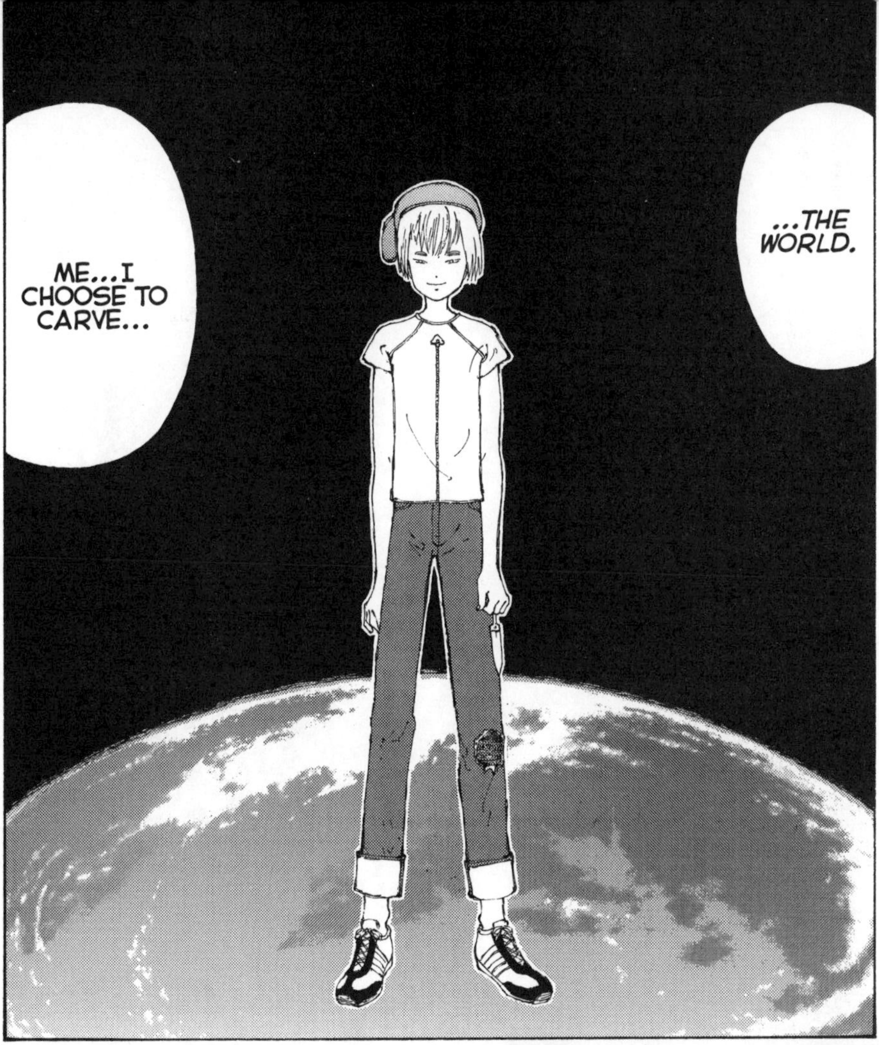
ME...I CHOOSE TO CARVE...
...THE WORLD.
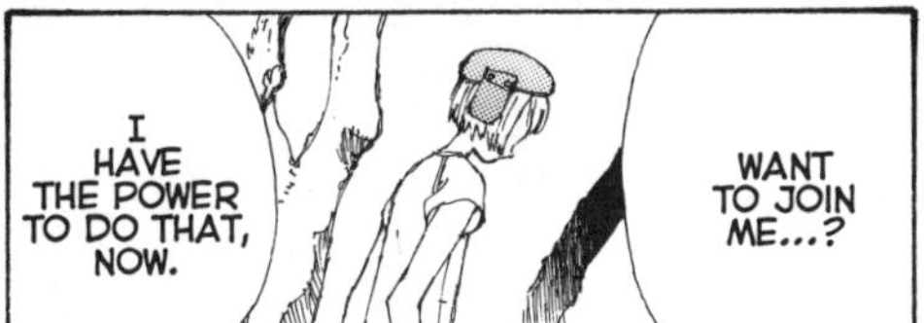
I HAVE THE POWER TO DO THAT, NOW.
WANT TO JOIN ME...?
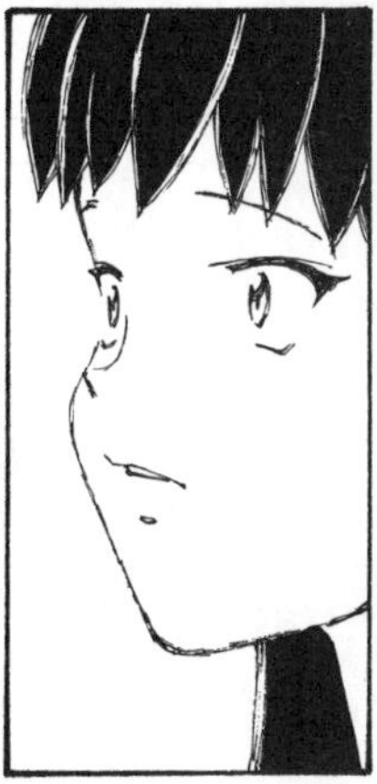
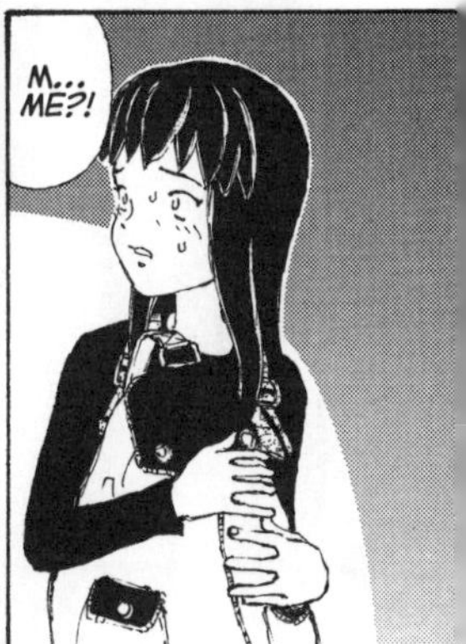
M... ME?!

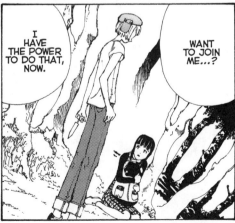

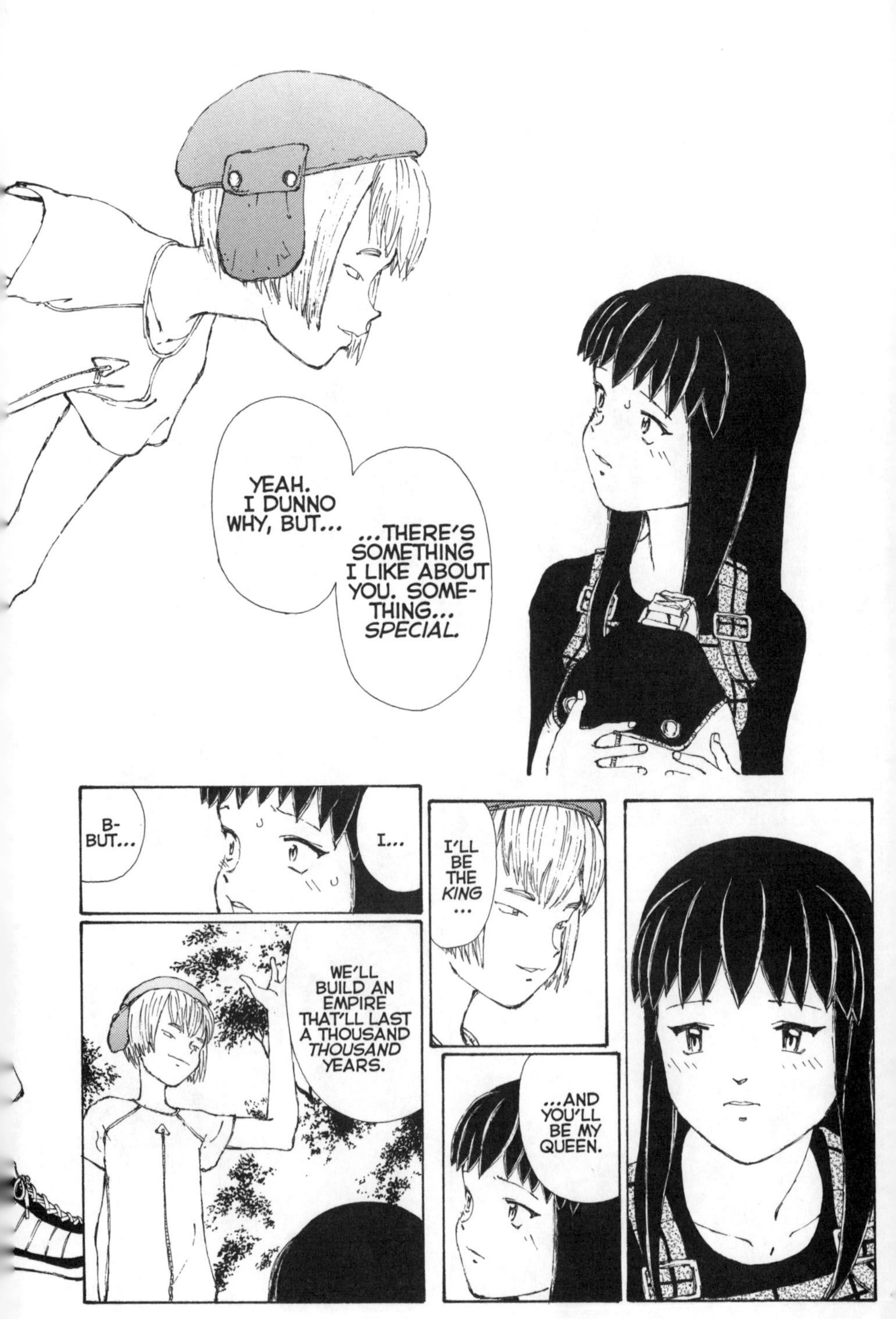
YEAH. I DUNNO WHY, BUT...
...THERE'S SOMETHING I LIKE ABOUT YOU. SOME-THING... *SPECIAL.*
B- BUT...
I...
I'LL BE THE *KING*...
WE'LL BUILD AN EMPIRE THAT'LL LAST A THOUSAND *THOUSAND* YEARS.
...AND YOU'LL BE MY QUEEN.

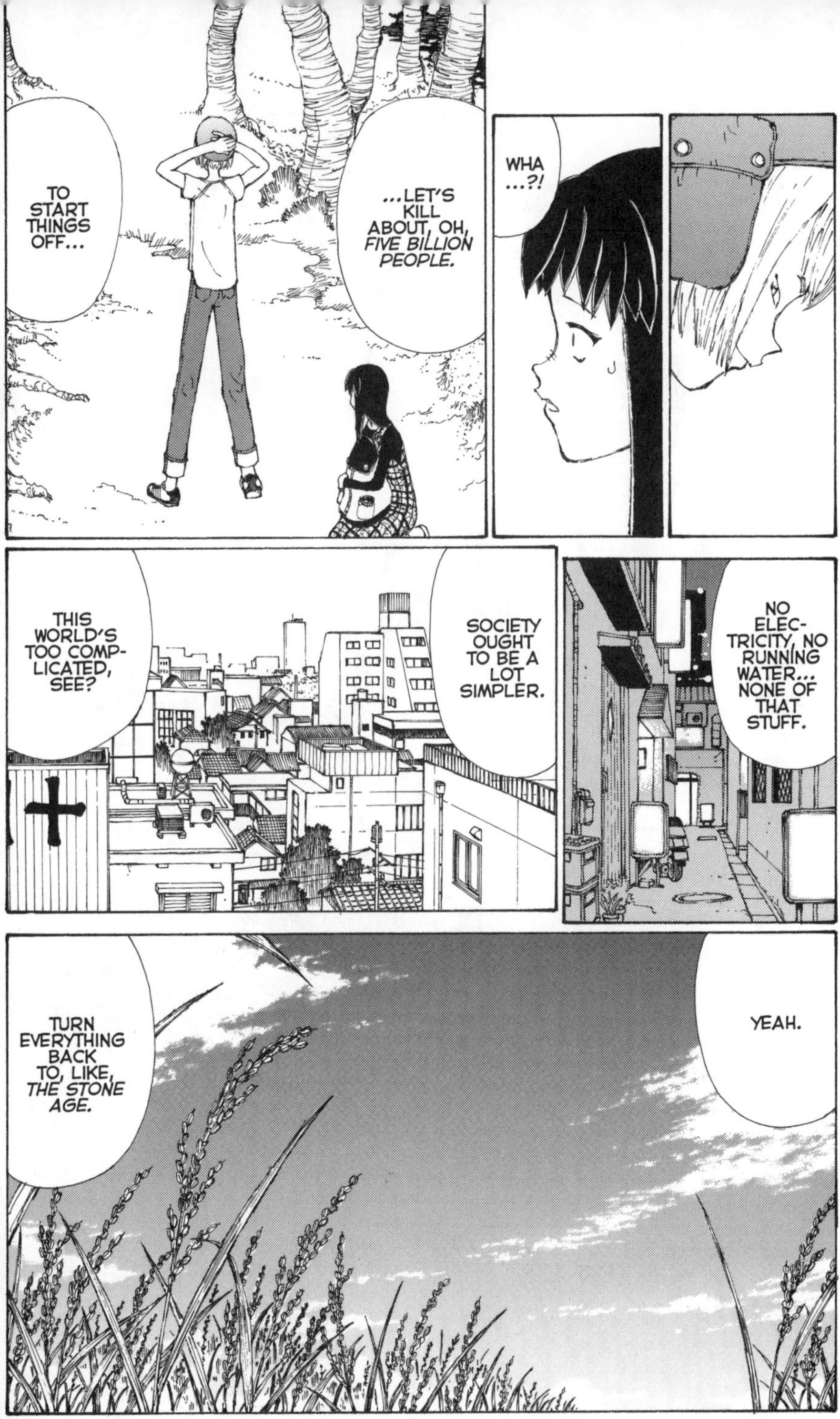
TO START THINGS OFF...
...LET'S KILL ABOUT, OH, *FIVE BILLION PEOPLE.*
WHA ...?!
THIS WORLD'S TOO COMPLICATED, SEE?
SOCIETY OUGHT TO BE A LOT SIMPLER.
NO ELECTRICITY, NO RUNNING WATER... NONE OF THAT STUFF.
TURN EVERYTHING BACK TO, LIKE, *THE STONE AGE.*
YEAH.

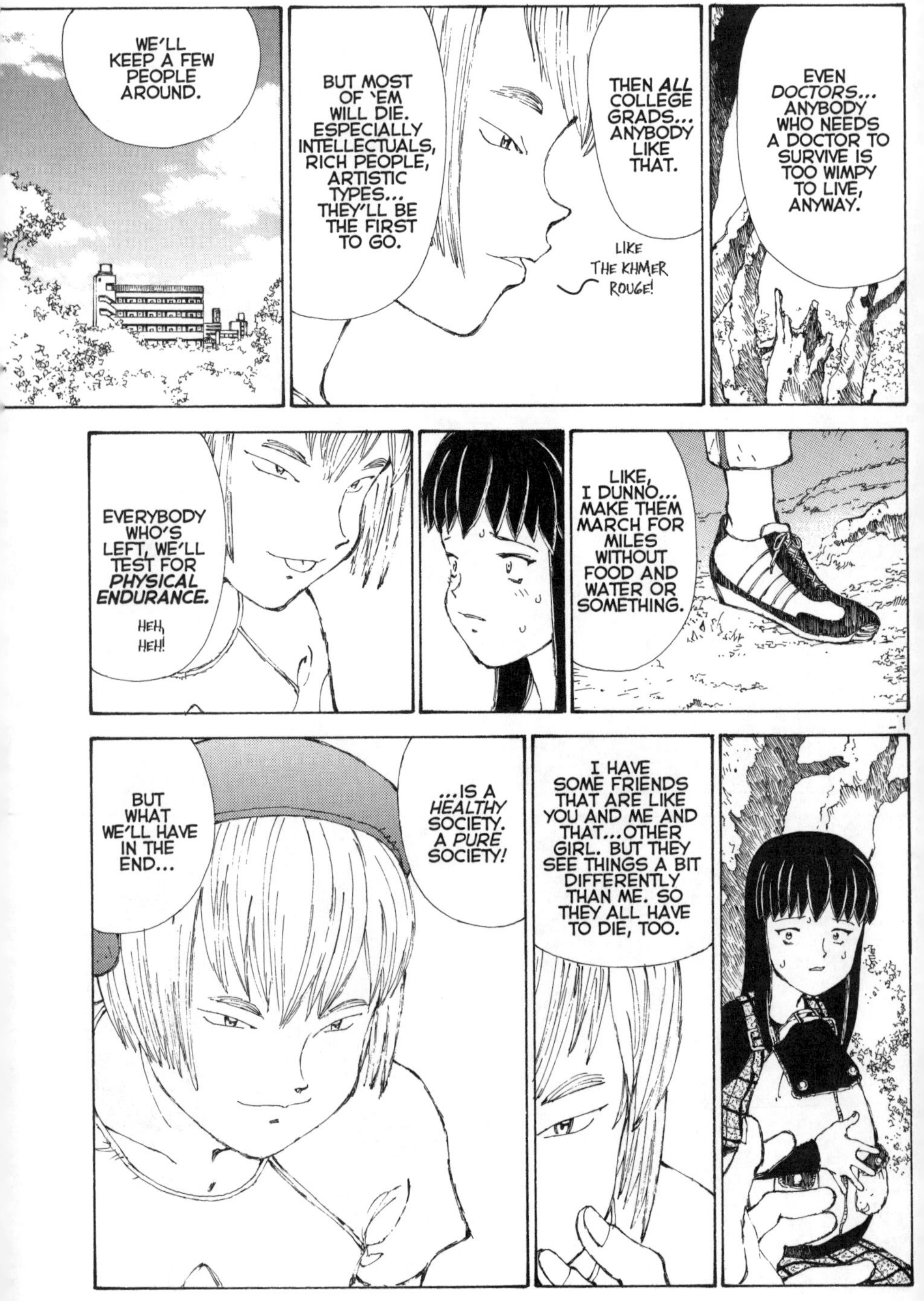
WE'LL KEEP A FEW PEOPLE AROUND.
BUT MOST OF 'EM WILL DIE. ESPECIALLY INTELLECTUALS, RICH PEOPLE, ARTISTIC TYPES... THEY'LL BE THE FIRST TO GO.
THEN ALL COLLEGE GRADS... ANYBODY LIKE THAT.
LIKE THE KHMER ROUGE!
EVEN DOCTORS... ANYBODY WHO NEEDS A DOCTOR TO SURVIVE IS TOO WIMPY TO LIVE, ANYWAY.
EVERYBODY WHO'S LEFT, WE'LL TEST FOR PHYSICAL ENDURANCE.
HEH, HEH!
LIKE, I DUNNO... MAKE THEM MARCH FOR MILES WITHOUT FOOD AND WATER OR SOMETHING.
BUT WHAT WE'LL HAVE IN THE END...
...IS A HEALTHY SOCIETY. A PURE SOCIETY!
I HAVE SOME FRIENDS THAT ARE LIKE YOU AND ME AND THAT...OTHER GIRL. BUT THEY SEE THINGS A BIT DIFFERENTLY THAN ME. SO THEY ALL HAVE TO DIE, TOO.

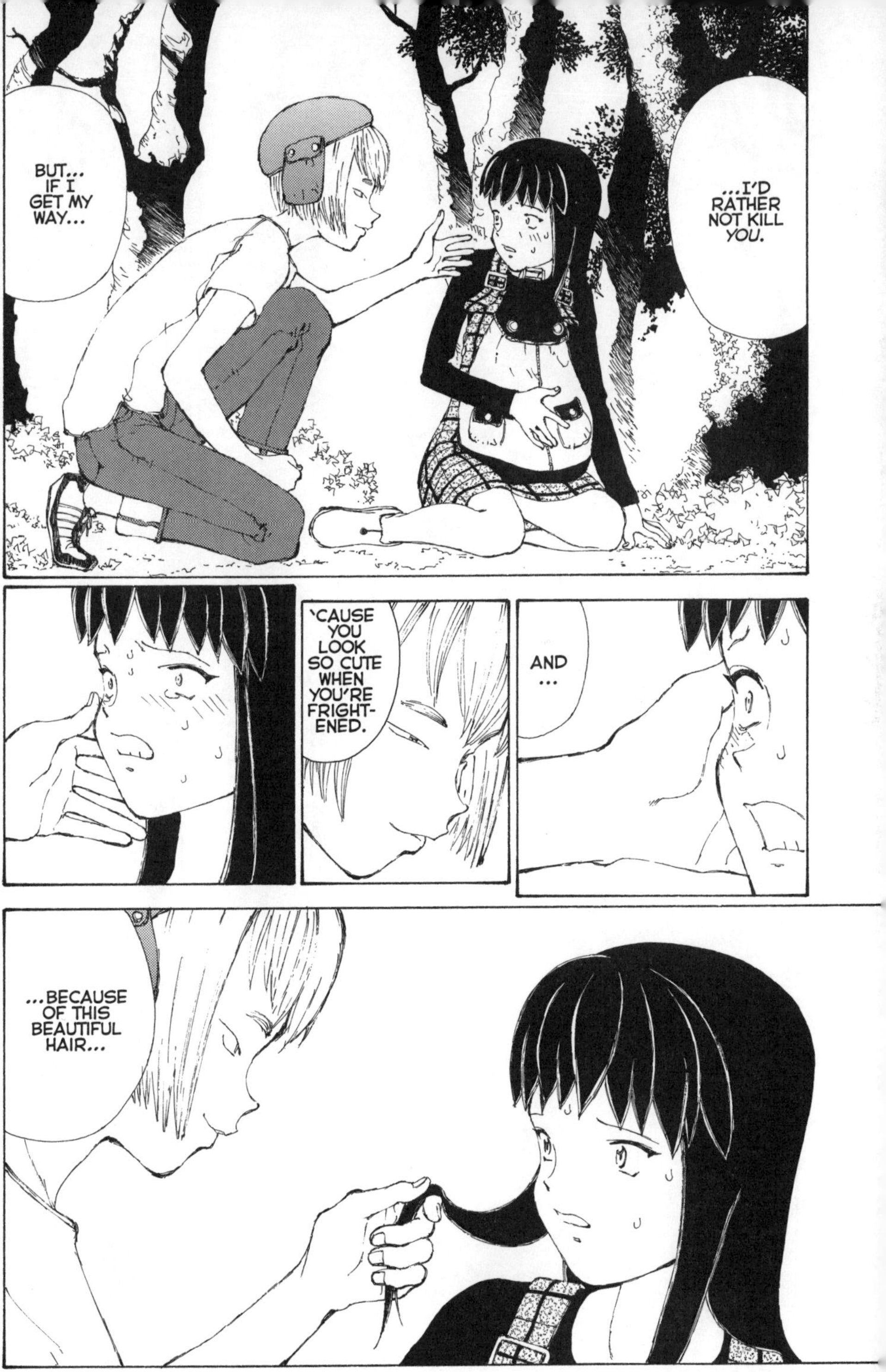
BUT... IF I GET MY WAY...
...I'D RATHER NOT KILL *YOU*.
'CAUSE YOU LOOK SO CUTE WHEN YOU'RE FRIGHT- ENED.
AND ...
...BECAUSE OF THIS BEAUTIFUL HAIR...

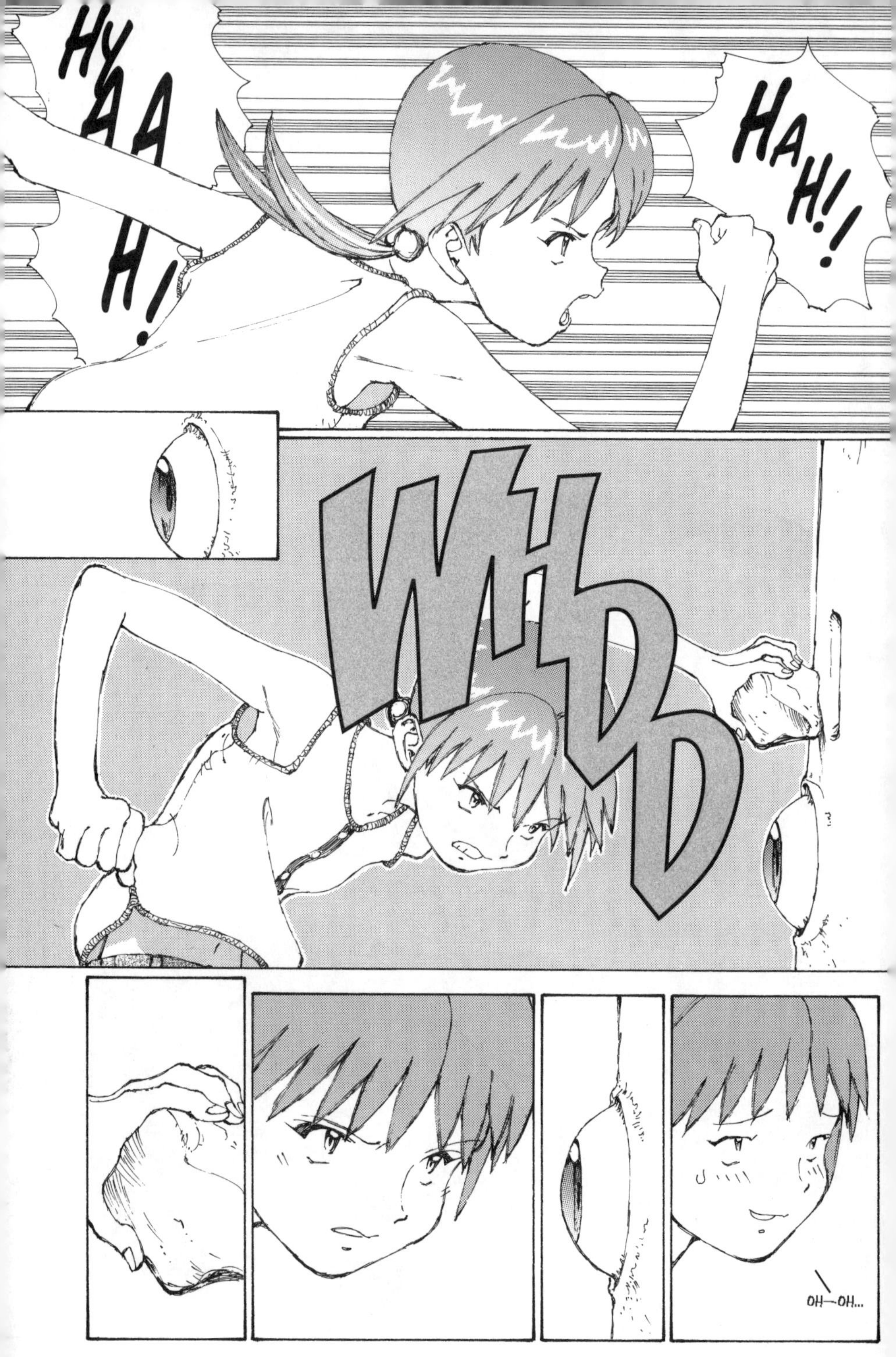
HAH!!
HYAAAH!!
WHUD
OH—OH...

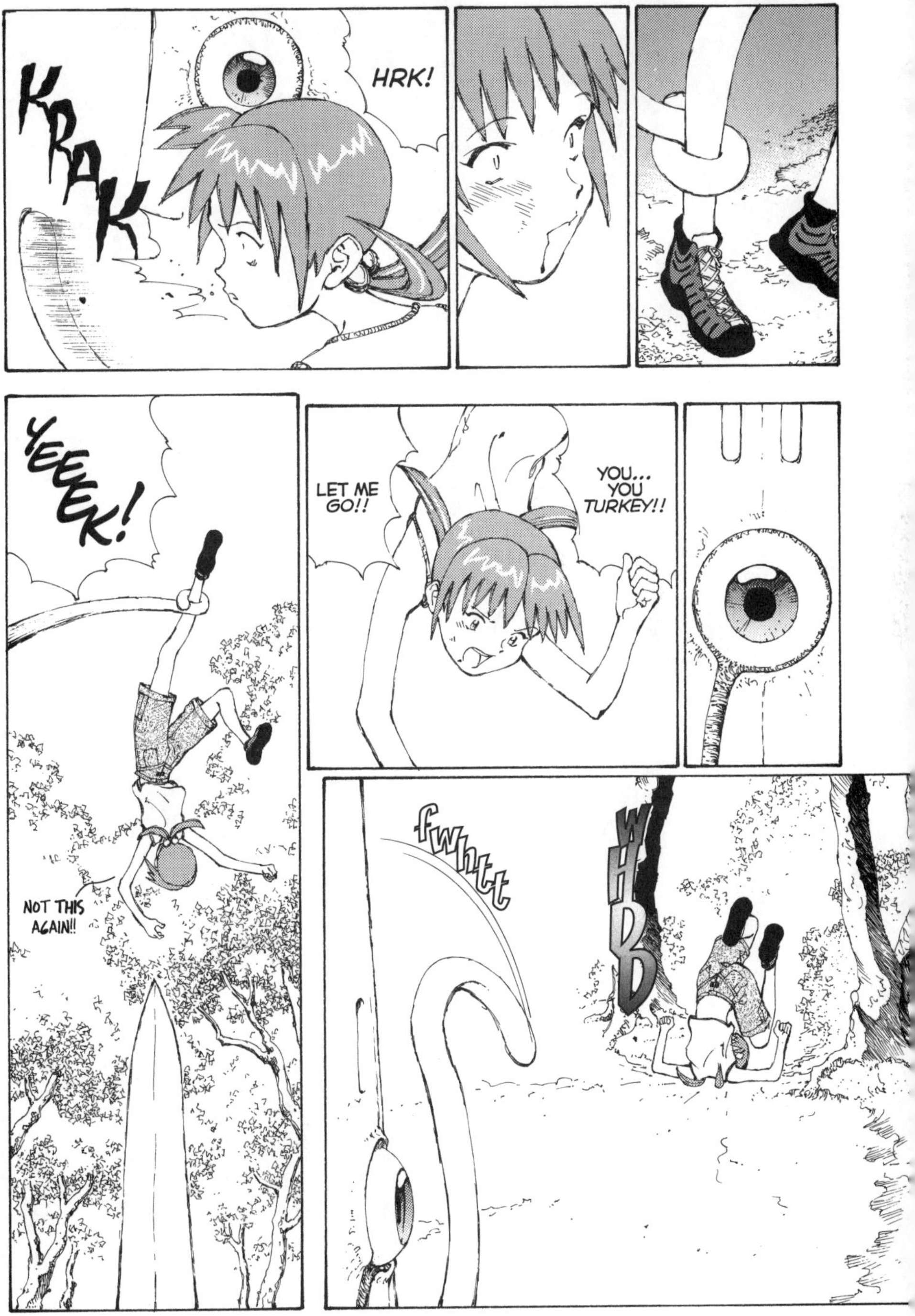
KRAK
HRK!
YEEEK!
NOT THIS AGAIN!!
LET ME GO!!
YOU... YOU TURKEY!!
fwhtt
WHDB

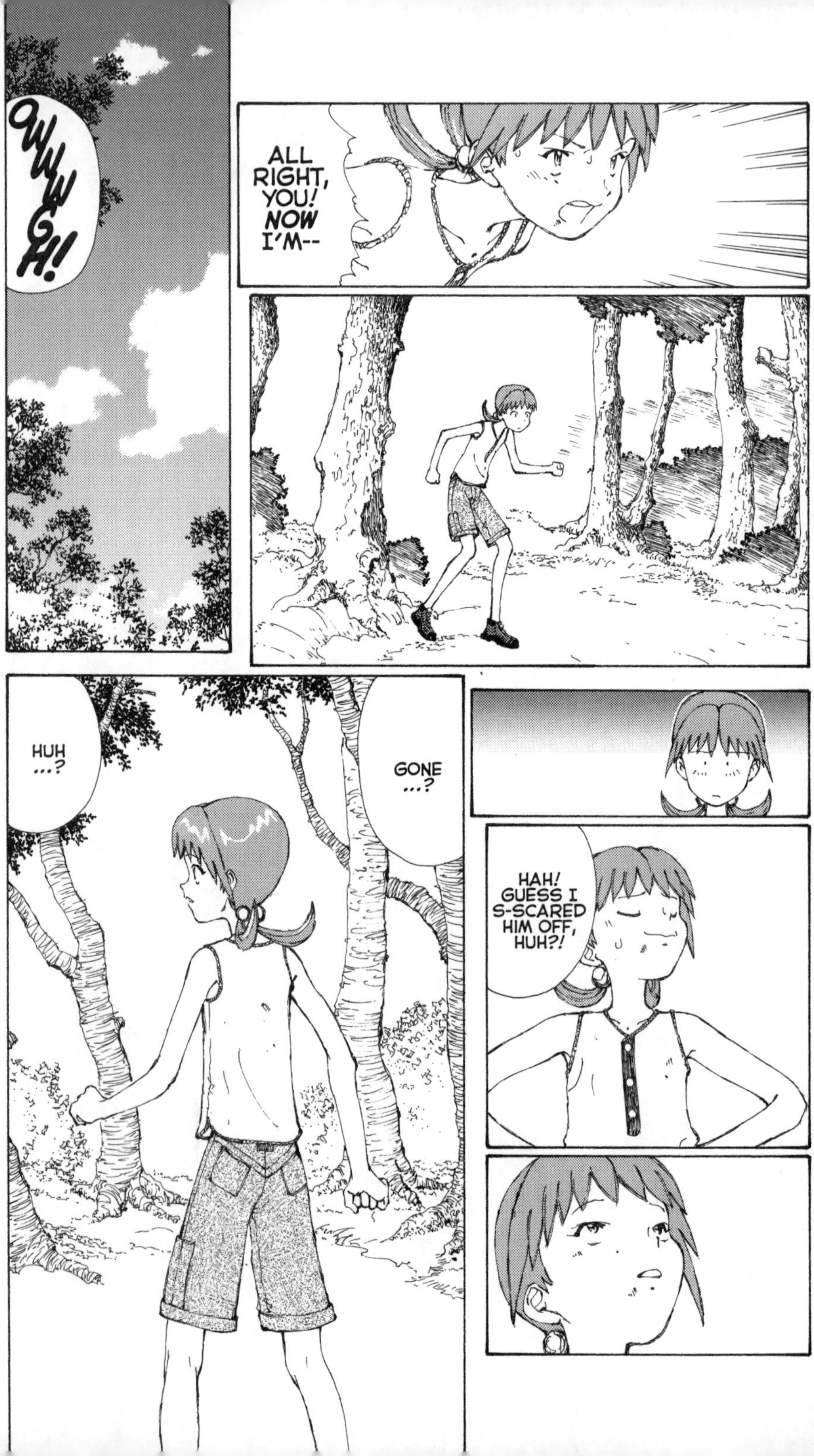
OWWWGH!
ALL RIGHT, YOU! NOW I'M--
HUH ...?
GONE ...?
HAH! GUESS I S-SCARED HIM OFF, HUH?!

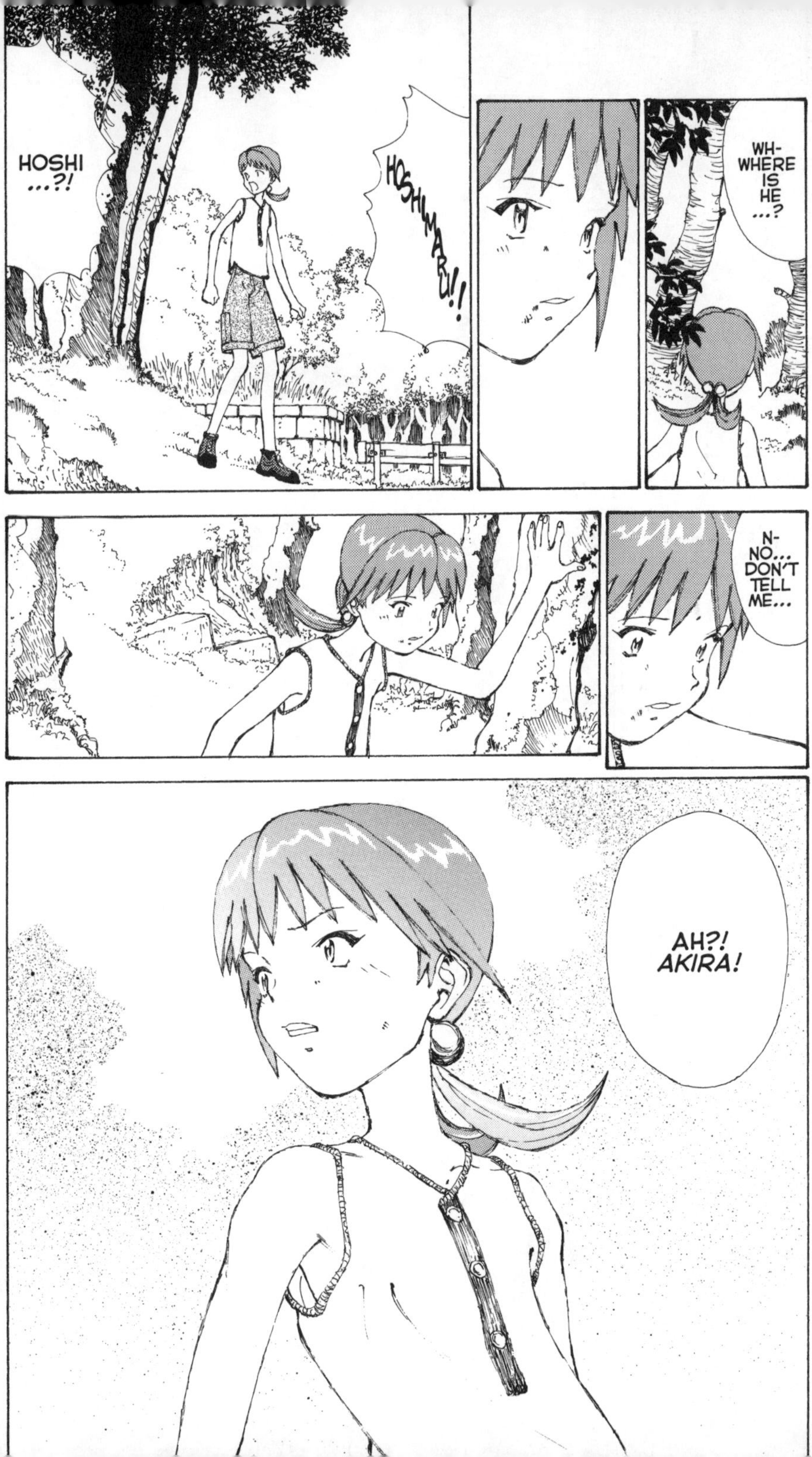
WH- WHERE IS HE ...?
HOSHI ...?!
HOSHIMARU!!
N- NO... DON'T TELL ME...
AH?! AKIRA!

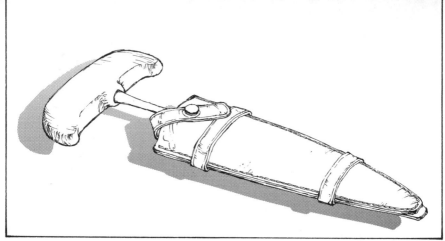

HERE. A
PRESENT.

BEND
YOUR
WRIST *IN*,
THEN
CUT
HARD...

...AND
YOU'LL
*DEFINITE-
LY* DIE.

CARVE
THE WORLD
WITH ME.

OR
CARVE
YOURSELF
ALONE.

CHOOSE.

I'LL
GIVE
YOU SOME
TIME. NOT
MUCH.

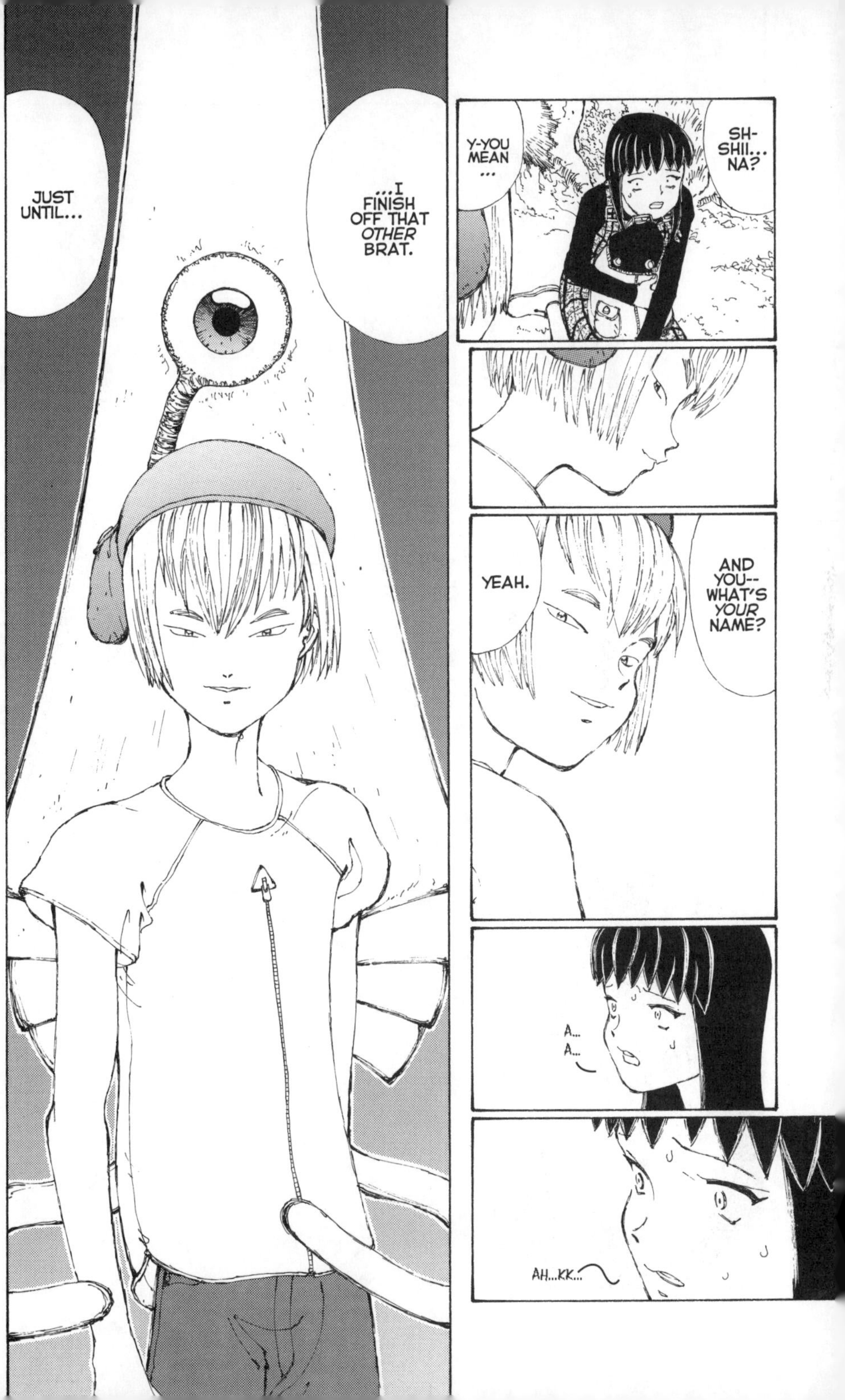
JUST UNTIL...
...I FINISH OFF THAT *OTHER* BRAT.
Y-YOU MEAN ...
SH-SHII... NA?
YEAH.
AND YOU-- WHAT'S *YOUR* NAME?
A... A...
AH...KK...

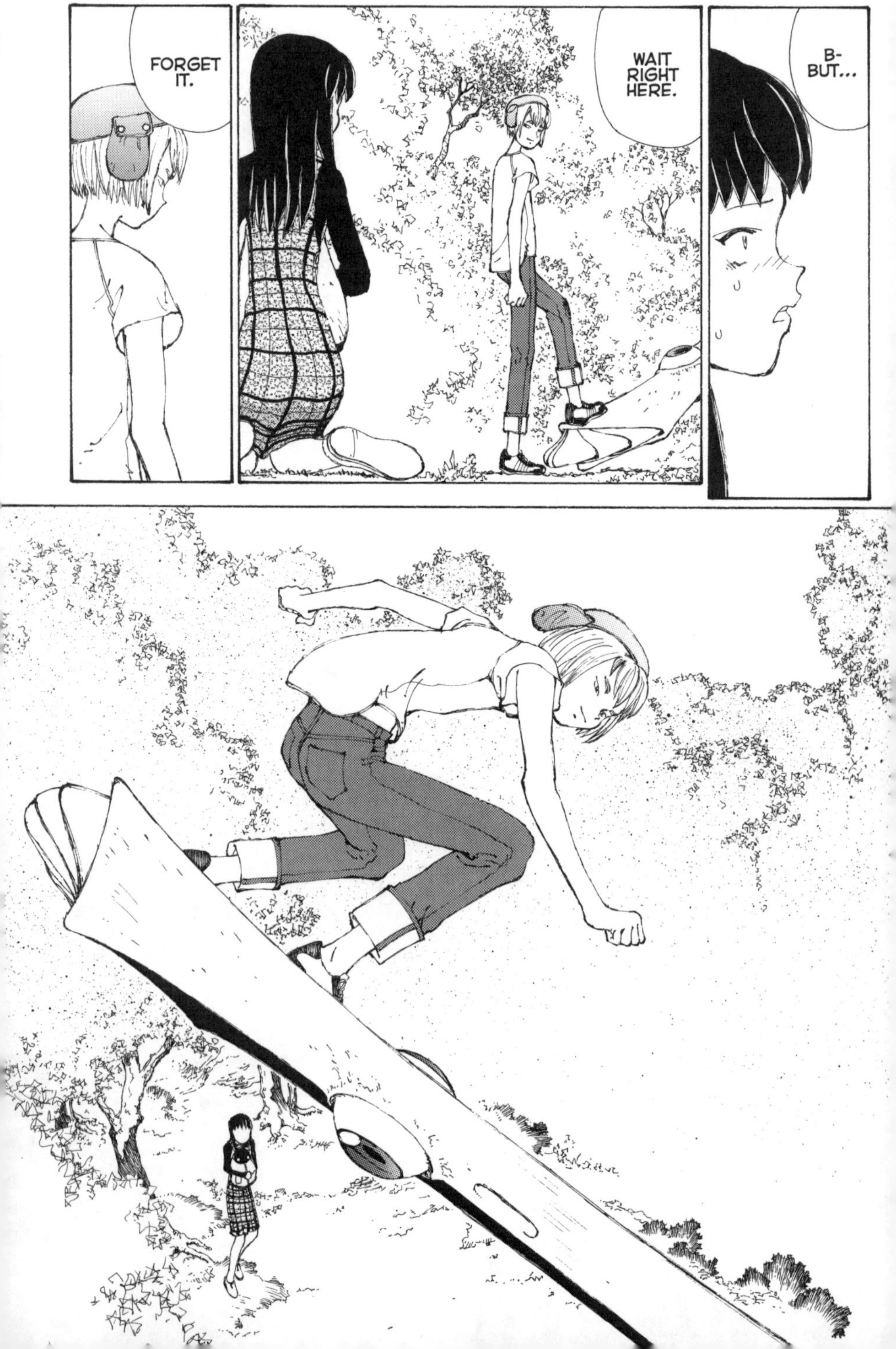
B- BUT...
WAIT RIGHT HERE.
FORGET IT.

OH...
OH...

WH...

WHAT
SHOULD
I...
D-*DO?!*

AH
....!

SH-
SHIINA'S
IN...
T-
TROUBLE!

BUT
I...I...HE
SAID...

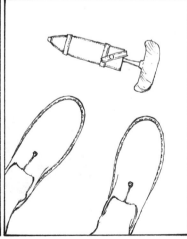

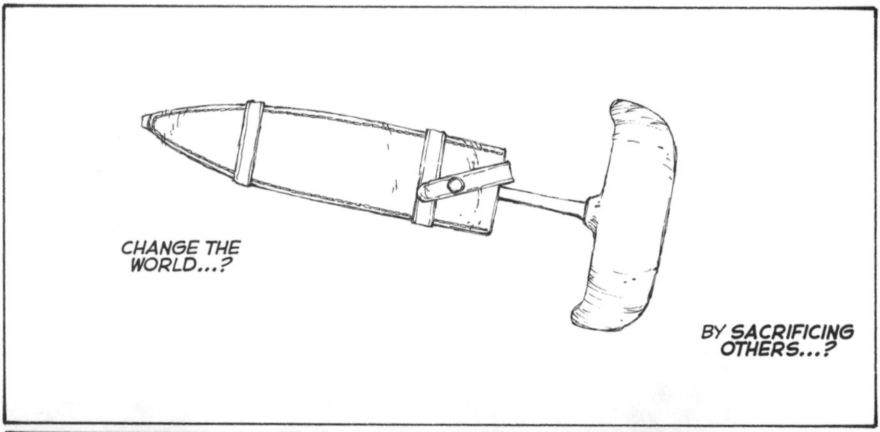
BY SACRIFICING OTHERS...?
CHANGE THE WORLD...?
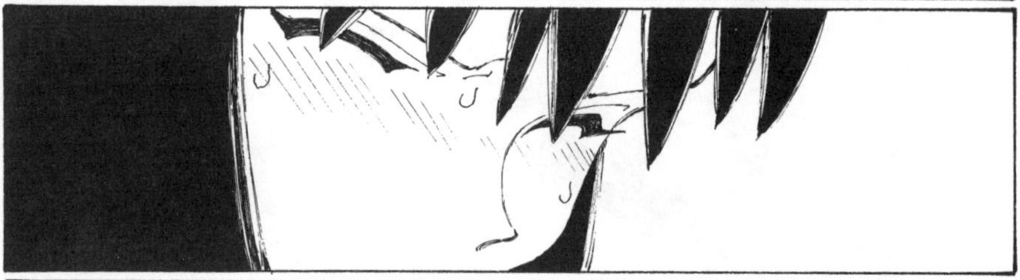
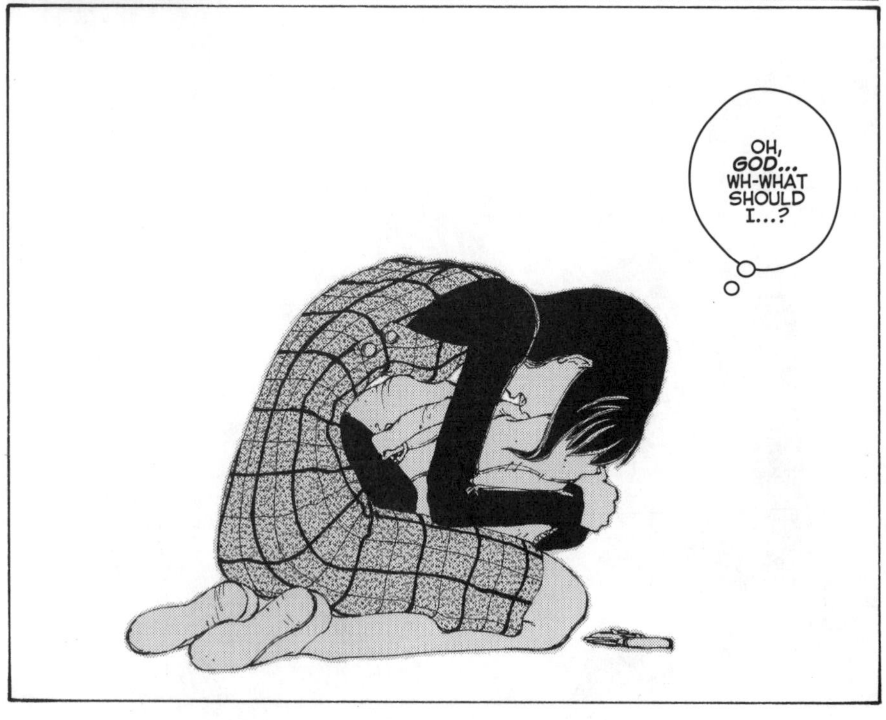
OH, GOD... WH-WHAT SHOULD I...?

BLOOD SACRIFICE

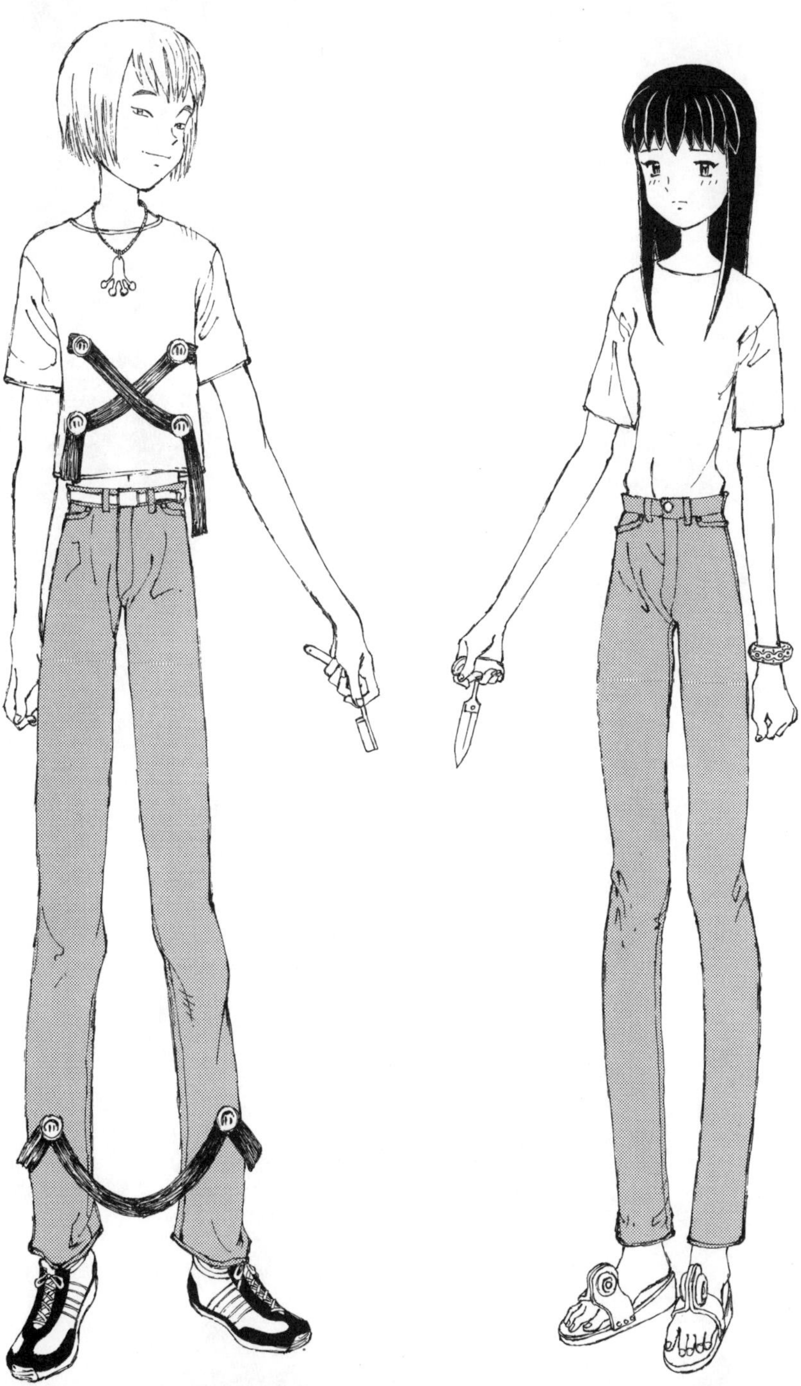

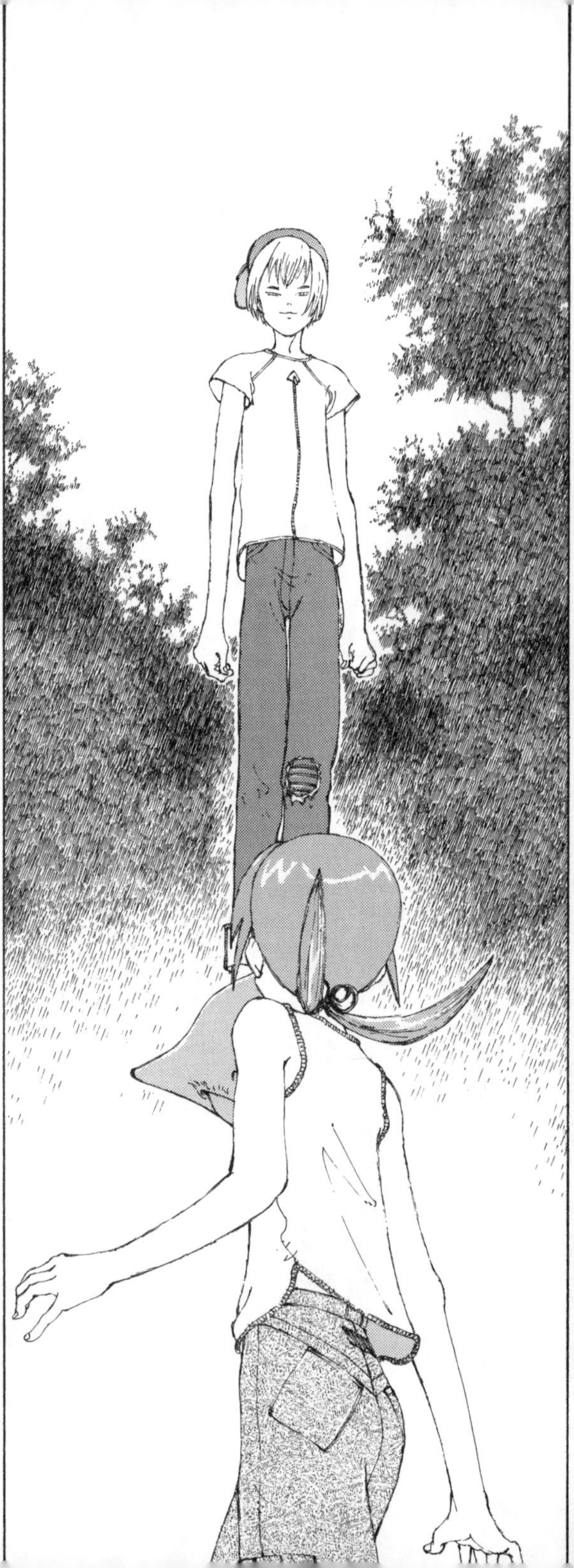

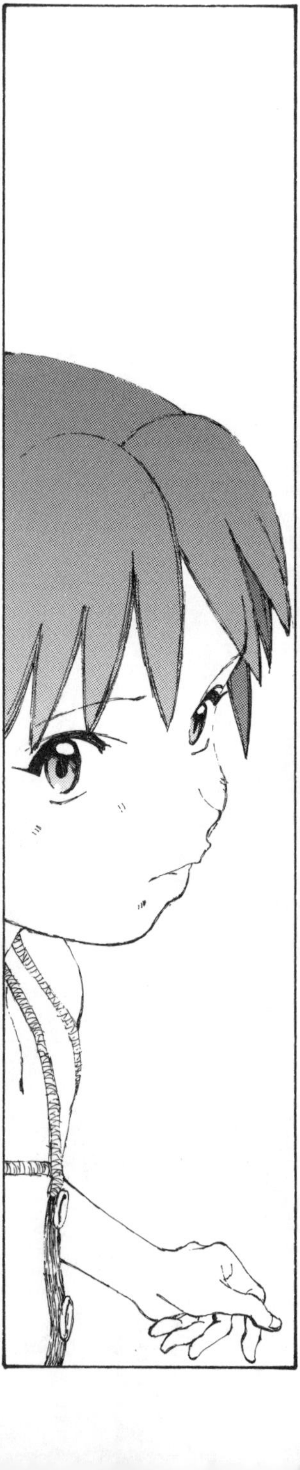

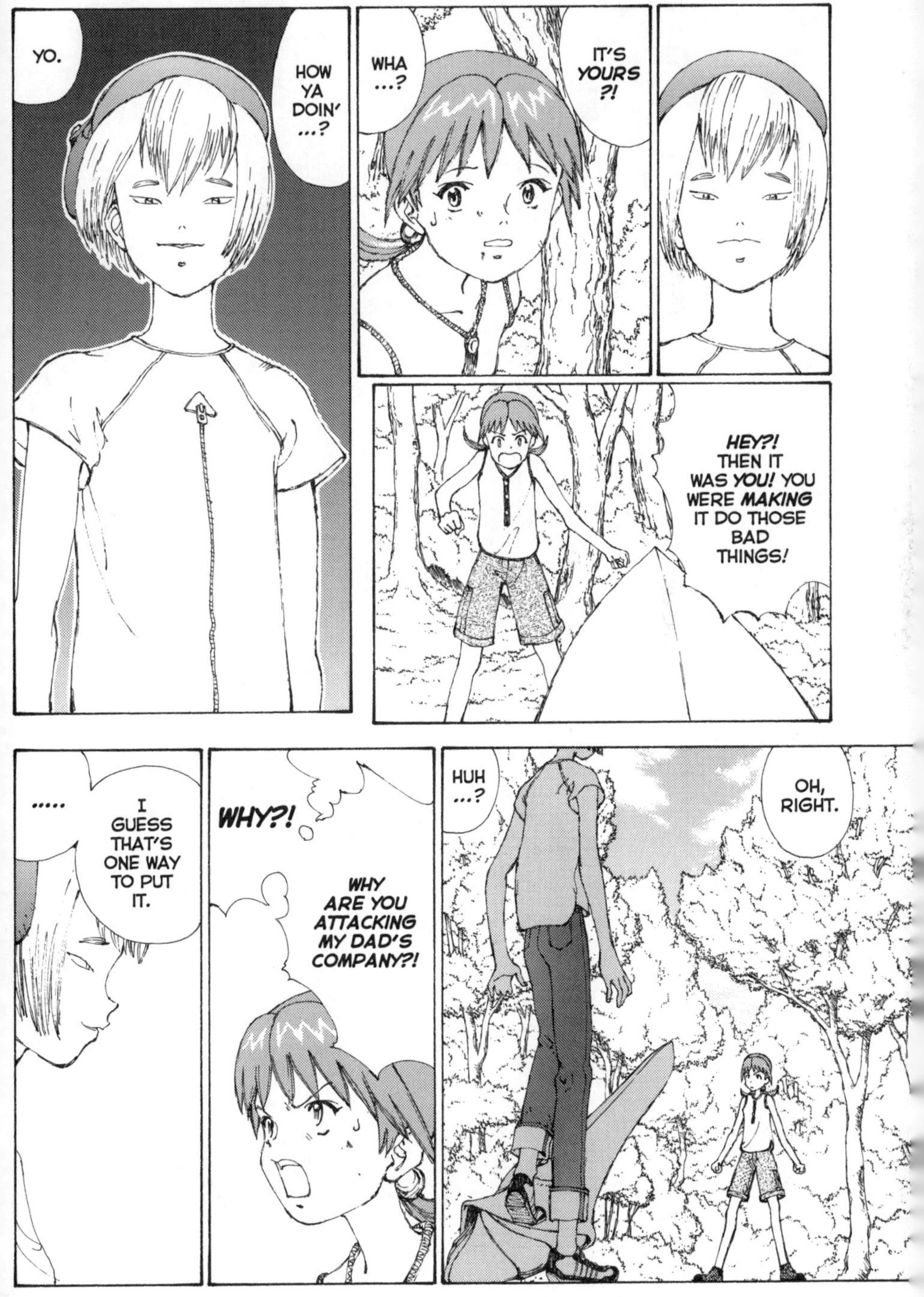
YO.
HOW YA DOIN' ...?
WHA ...?
IT'S *YOURS* ?!
HEY?! THEN IT WAS *YOU!* YOU WERE *MAKING* IT DO THOSE BAD THINGS*!*
.....
I GUESS THAT'S ONE WAY TO PUT IT.
WHY?!
WHY ARE YOU ATTACKING MY DAD'S COMPANY?!
HUH ...?
OH, RIGHT.

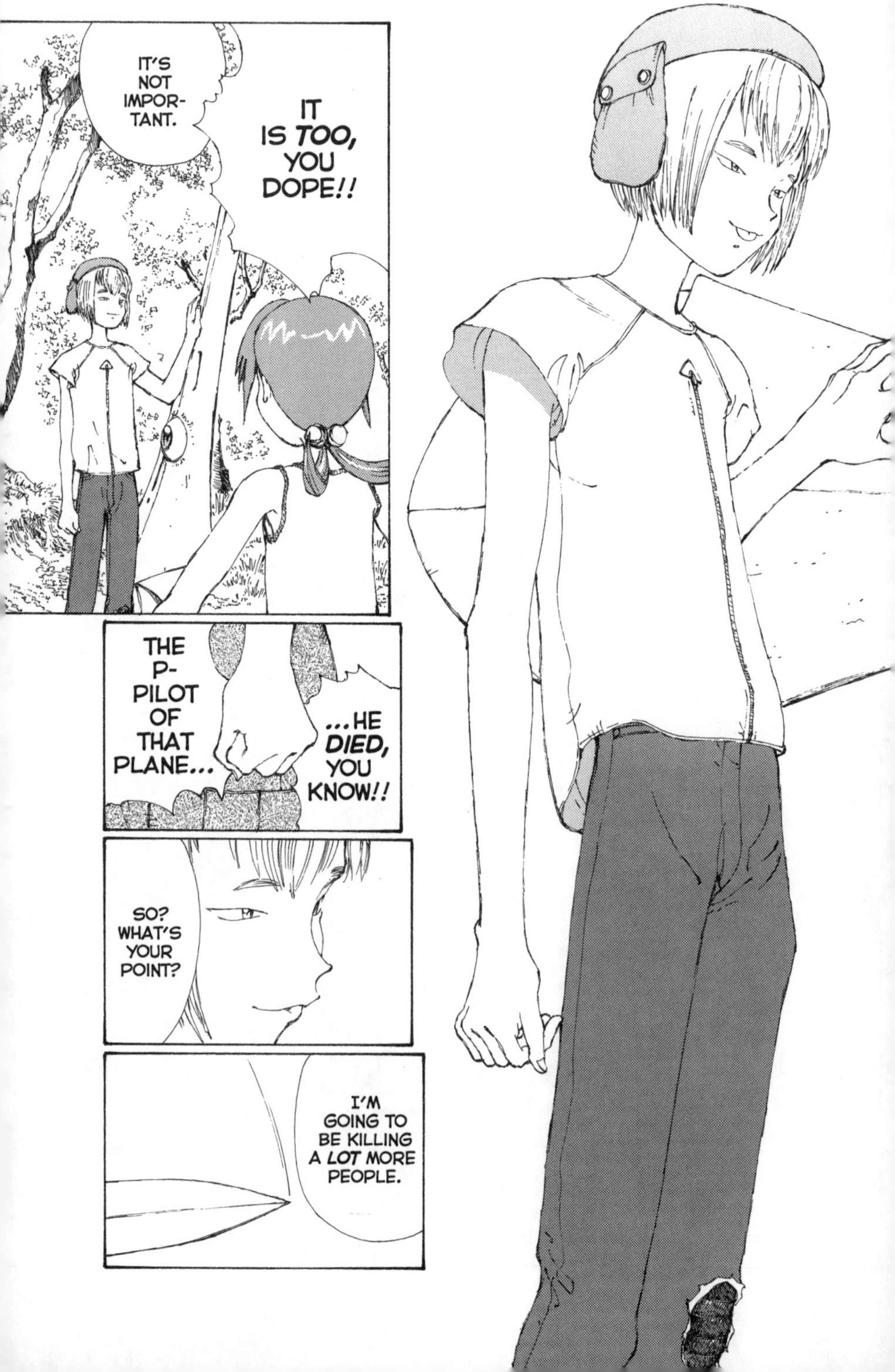
IT'S NOT IMPORTANT.
IT IS *TOO*, YOU DOPE!!
THE P-PILOT OF THAT PLANE...
...HE *DIED*, YOU KNOW!!
SO? WHAT'S YOUR POINT?
I'M GOING TO BE KILLING A *LOT* MORE PEOPLE.

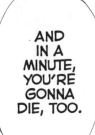

AND IN A MINUTE, YOU'RE GONNA DIE, TOO.
YOU UNDERSTAND ME, RIGHT? YOU'RE LINKED WITH A DRAGONCHILD, TOO, SO...
BECAUSE THAT'S THE KIND OF WORLD I WANT, I GUESS.
WH... WHY ARE YOU DOING THIS?!

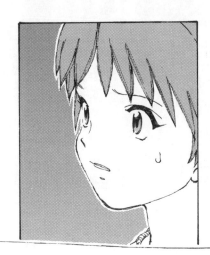

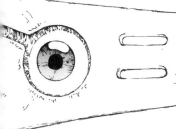

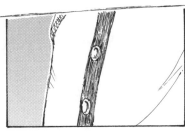

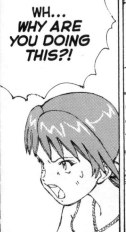

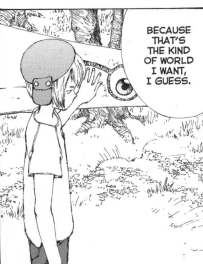

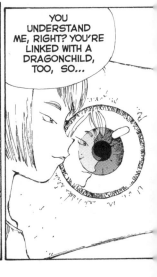

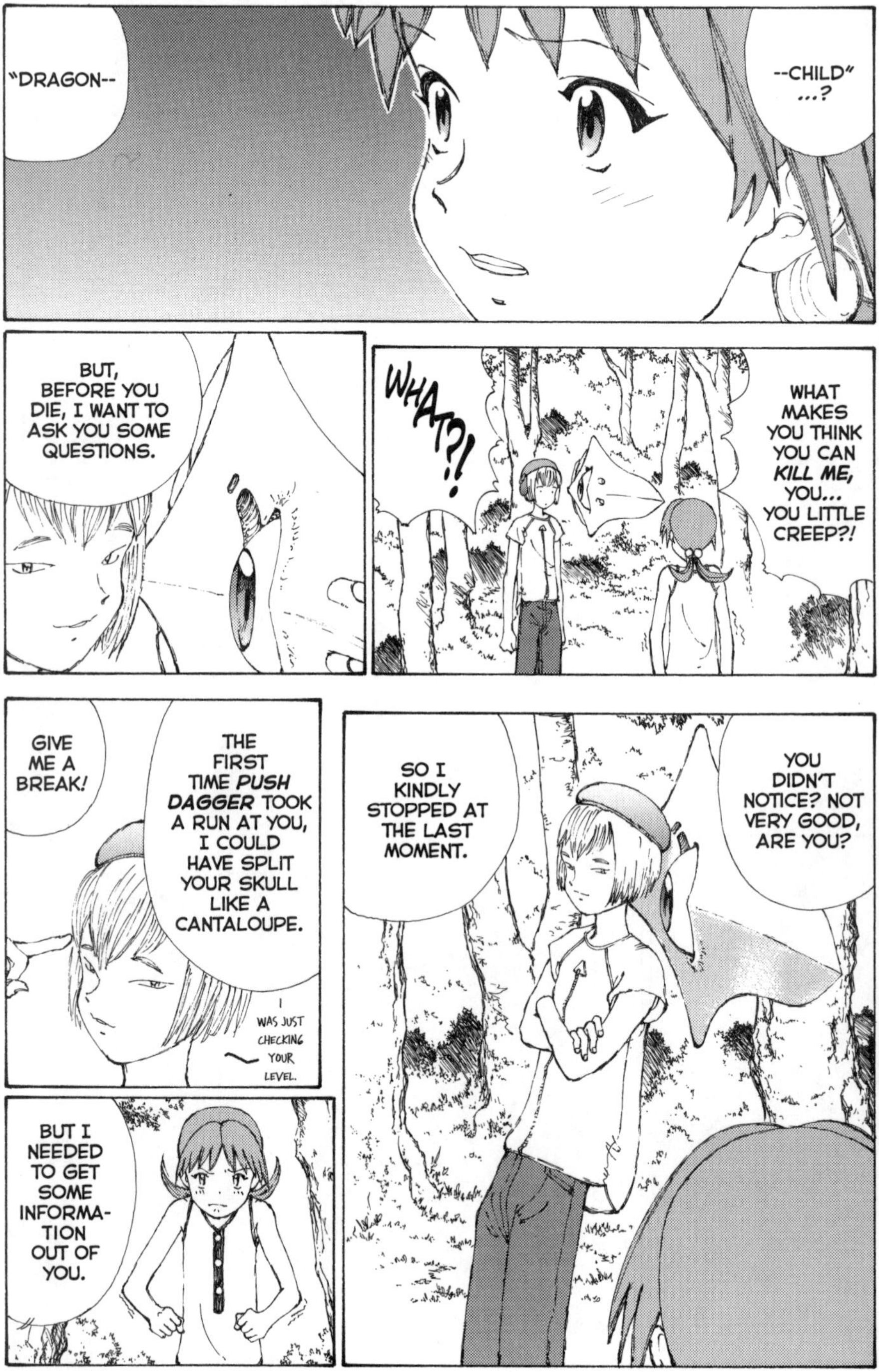

"DRAGON--
--CHILD" ...?
BUT, BEFORE YOU DIE, I WANT TO ASK YOU SOME QUESTIONS.
WHAT?!
WHAT MAKES YOU THINK YOU CAN KILL ME, YOU... YOU LITTLE CREEP?!
GIVE ME A BREAK!
THE FIRST TIME PUSH DAGGER TOOK A RUN AT YOU, I COULD HAVE SPLIT YOUR SKULL LIKE A CANTALOUPE.
I WAS JUST CHECKING YOUR LEVEL.
BUT I NEEDED TO GET SOME INFORMATION OUT OF YOU.
SO I KINDLY STOPPED AT THE LAST MOMENT.
YOU DIDN'T NOTICE? NOT VERY GOOD, ARE YOU?

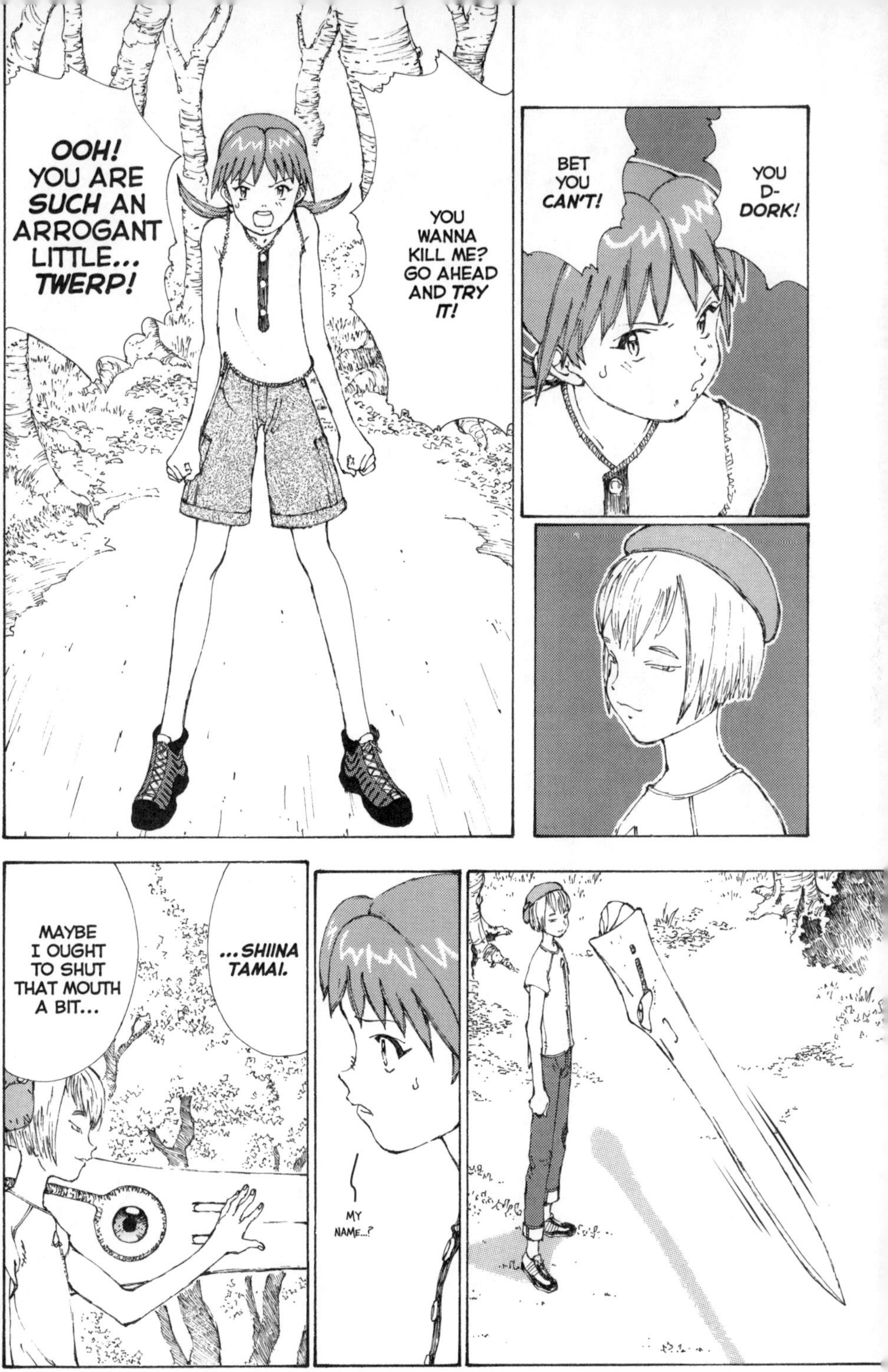
OOH! YOU ARE SUCH AN ARROGANT LITTLE... TWERP!
YOU WANNA KILL ME? GO AHEAD AND TRY IT!
BET YOU CAN'T!
YOU D-DORK!
MAYBE I OUGHT TO SHUT THAT MOUTH A BIT...
...SHIINA TAMAI.
MY NAME...?

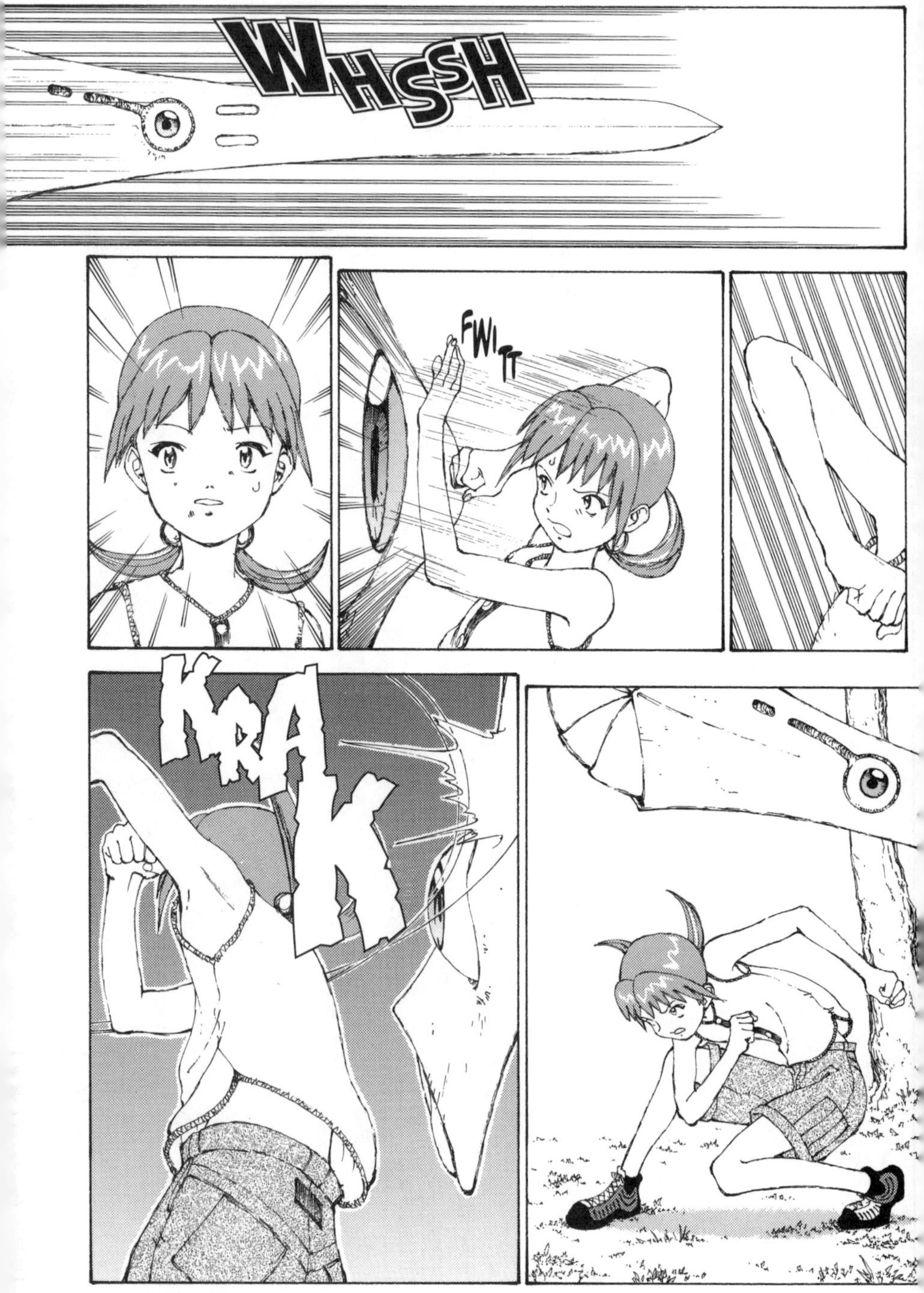
WHSSH
FWITT
KRAK

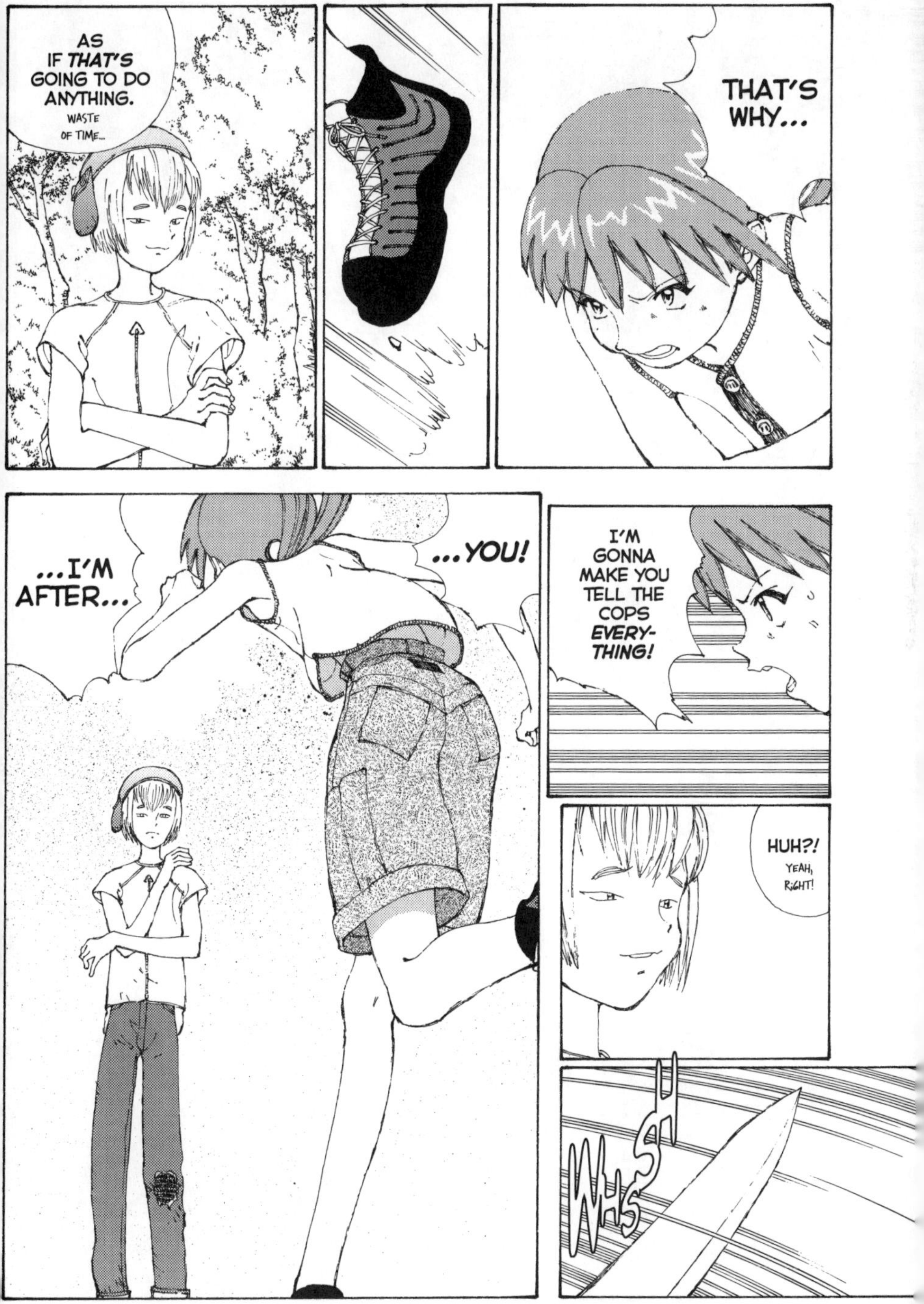
AS IF *THAT'S* GOING TO DO ANYTHING.
WASTE OF TIME...
THAT'S WHY...
...I'M AFTER...
...YOU!
I'M GONNA MAKE YOU TELL THE COPS *EVERY-THING!*
HUH?!
YEAH, RIGHT!
WHSH

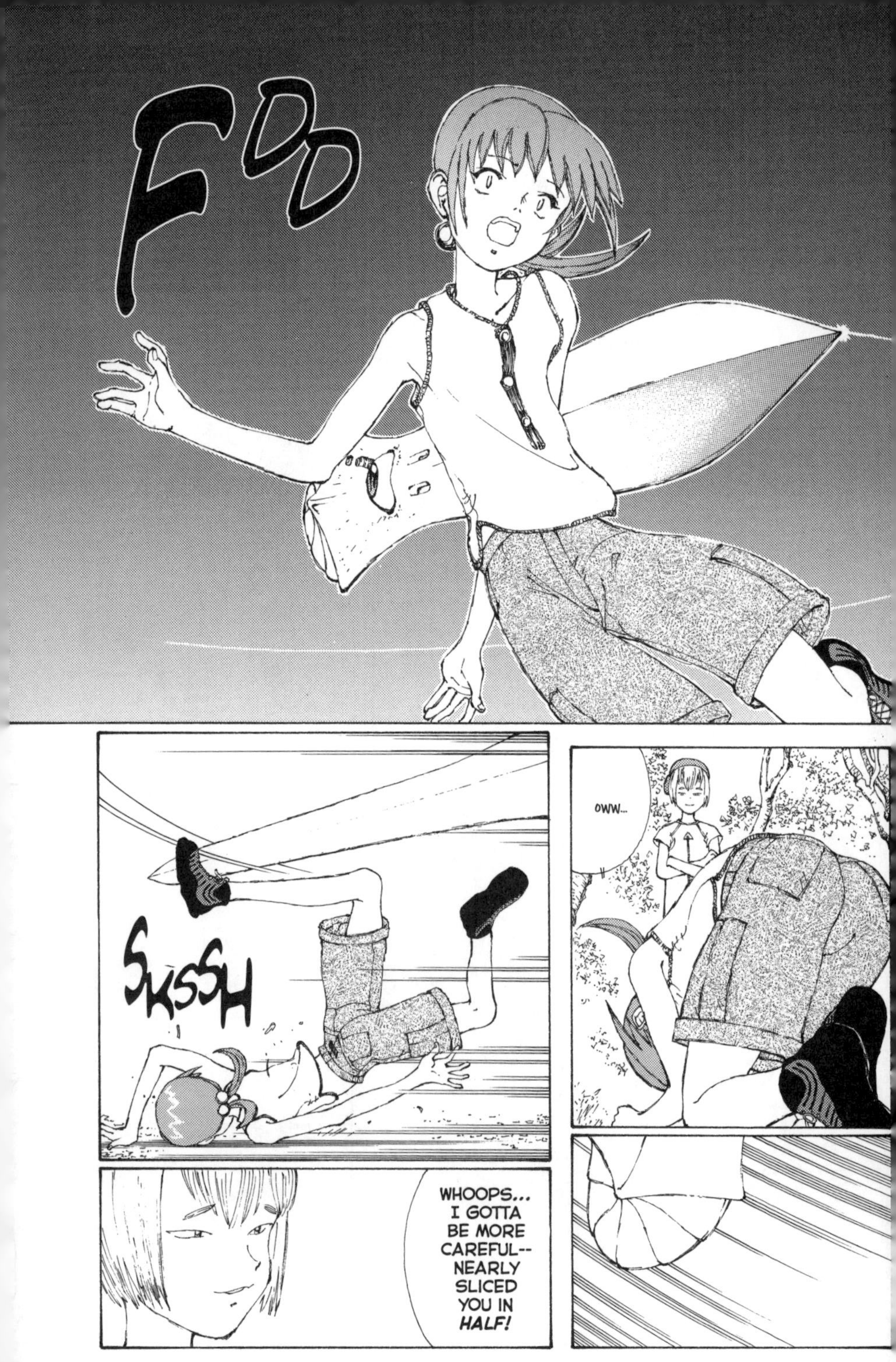
FDD
OWW...
SKSSH
WHOOPS... I GOTTA BE MORE CAREFUL-- NEARLY SLICED YOU IN HALF!

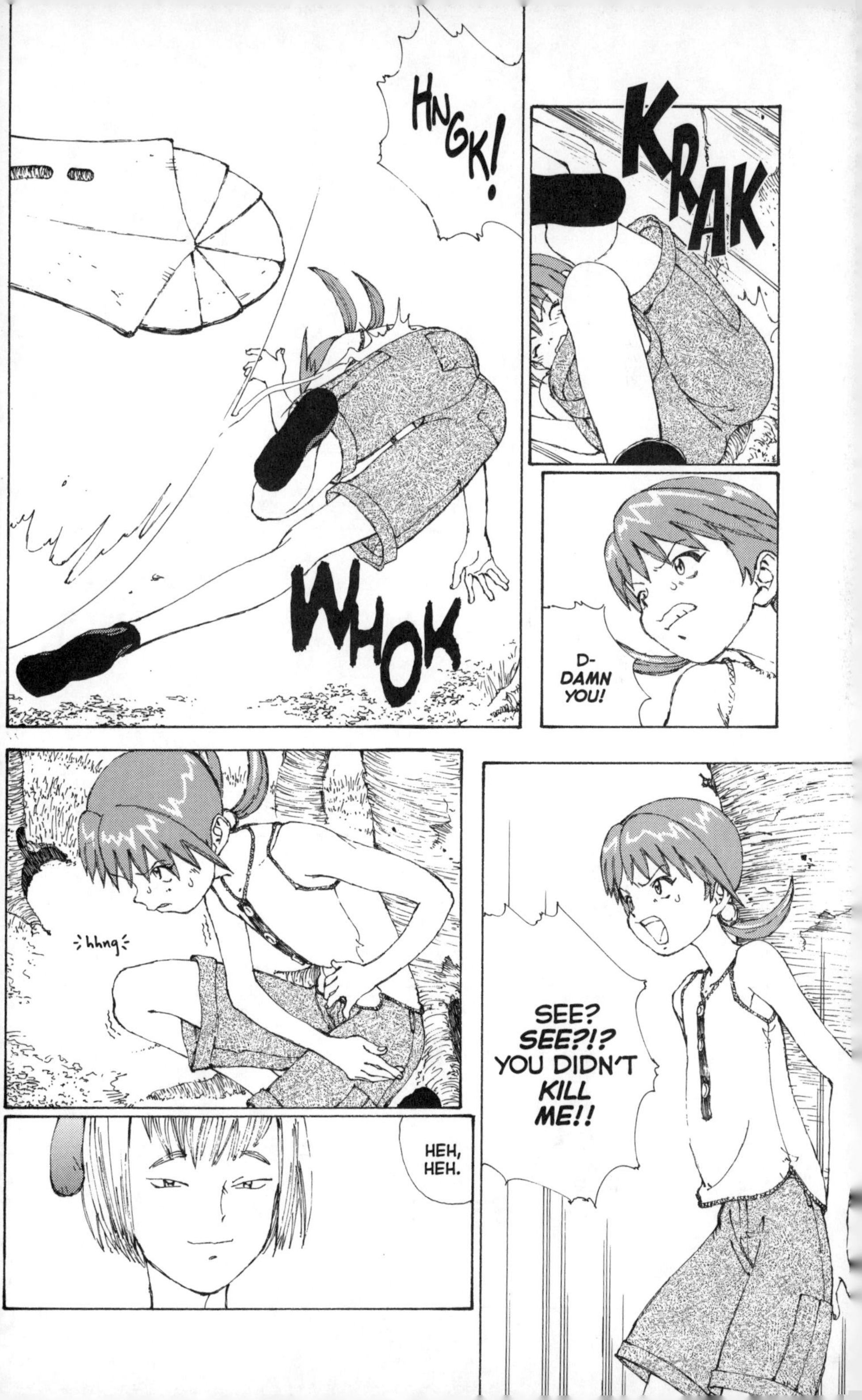
KRAK
D-
DAMN
YOU!
HNGK!
WHOK
SEE?
SEE?!?
YOU DIDN'T
KILL
ME!!
hhng
HEH,
HEH.

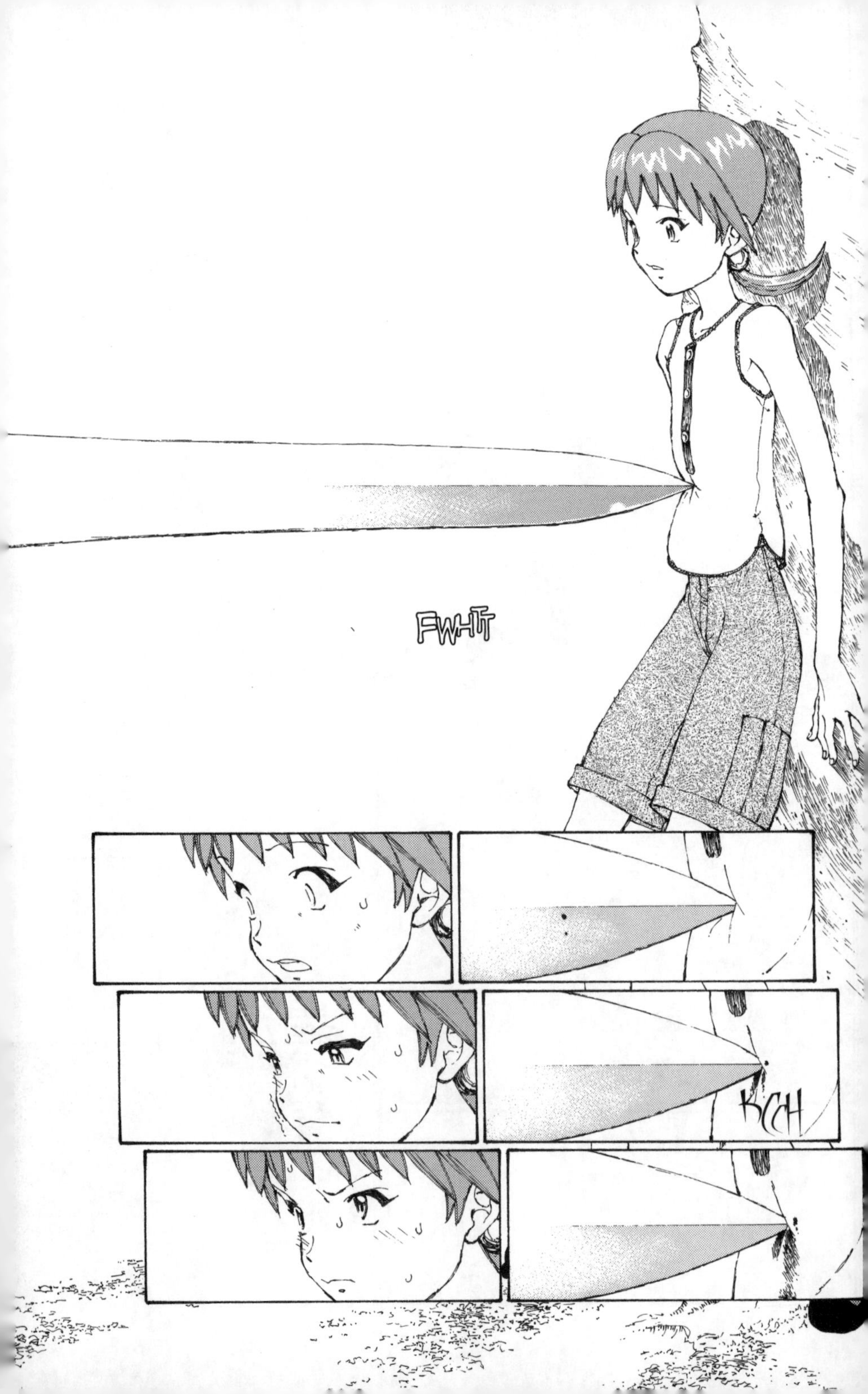
FWHTT
KCCH

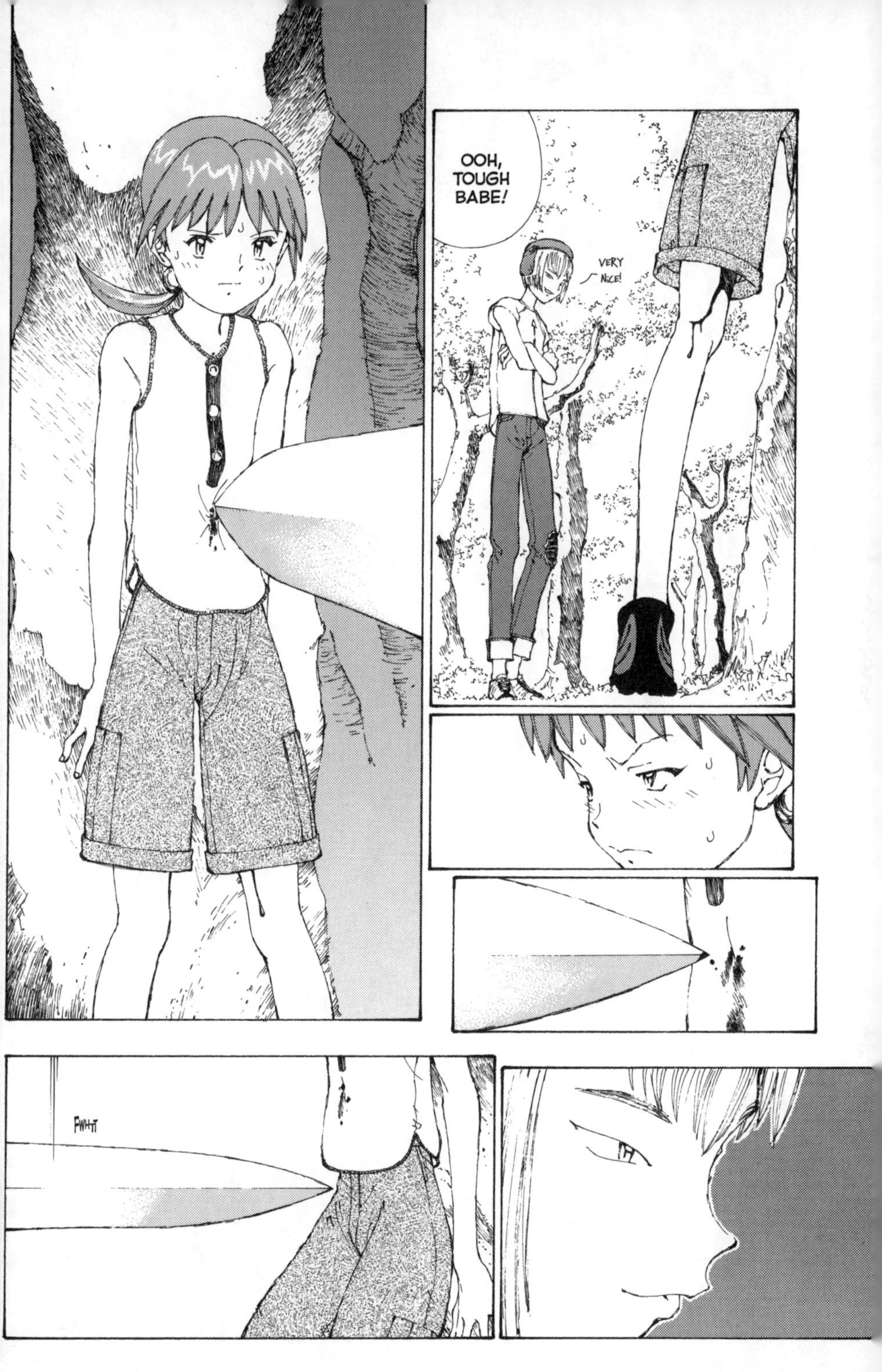
OOH, TOUGH BABE!
VERY NICE!
FWHTT

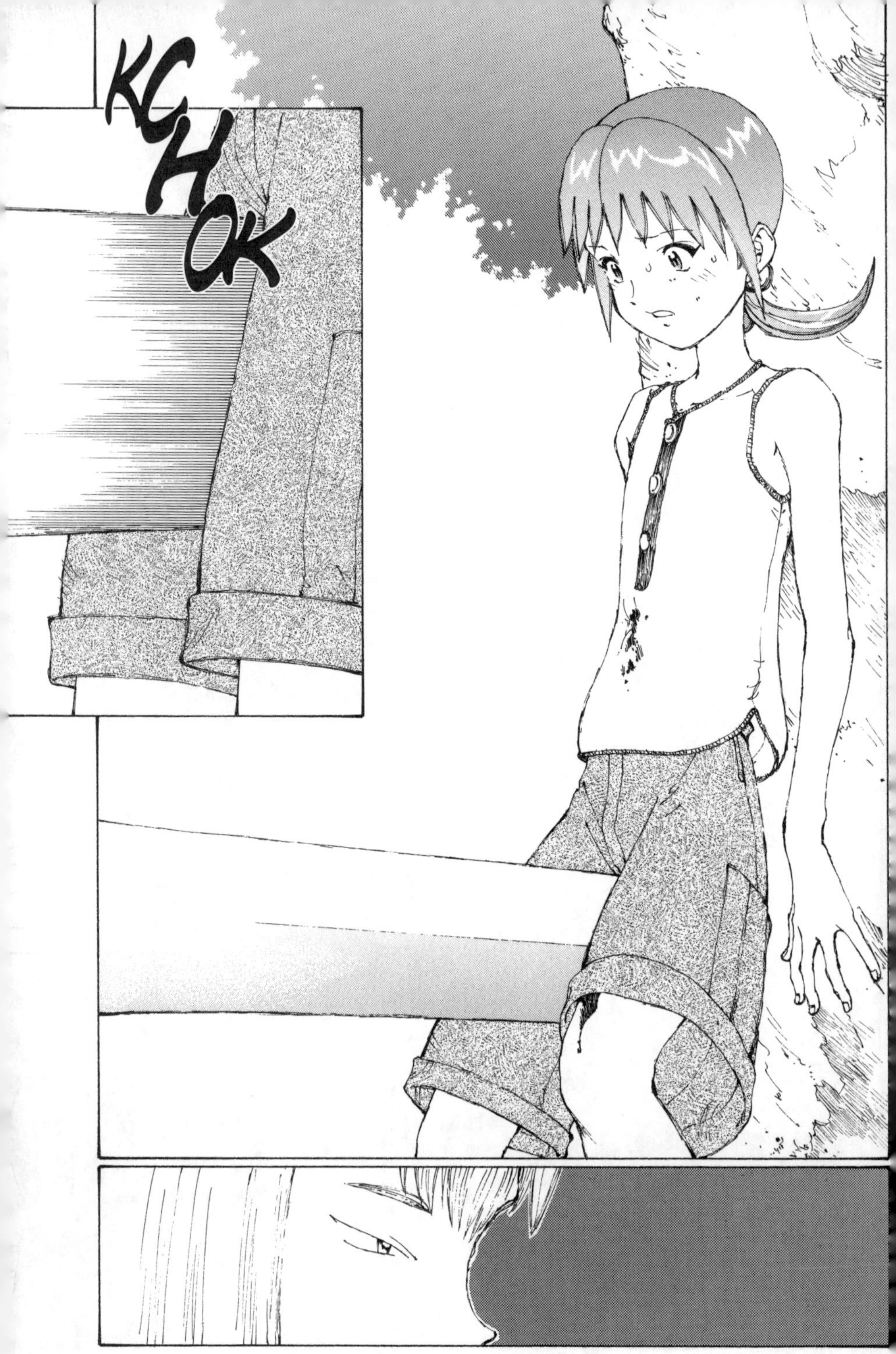
KCHOK

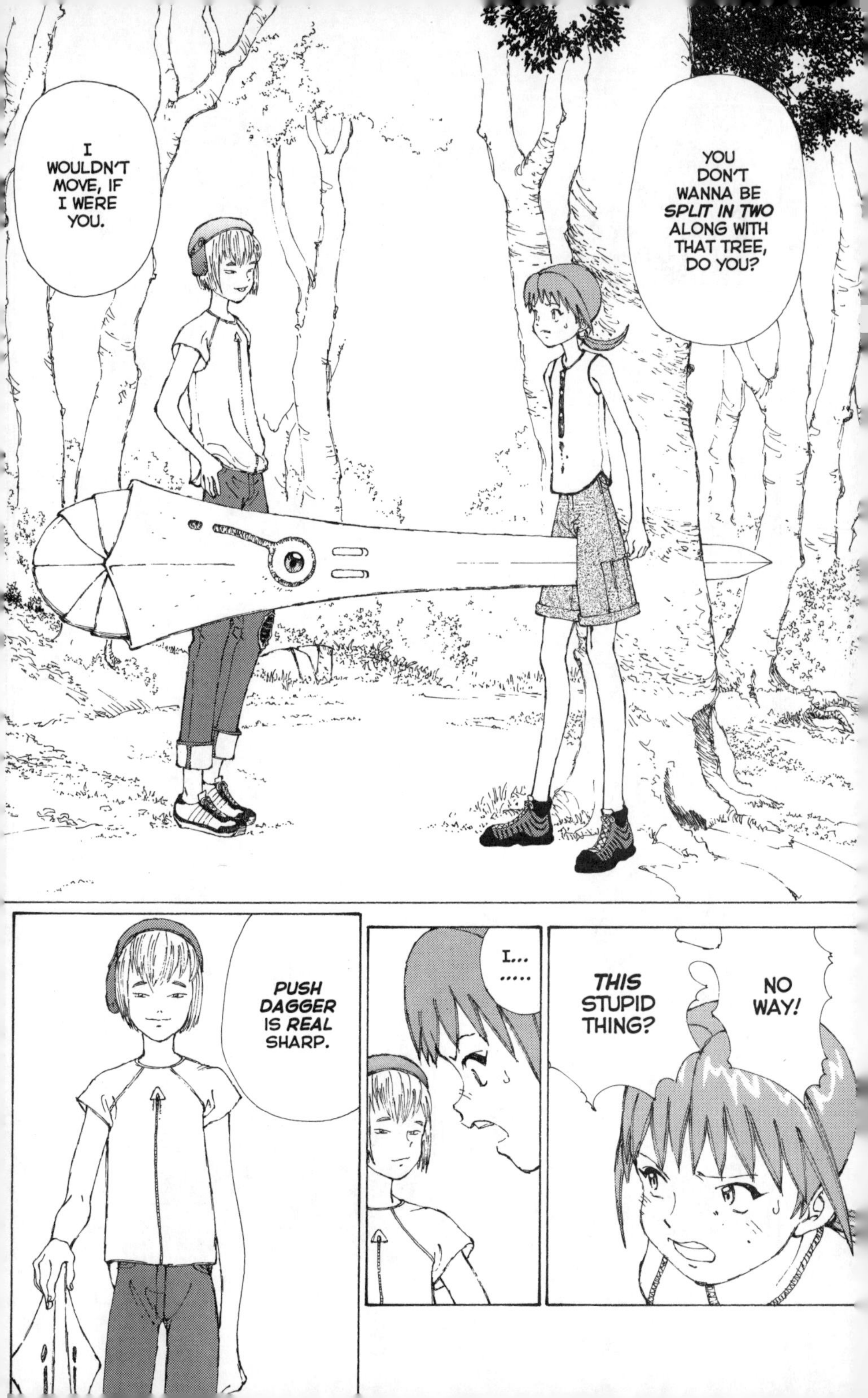
I WOULDN'T MOVE, IF I WERE YOU.
YOU DON'T WANNA BE *SPLIT IN TWO* ALONG WITH THAT TREE, DO YOU?
PUSH DAGGER IS *REAL* SHARP.
I... .....
THIS STUPID THING?
NO WAY!

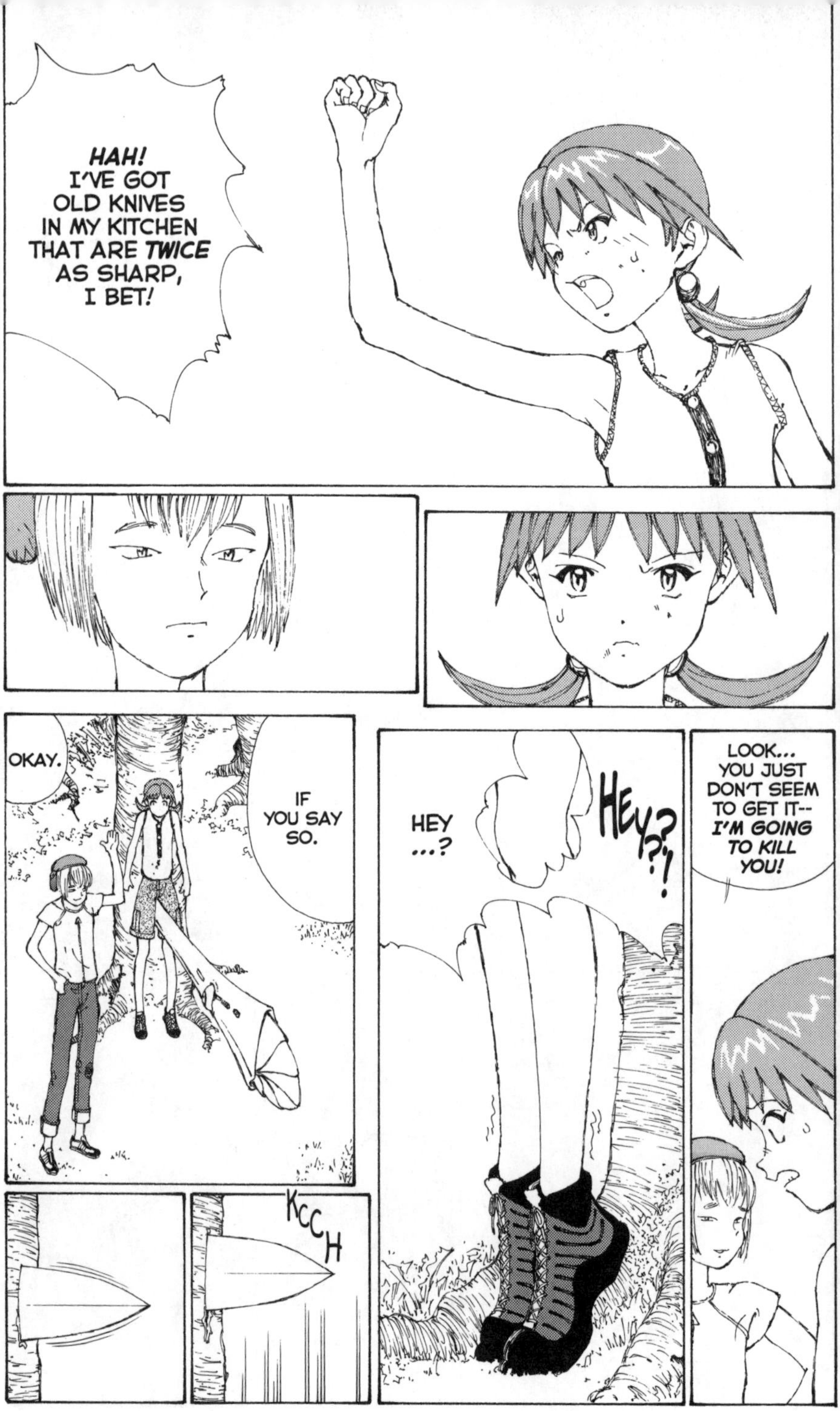
HAH! I'VE GOT OLD KNIVES IN MY KITCHEN THAT ARE TWICE AS SHARP, I BET!
LOOK... YOU JUST DON'T SEEM TO GET IT-- I'M GOING TO KILL YOU!
HEY ...?
HEY?!
OKAY.
IF YOU SAY SO.
KCCH

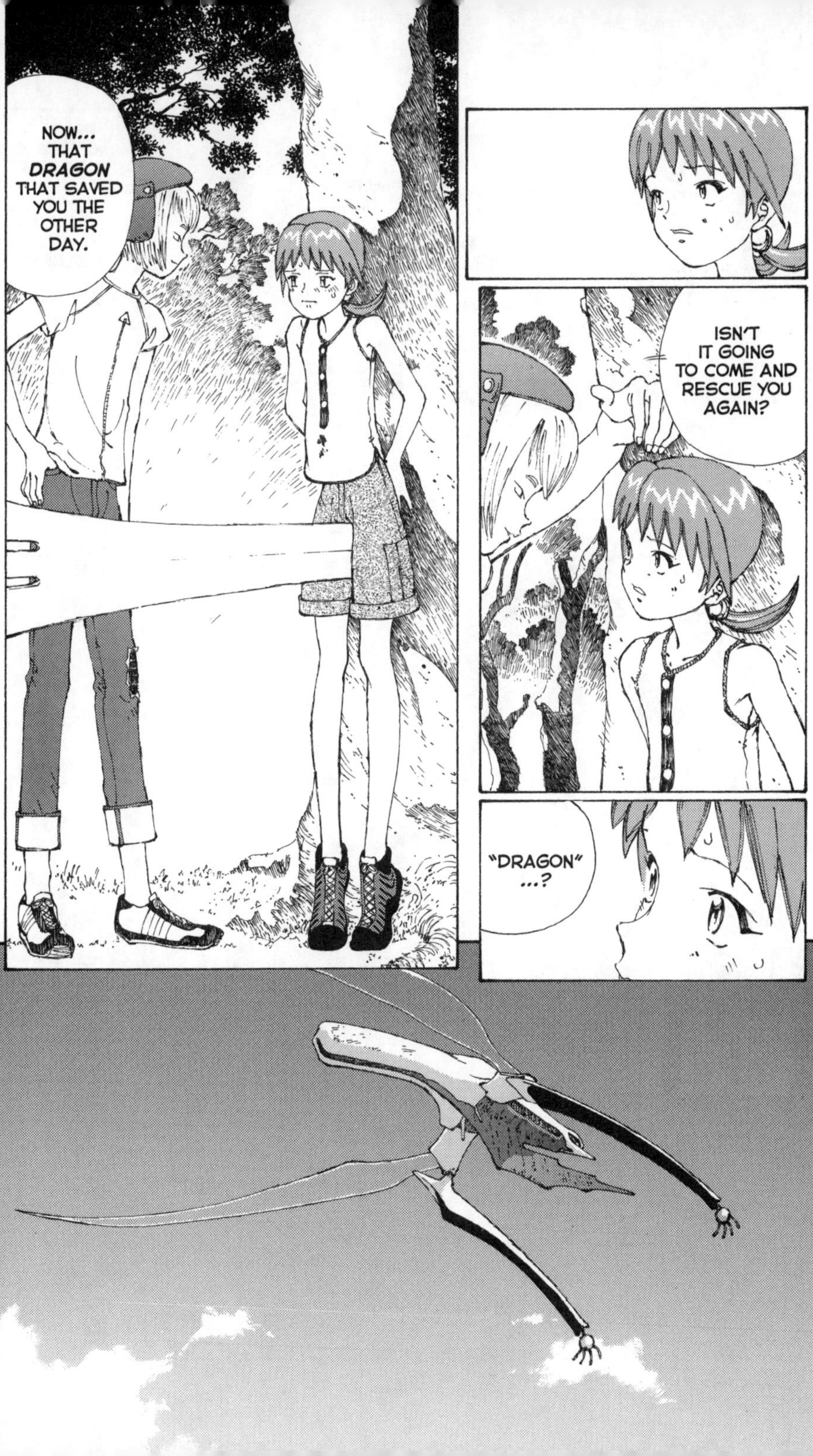
NOW... THAT *DRAGON* THAT SAVED YOU THE OTHER DAY.
ISN'T IT GOING TO COME AND RESCUE YOU AGAIN?
"DRAGON" ...?

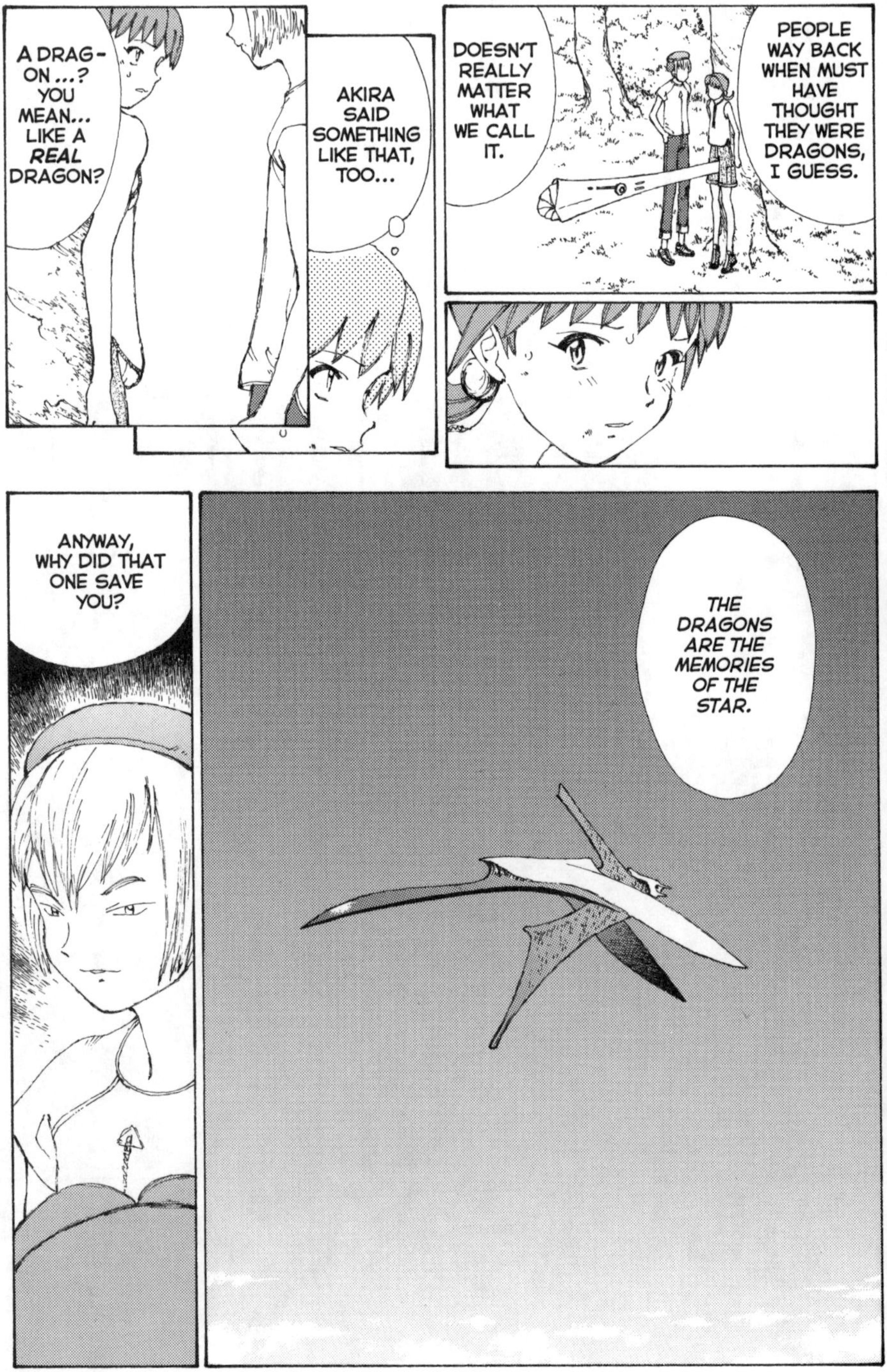
A DRAG-ON...? YOU MEAN... LIKE A *REAL* DRAGON?
AKIRA SAID SOMETHING LIKE THAT, TOO...
DOESN'T REALLY MATTER WHAT WE CALL IT.
PEOPLE WAY BACK WHEN MUST HAVE THOUGHT THEY WERE DRAGONS, I GUESS.
ANYWAY, WHY DID THAT ONE SAVE YOU?
THE DRAGONS ARE THE MEMORIES OF THE STAR.

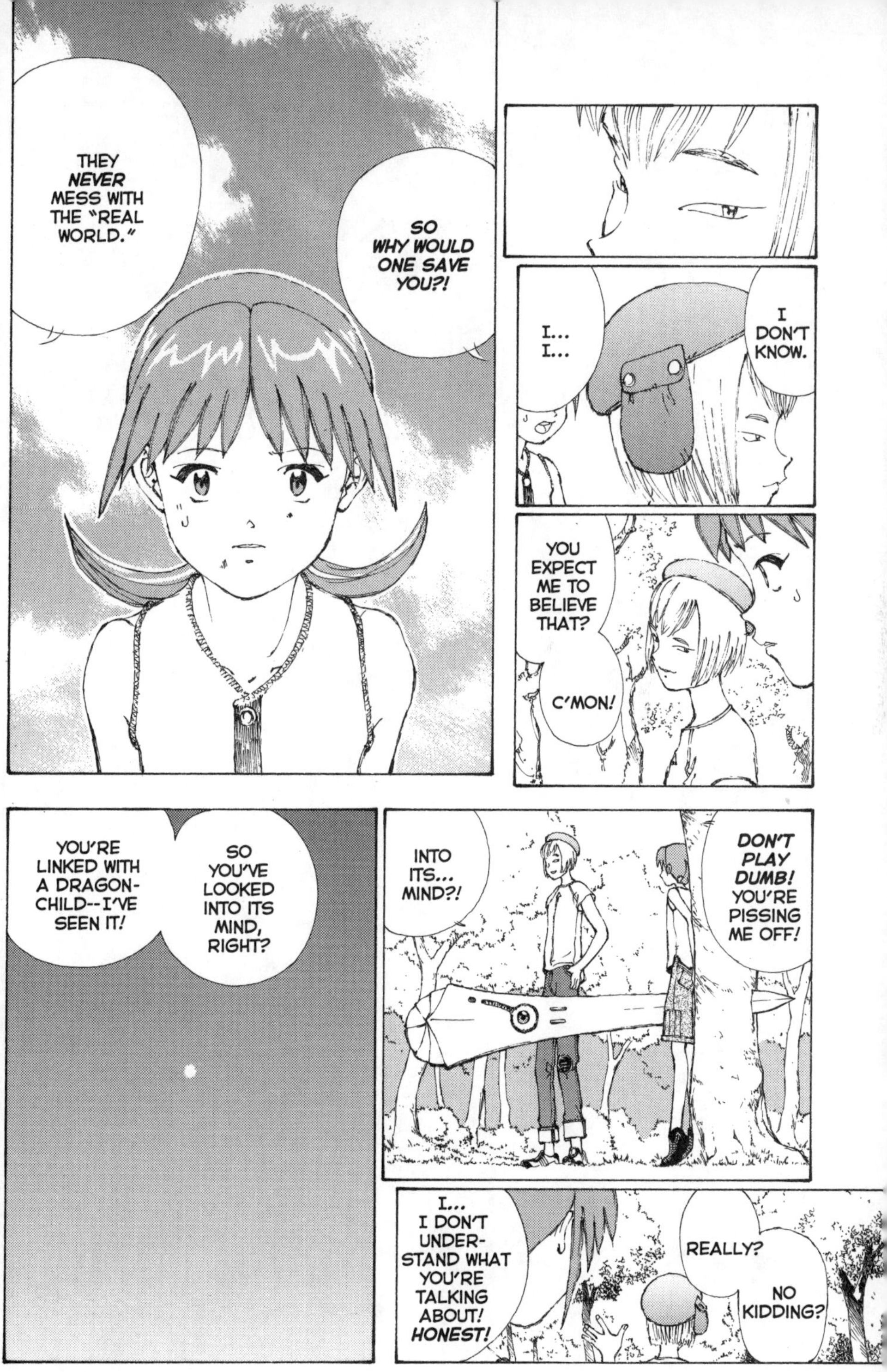
THEY NEVER MESS WITH THE "REAL WORLD."
SO WHY WOULD ONE SAVE YOU?!
I... I...
I DON'T KNOW.
YOU EXPECT ME TO BELIEVE THAT?
C'MON!
YOU'RE LINKED WITH A DRAGON-CHILD--I'VE SEEN IT!
SO YOU'VE LOOKED INTO ITS MIND, RIGHT?
INTO ITS... MIND?!
DON'T PLAY DUMB! YOU'RE PISSING ME OFF!
I... I DON'T UNDER-STAND WHAT YOU'RE TALKING ABOUT! HONEST!
REALLY?
NO KIDDING?

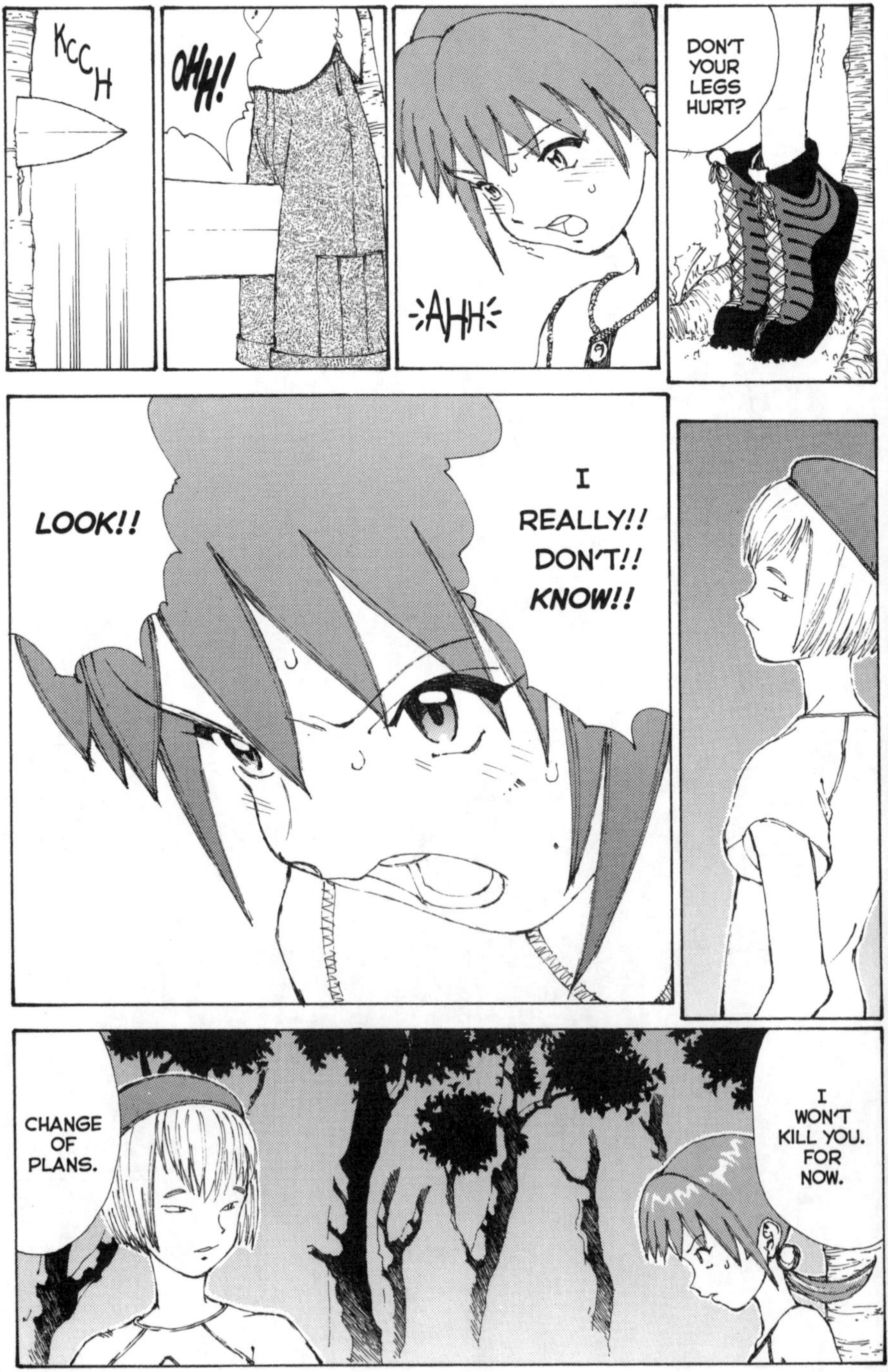
KCCH
OHH!
AHH
DON'T YOUR LEGS HURT?
LOOK!!
I REALLY!! DON'T!! KNOW!!
CHANGE OF PLANS.
I WON'T KILL YOU. FOR NOW.

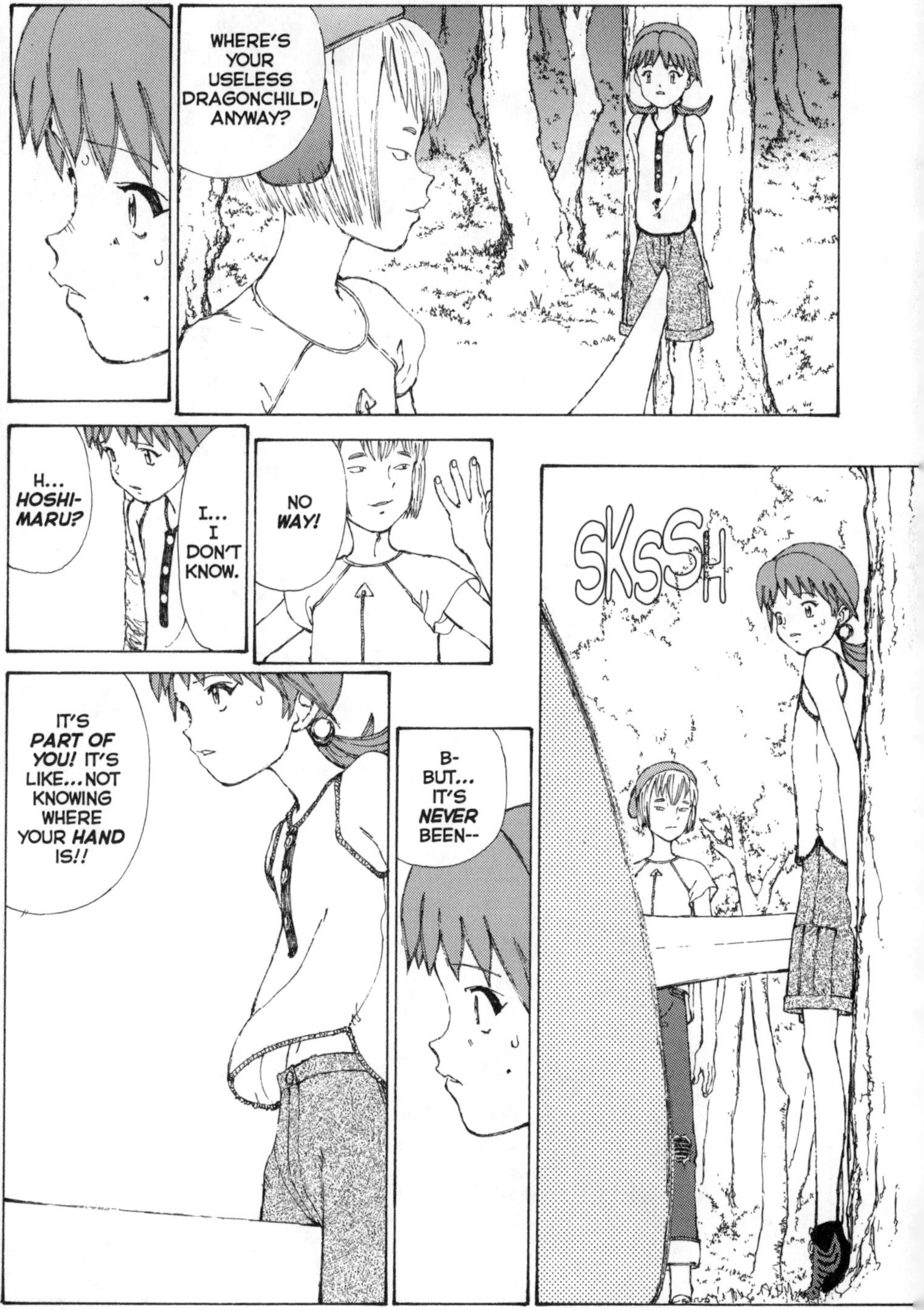
WHERE'S YOUR USELESS DRAGONCHILD, ANYWAY?
H... HOSHIMARU?
I... I DON'T KNOW.
NO WAY!
SKSSH
IT'S PART OF YOU! IT'S LIKE...NOT KNOWING WHERE YOUR HAND IS!!
B-BUT... IT'S NEVER BEEN--

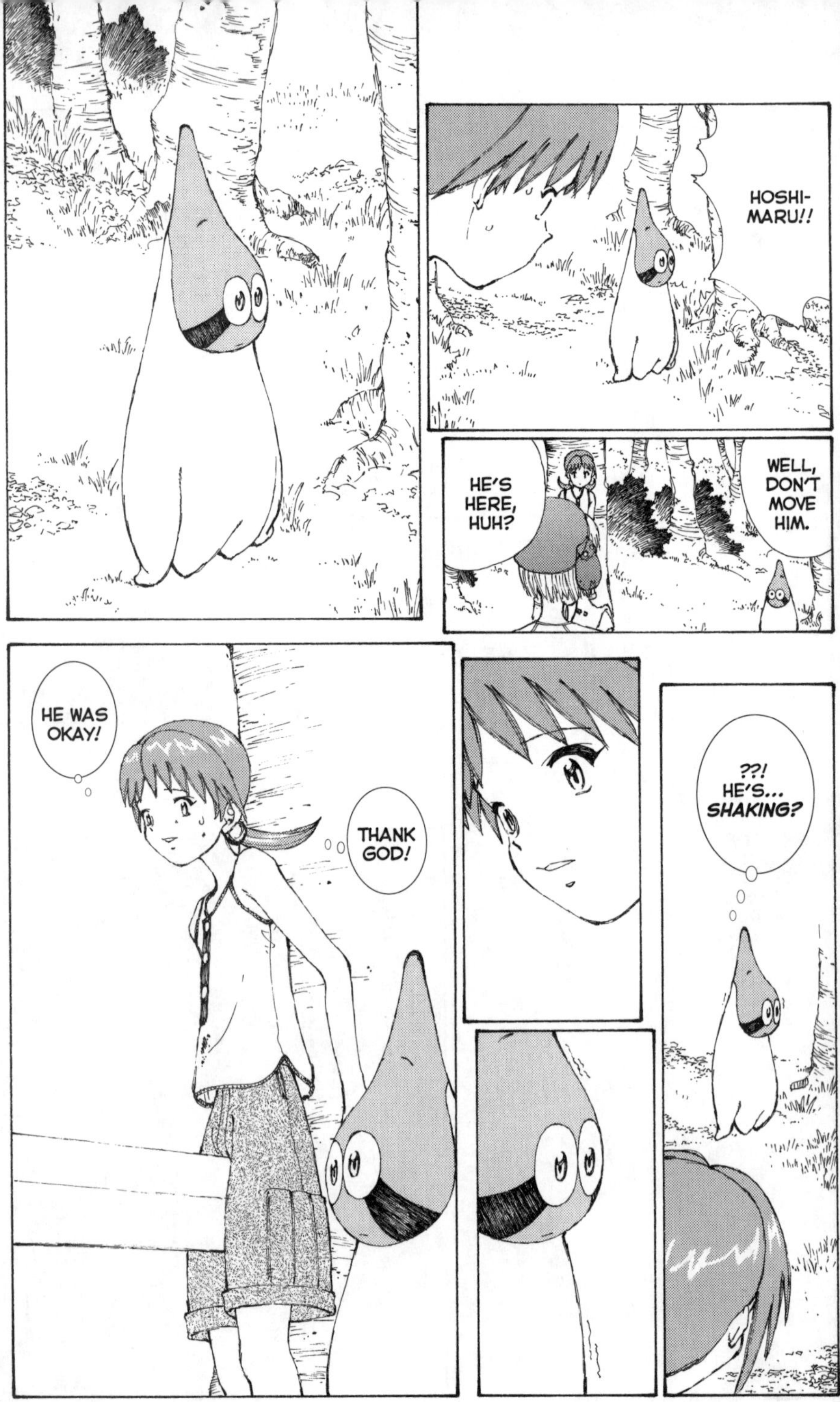
HOSHI-MARU!!
HE'S HERE, HUH?
WELL, DON'T MOVE HIM.
HE WAS OKAY!
THANK GOD!
??! HE'S... SHAKING?

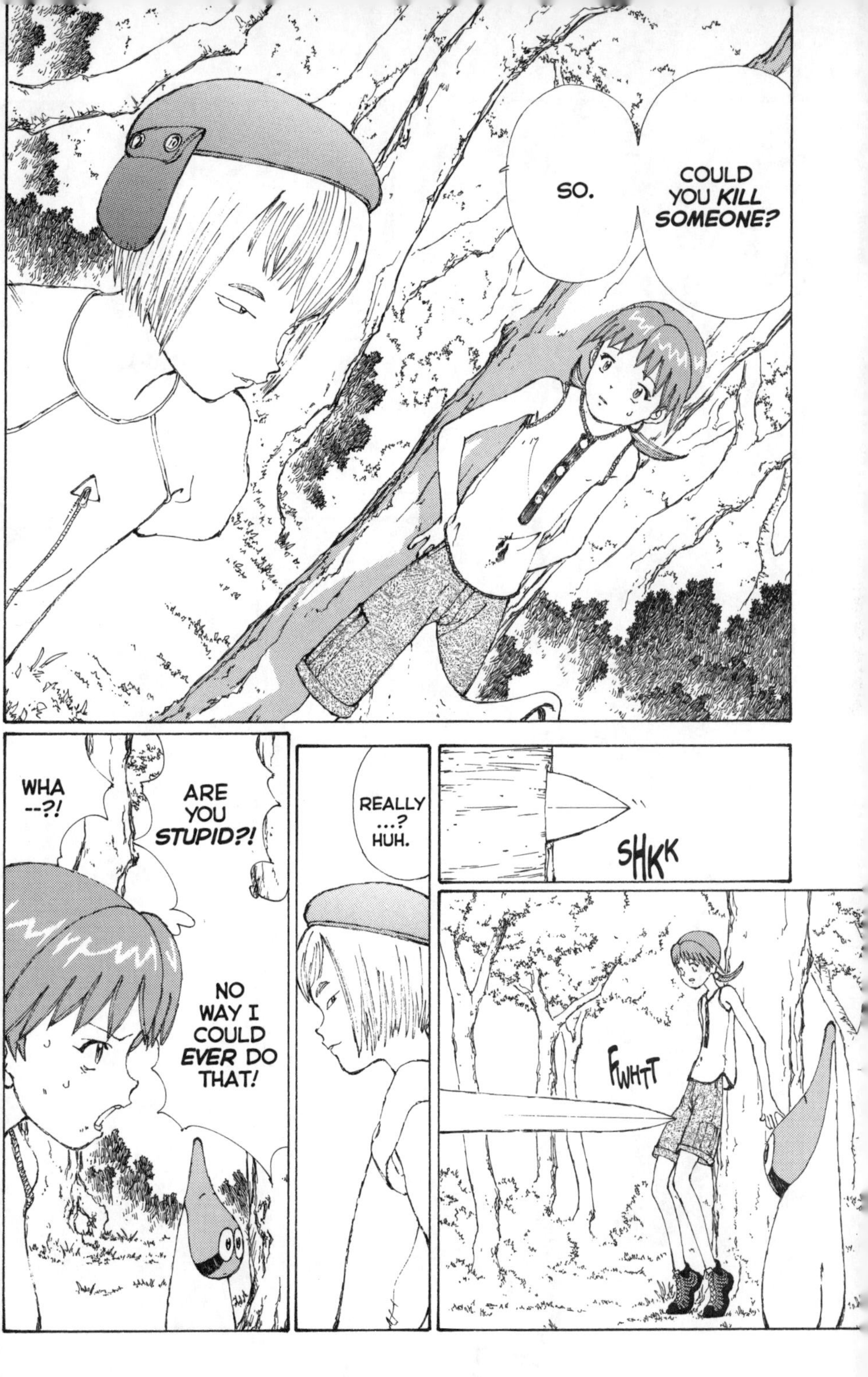
SO.
COULD YOU KILL SOMEONE?
WHA --?!
ARE YOU STUPID?!
NO WAY I COULD EVER DO THAT!
REALLY ...? HUH.
SHKK
FWHTT

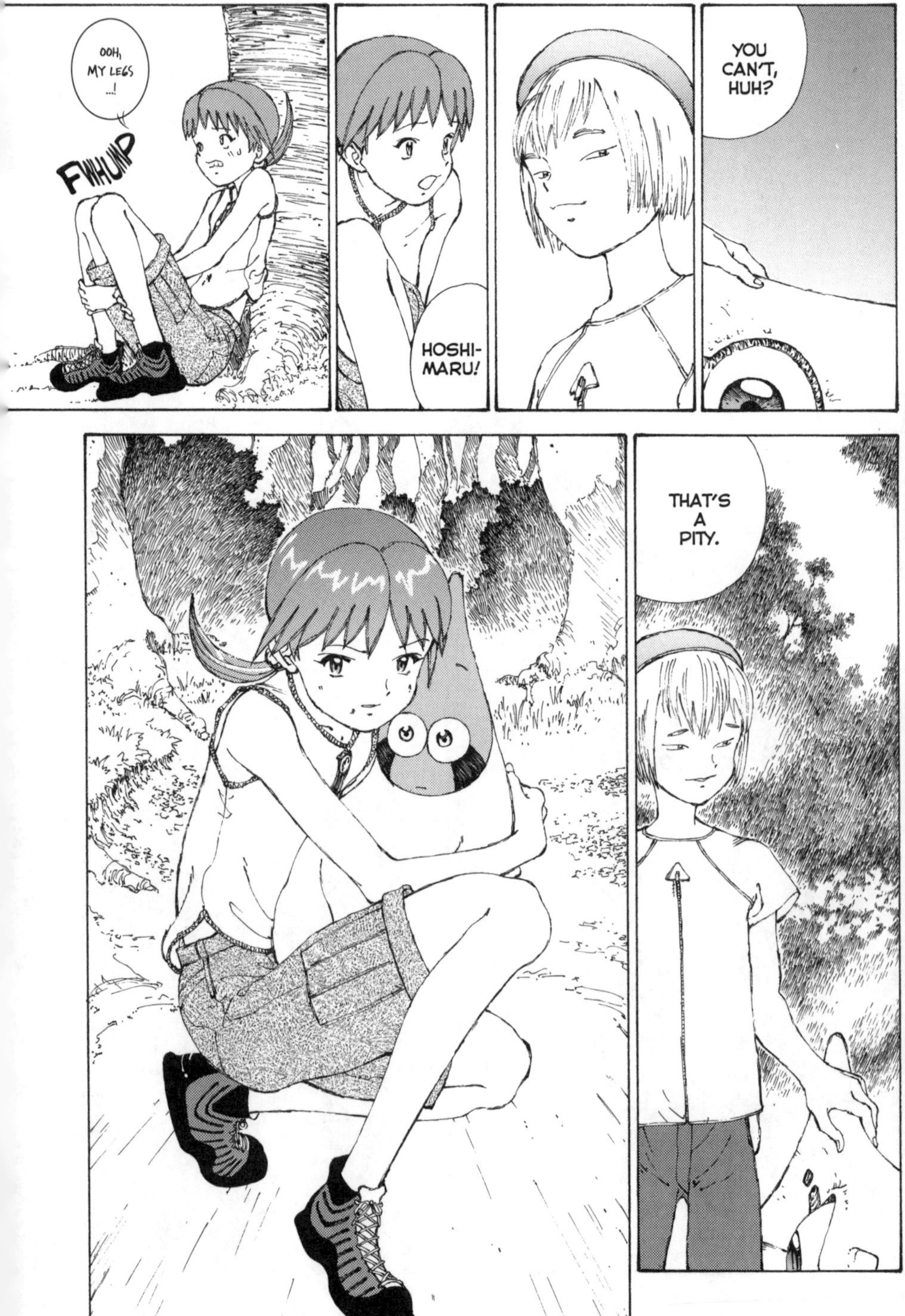
OOH, MY LEGS ...!
FWHUMP
HOSHI-MARU!
YOU CAN'T, HUH?
THAT'S A PITY.

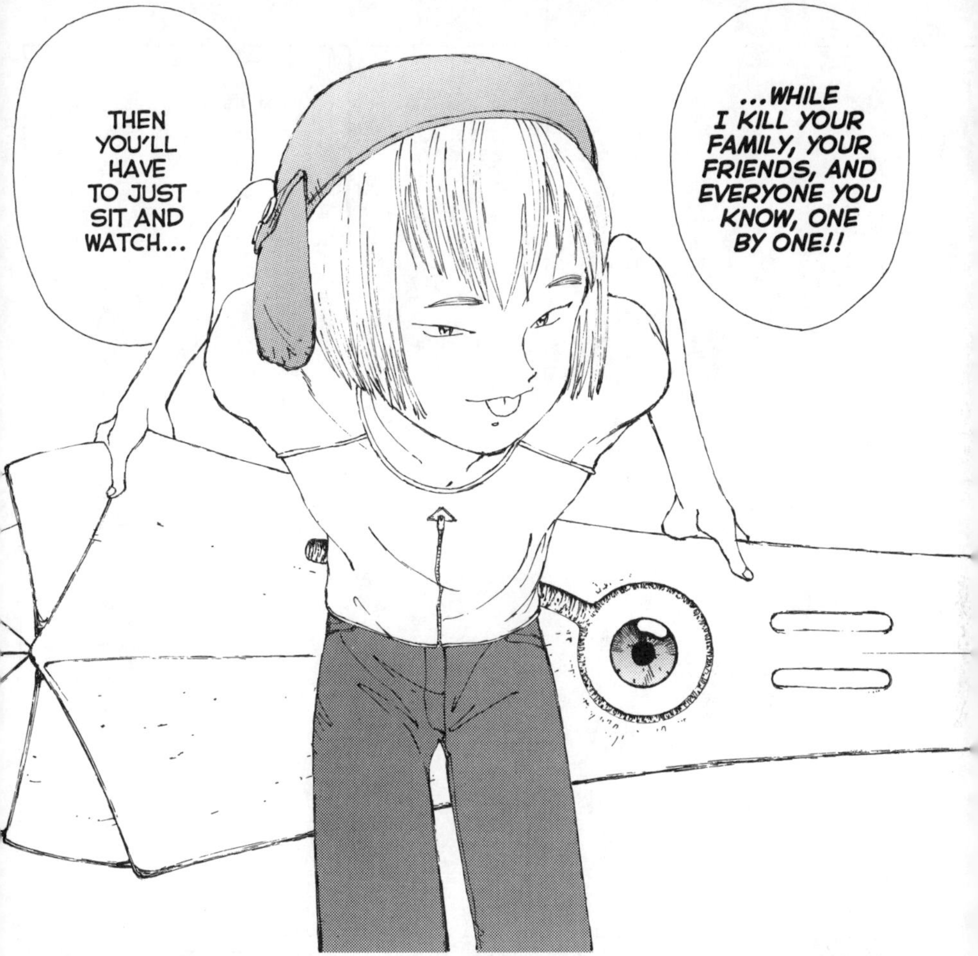
THEN YOU'LL HAVE TO JUST SIT AND WATCH...
...WHILE I KILL YOUR FAMILY, YOUR FRIENDS, AND EVERYONE YOU KNOW, ONE BY ONE!!
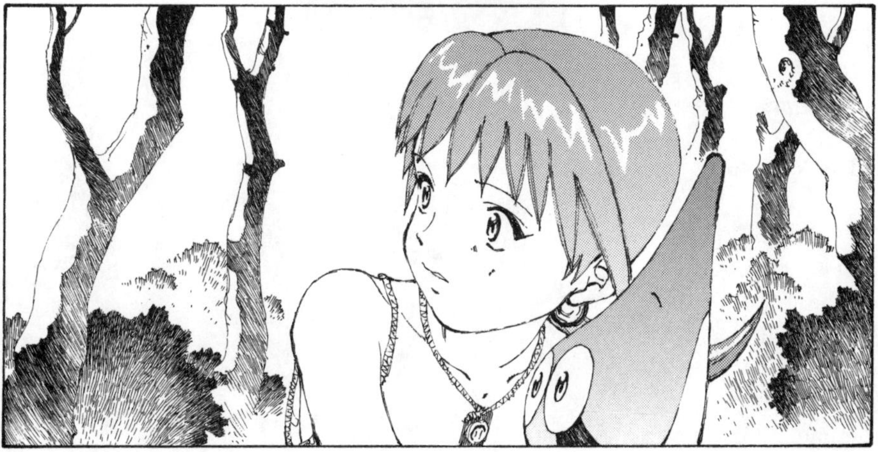

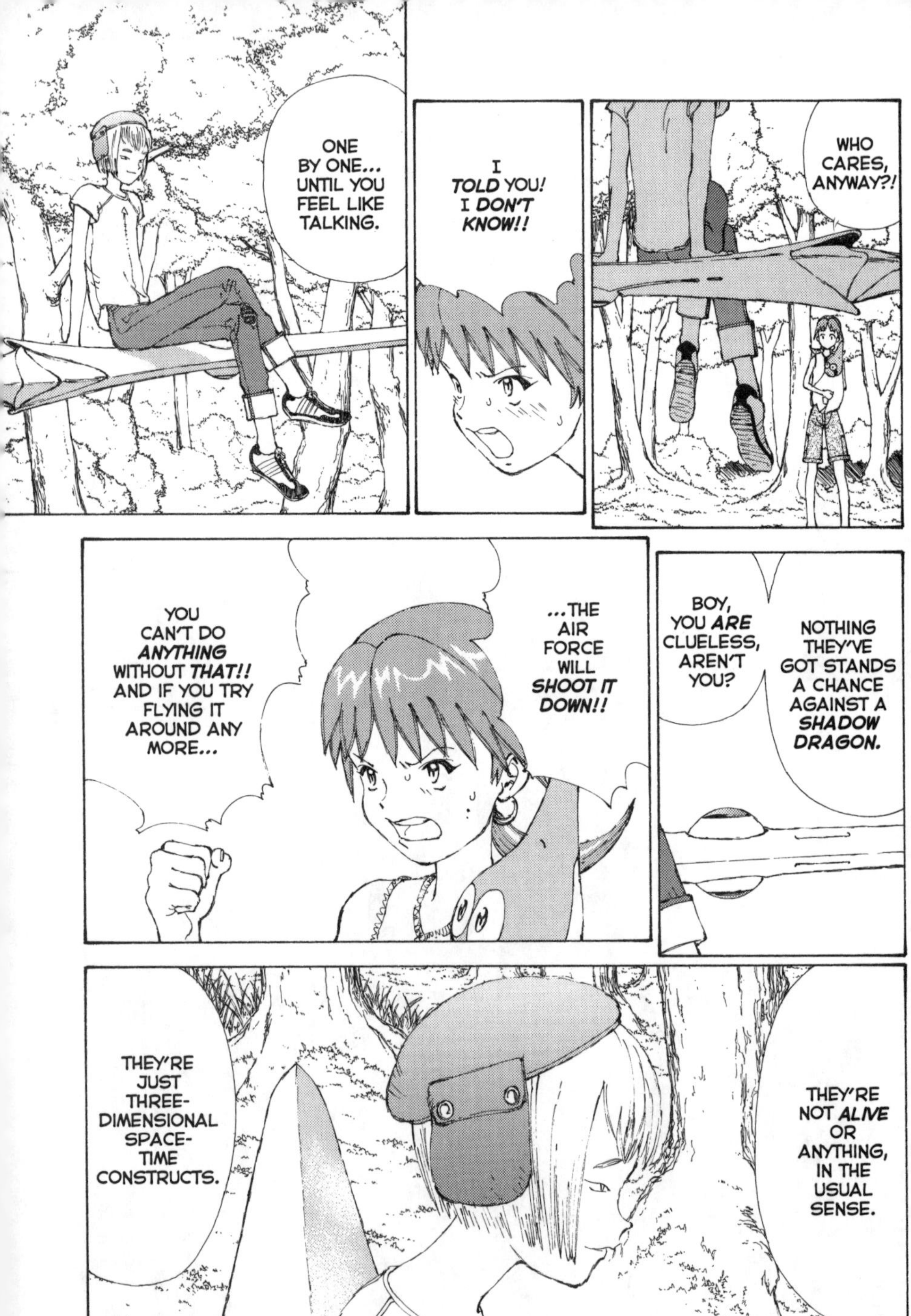
ONE BY ONE... UNTIL YOU FEEL LIKE TALKING.
I TOLD YOU! I DON'T KNOW!!
WHO CARES, ANYWAY?!
YOU CAN'T DO ANYTHING WITHOUT THAT!! AND IF YOU TRY FLYING IT AROUND ANY MORE...
...THE AIR FORCE WILL SHOOT IT DOWN!!
BOY, YOU ARE CLUELESS, AREN'T YOU?
NOTHING THEY'VE GOT STANDS A CHANCE AGAINST A SHADOW DRAGON.
THEY'RE JUST THREE-DIMENSIONAL SPACE-TIME CONSTRUCTS.
THEY'RE NOT ALIVE OR ANYTHING, IN THE USUAL SENSE.

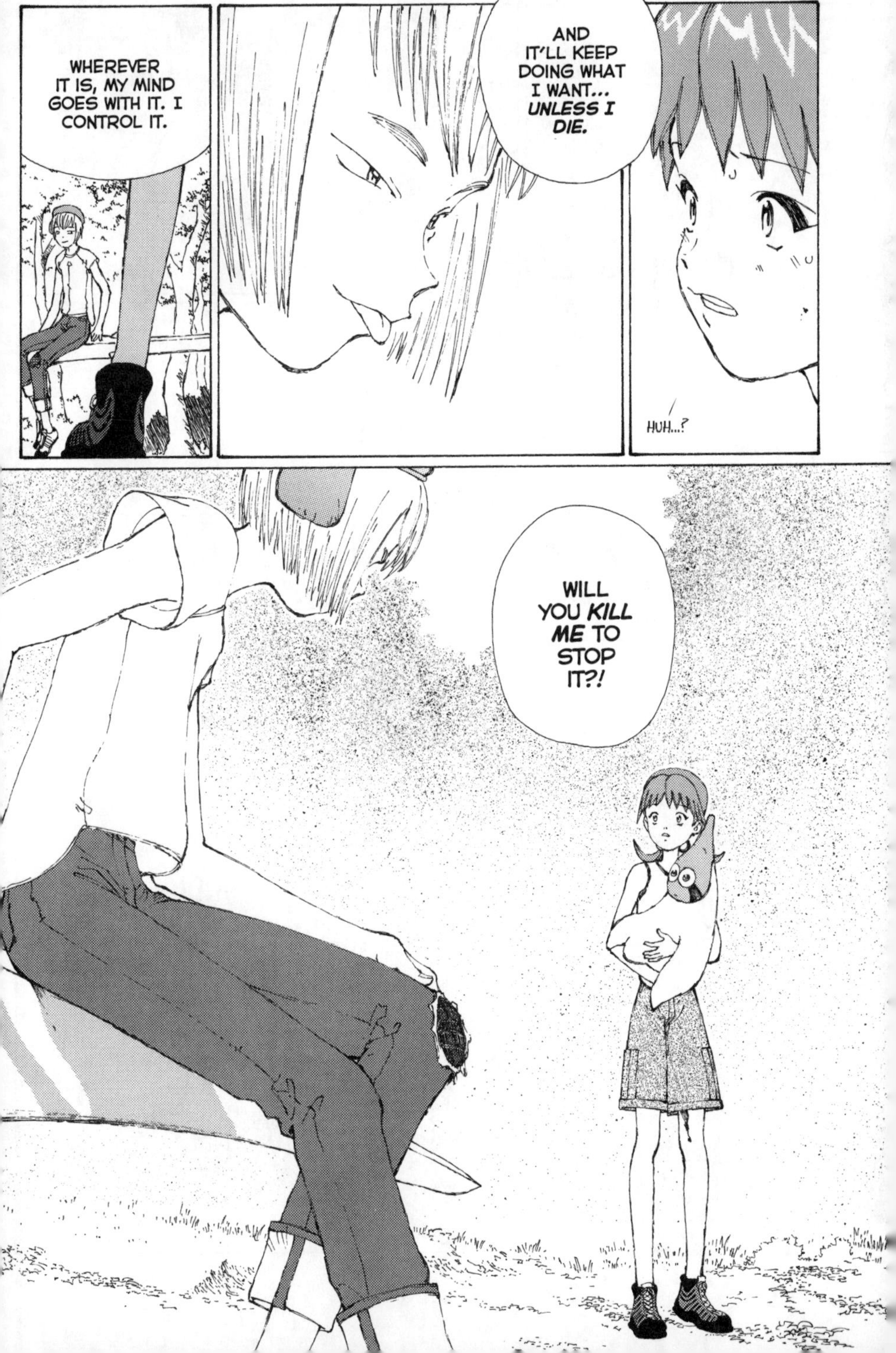
WHEREVER IT IS, MY MIND GOES WITH IT. I CONTROL IT.
AND IT'LL KEEP DOING WHAT I WANT... *UNLESS I DIE.*
HUH...?
WILL YOU *KILL ME* TO STOP IT?!

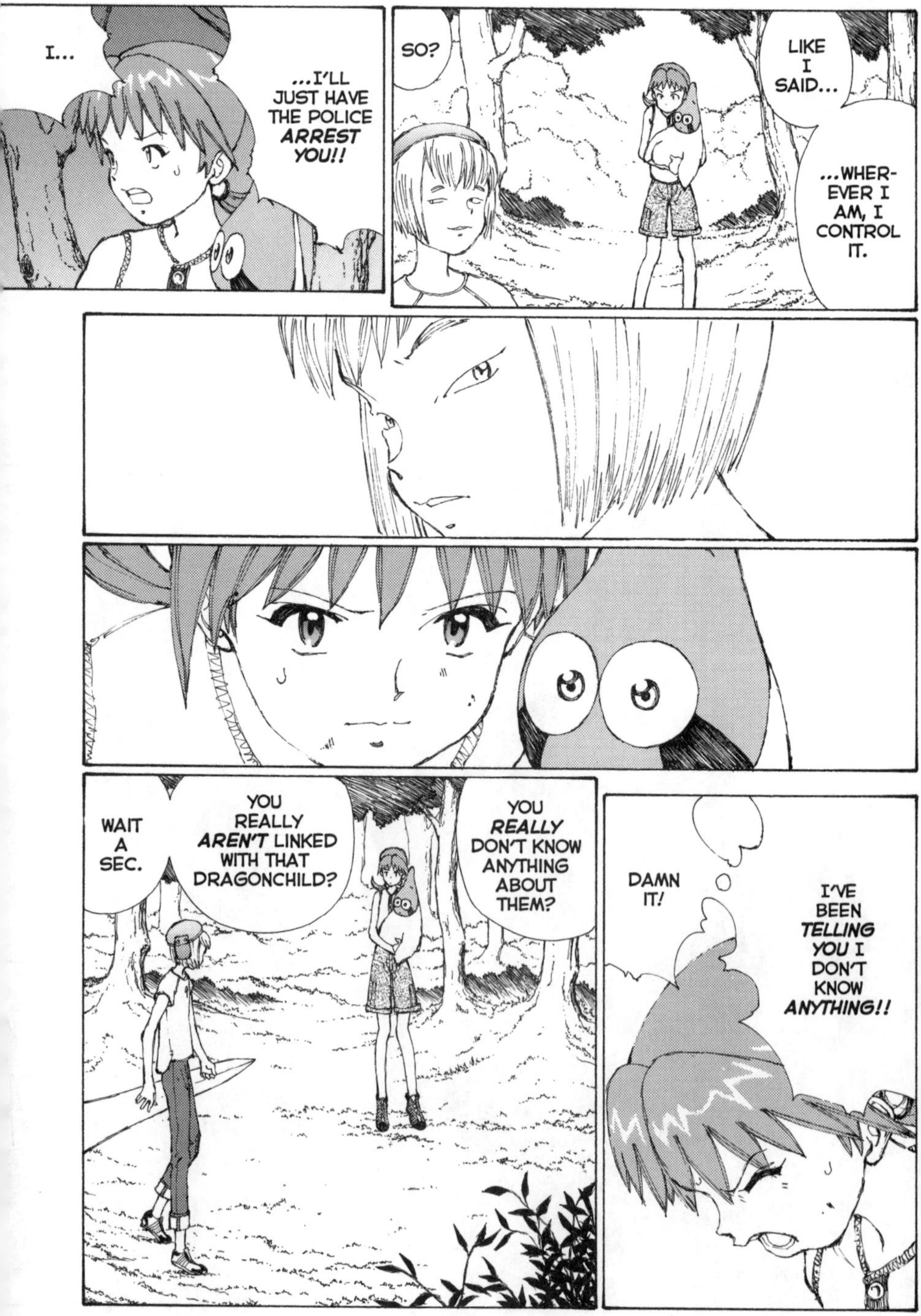
I...
...I'LL JUST HAVE THE POLICE ARREST YOU!!
SO?
LIKE I SAID...
...WHEREVER I AM, I CONTROL IT.
WAIT A SEC.
YOU REALLY AREN'T LINKED WITH THAT DRAGONCHILD?
YOU REALLY DON'T KNOW ANYTHING ABOUT THEM?
DAMN IT!
I'VE BEEN TELLING YOU I DON'T KNOW ANYTHING!!

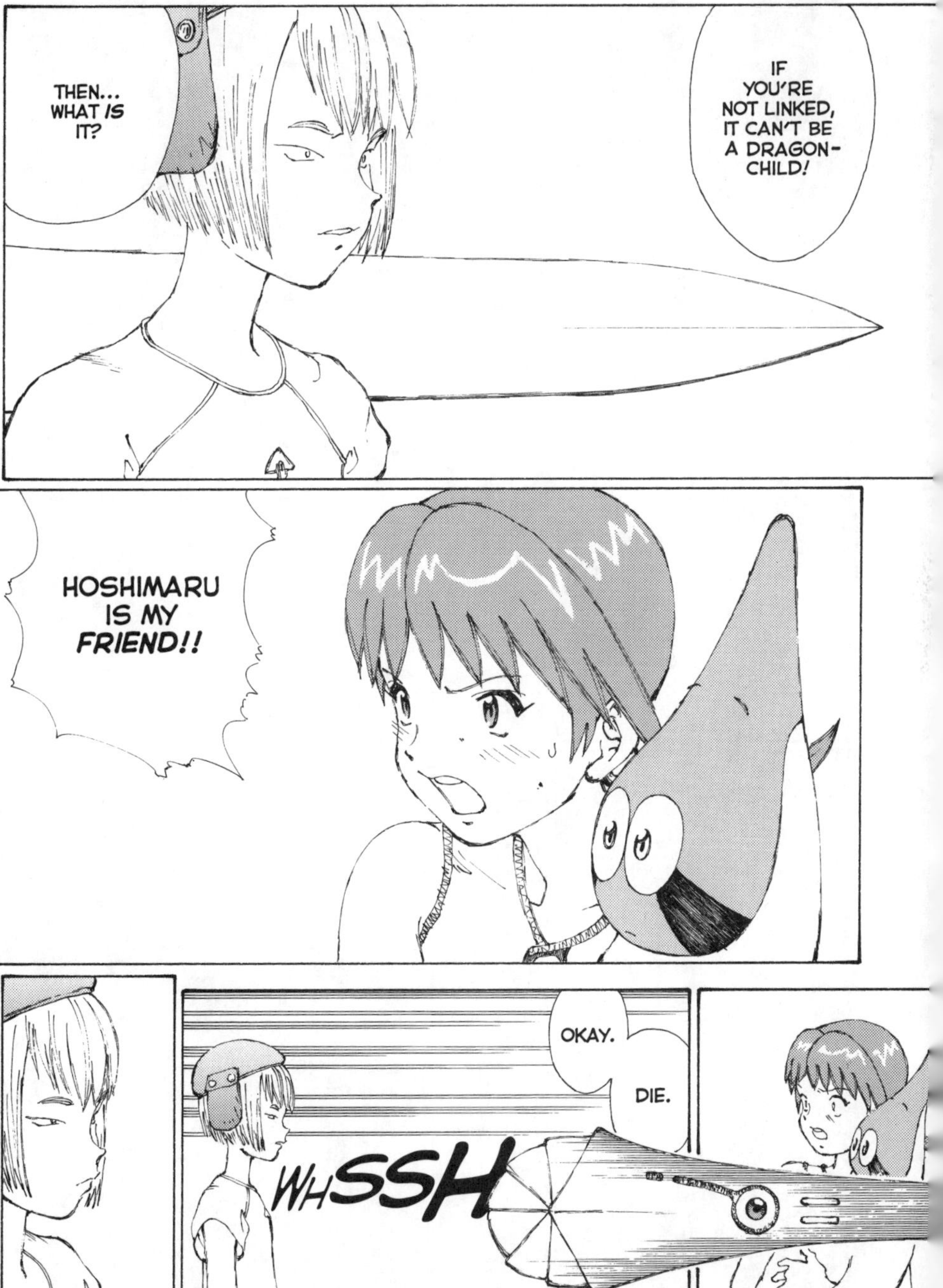
IF YOU'RE NOT LINKED, IT CAN'T BE A DRAGON-CHILD!
THEN... WHAT *IS* IT?
HOSHIMARU IS MY *FRIEND!!*
OKAY.
DIE.
WHSSH

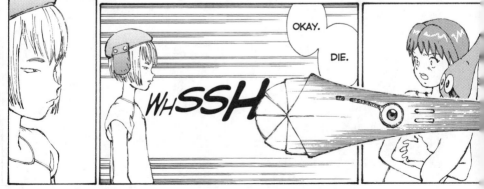

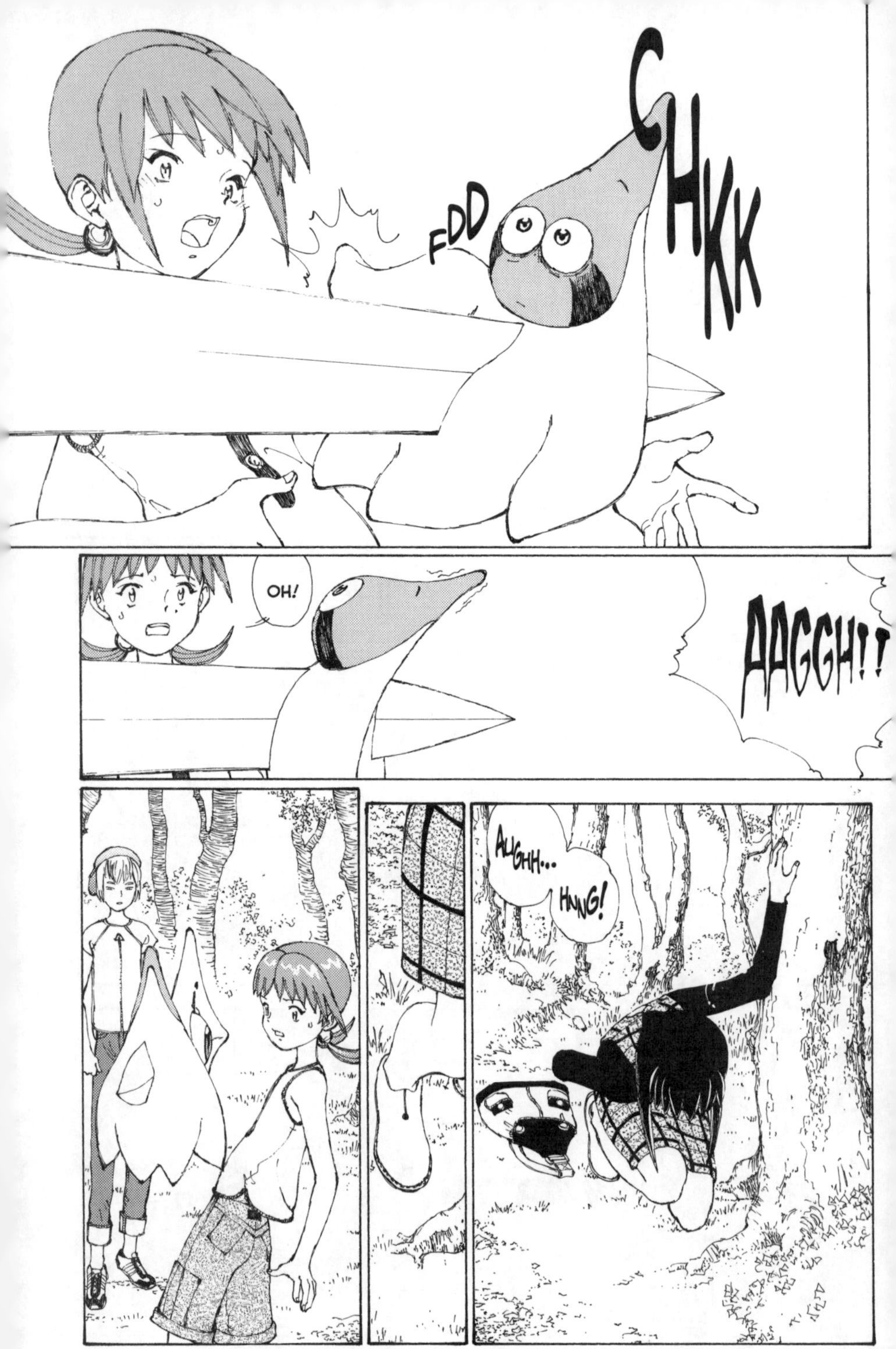
CHKK
FDD
AAGGH!!
OH!
AUGHH...
HNNG!

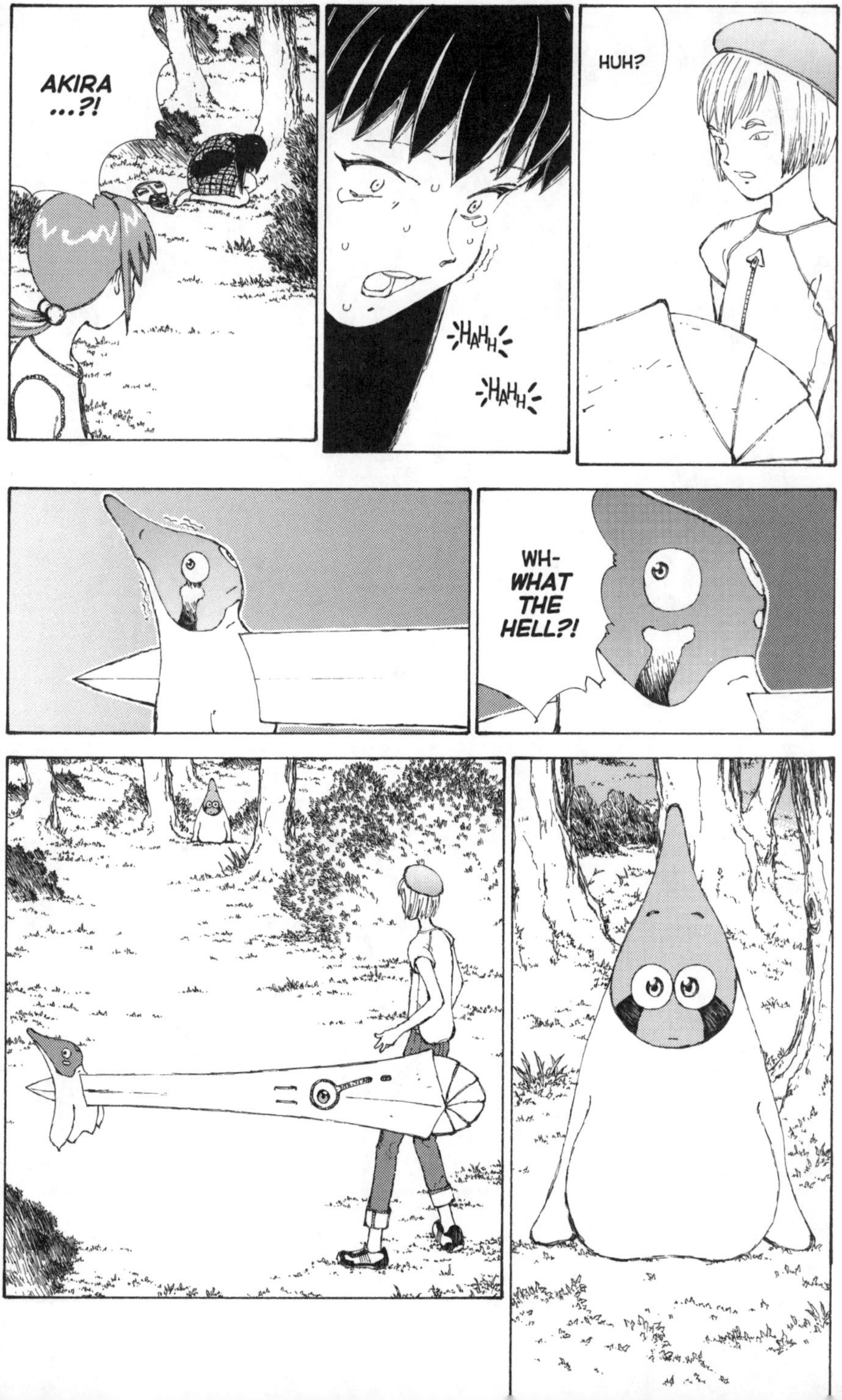
HUH?
HAHH
HAHH
AKIRA ...?!
WH- WHAT THE HELL?!

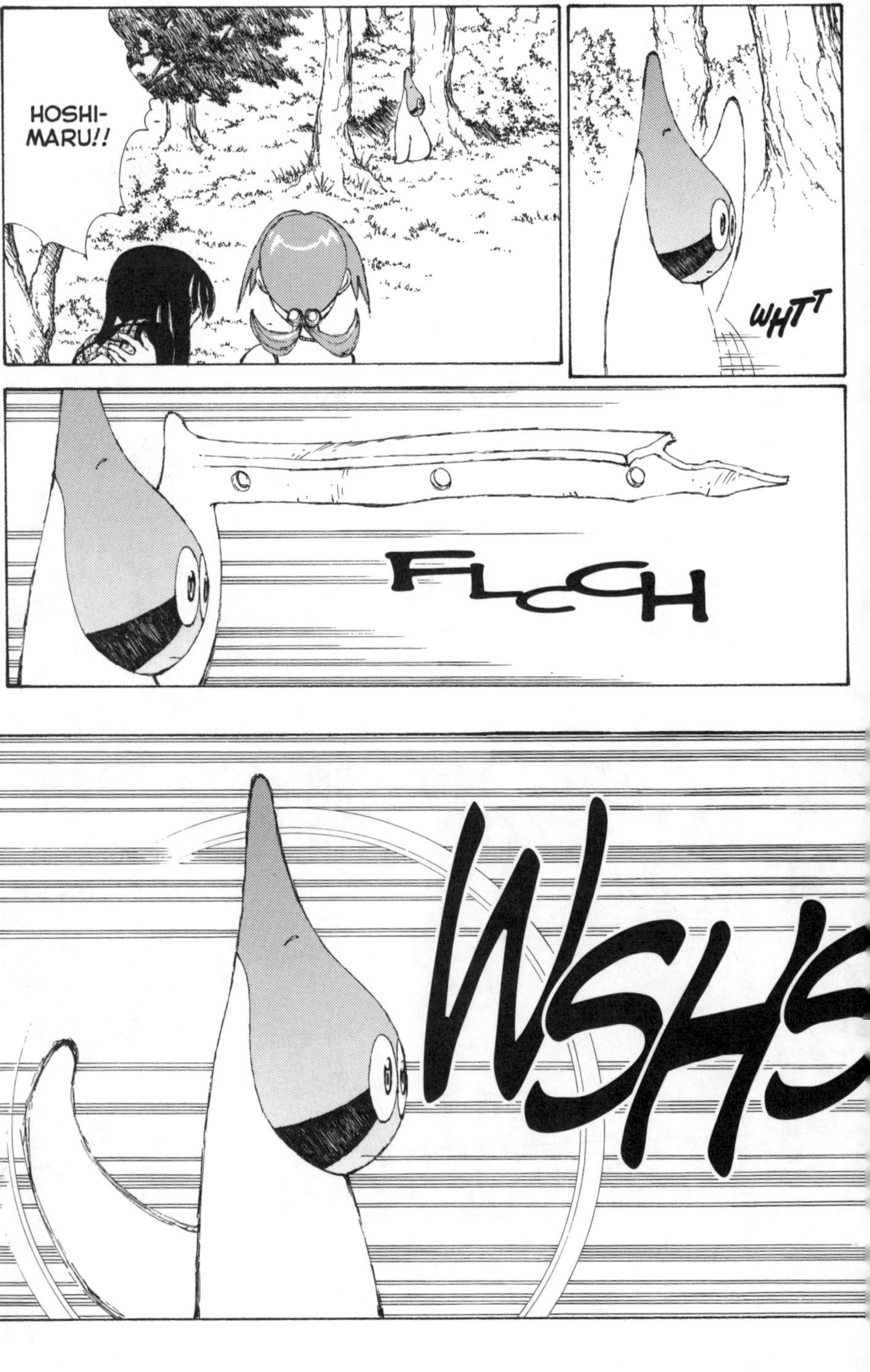
WHTT
HOSHI-
MARU!!
FLCCH
WSHS

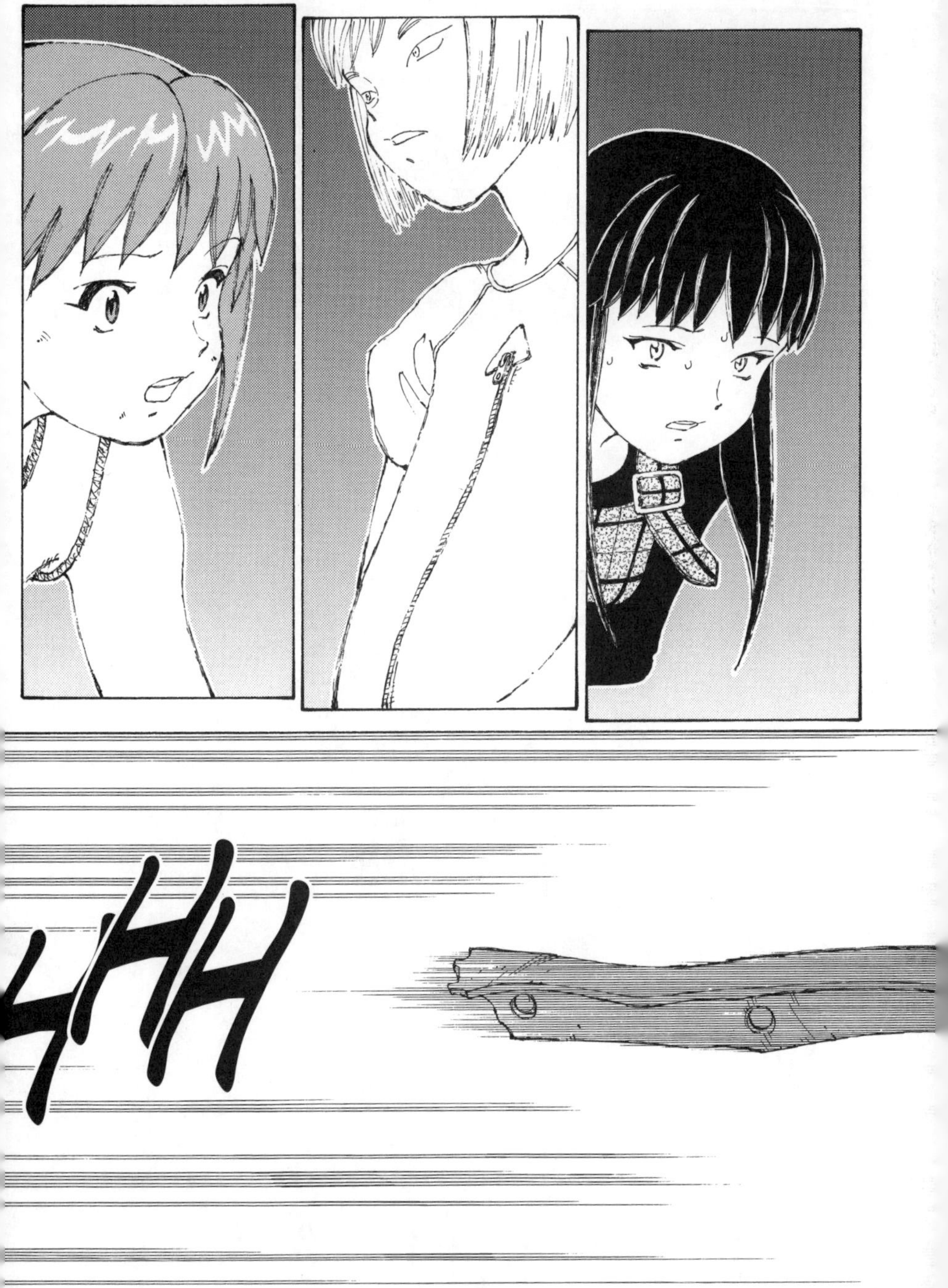

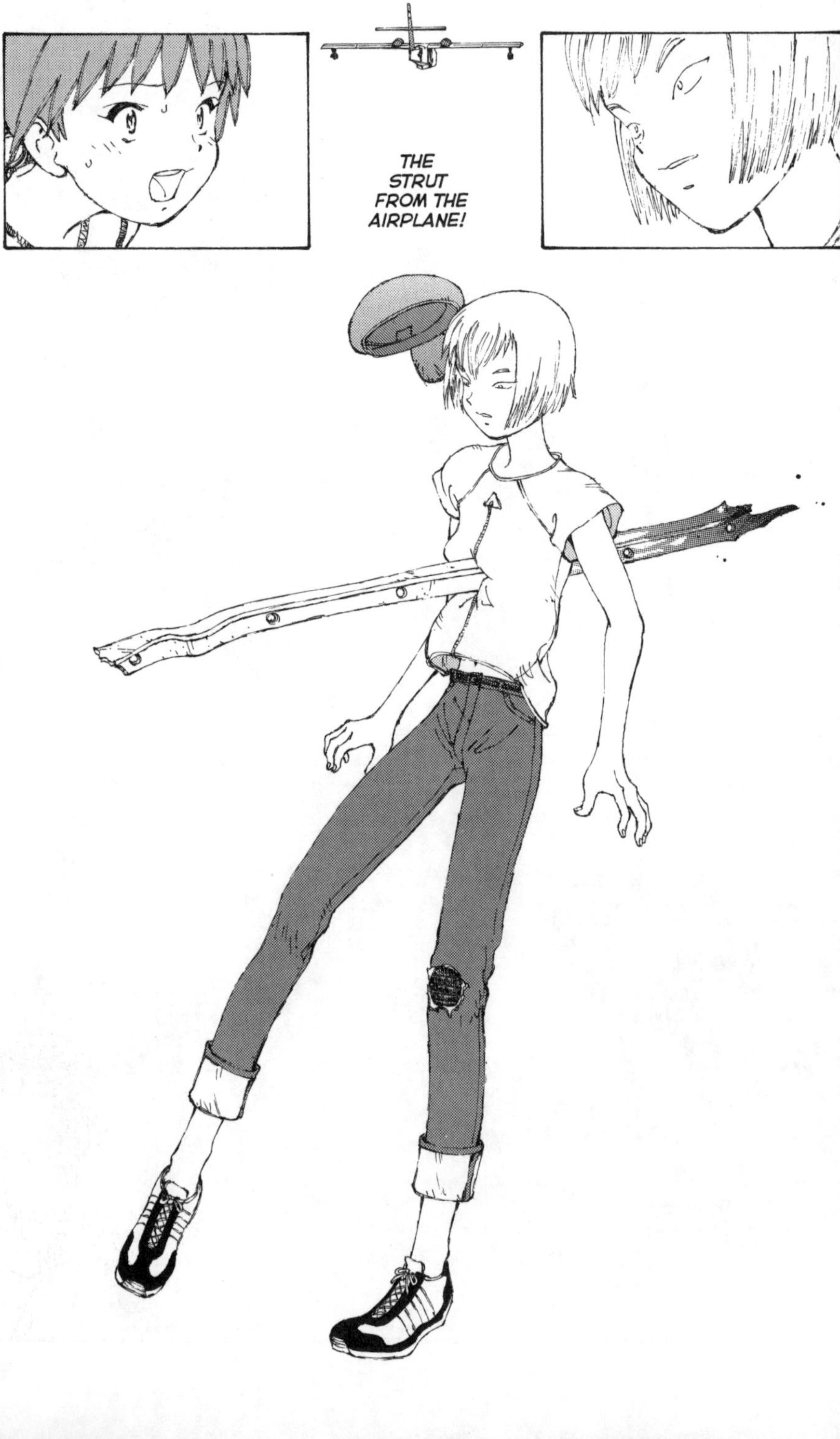
THE STRUT FROM THE AIRPLANE!

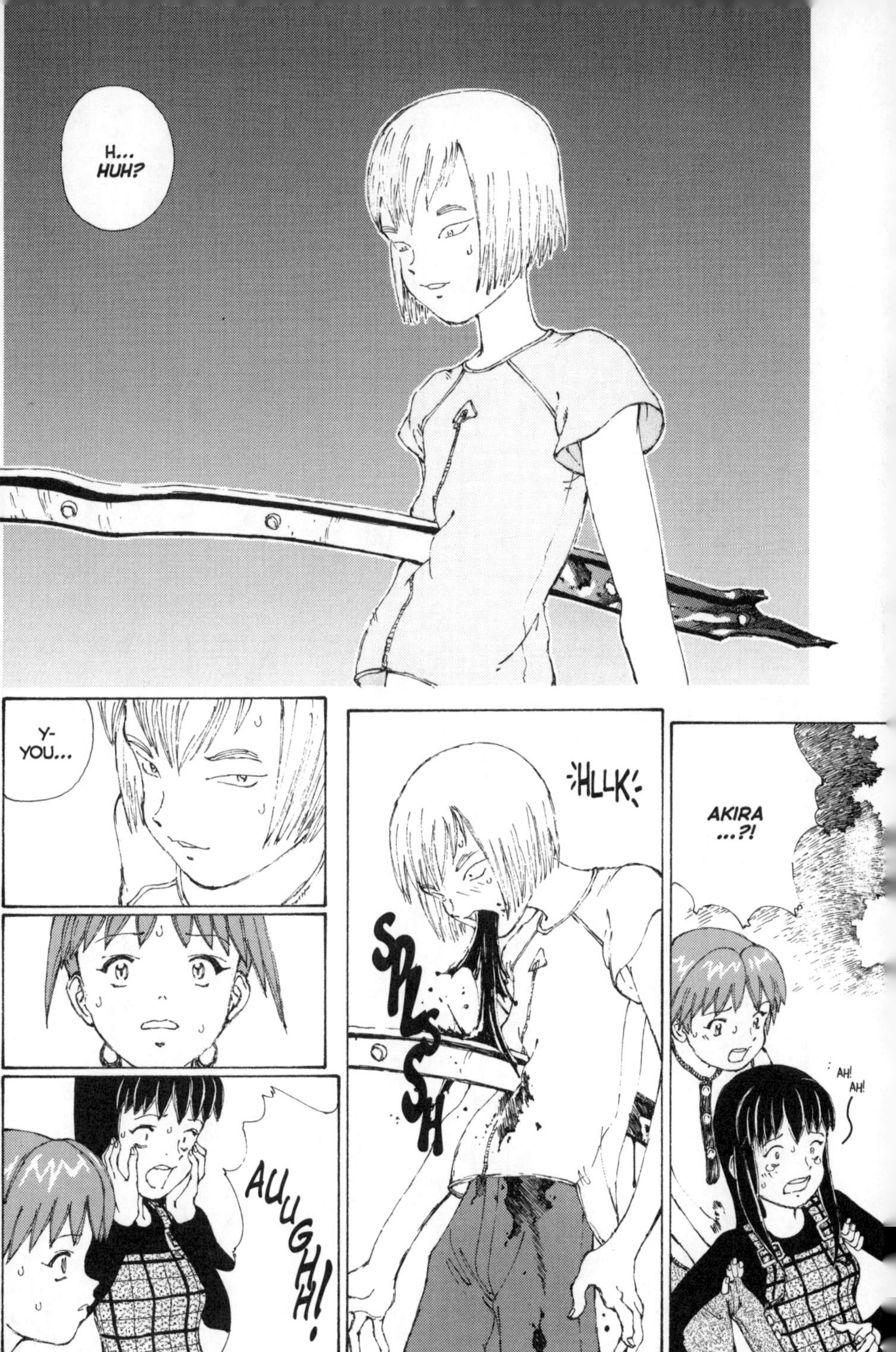
H... HUH?
AKIRA ...?!
AH! AH!
HLLK
SPLSSH
Y- YOU...
AUUGHH!

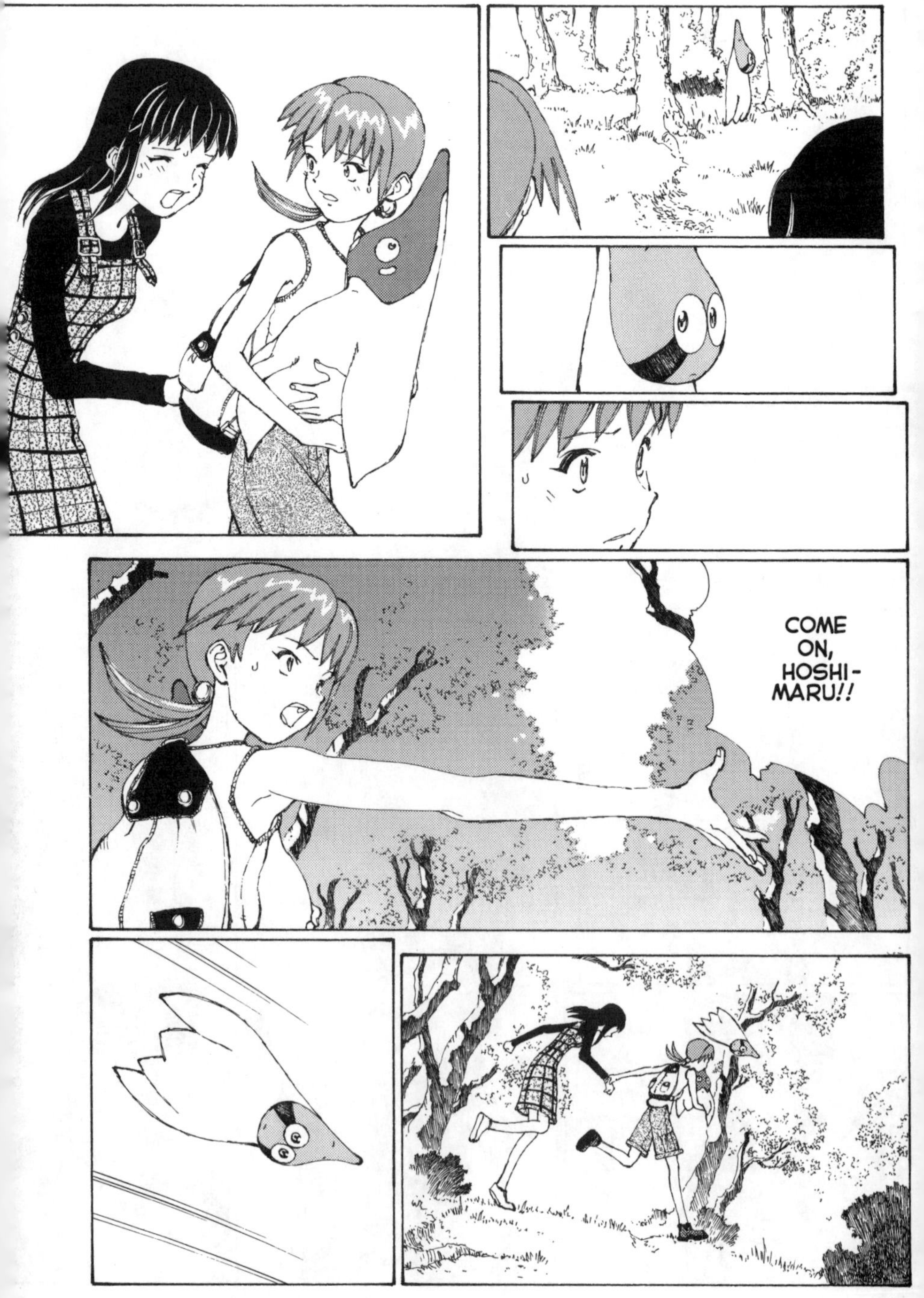
COME ON, HOSHI-MARU!!

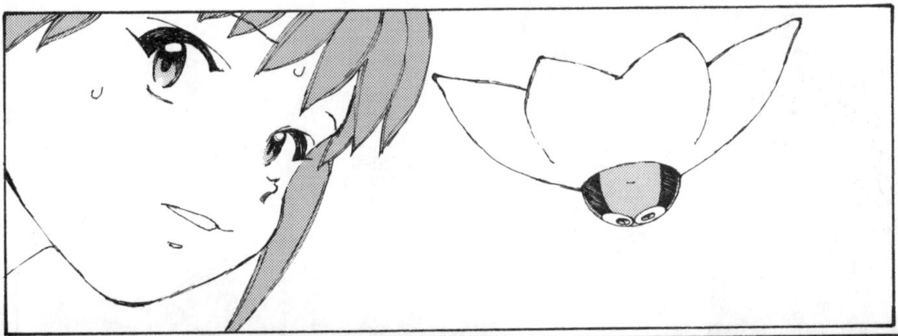
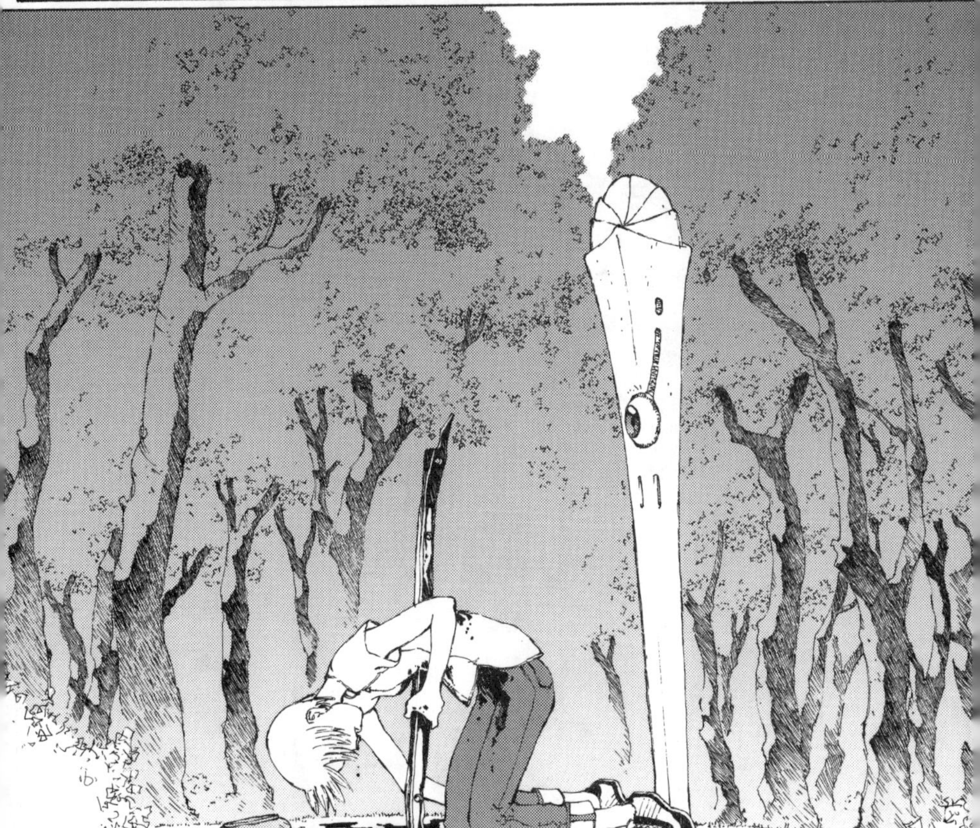

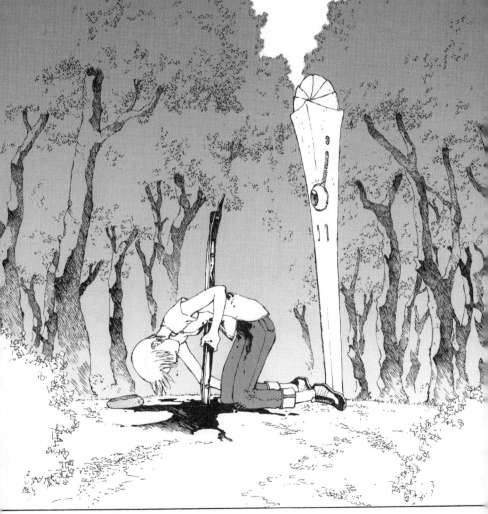

I...
I...I
THOUGHT M-
MAYBE I COULD
S-STAND UP
AGAINST HIM...
IF...IF I TRIED
BEING LIKE
YOU...SH-
SHIINA...

B-
BUT...

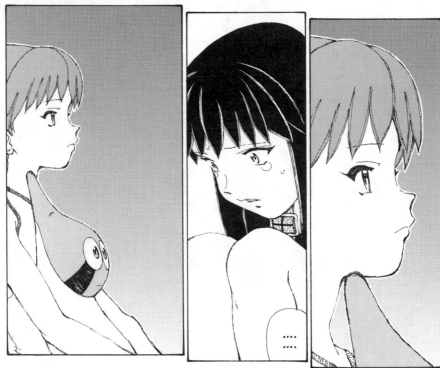

....
....

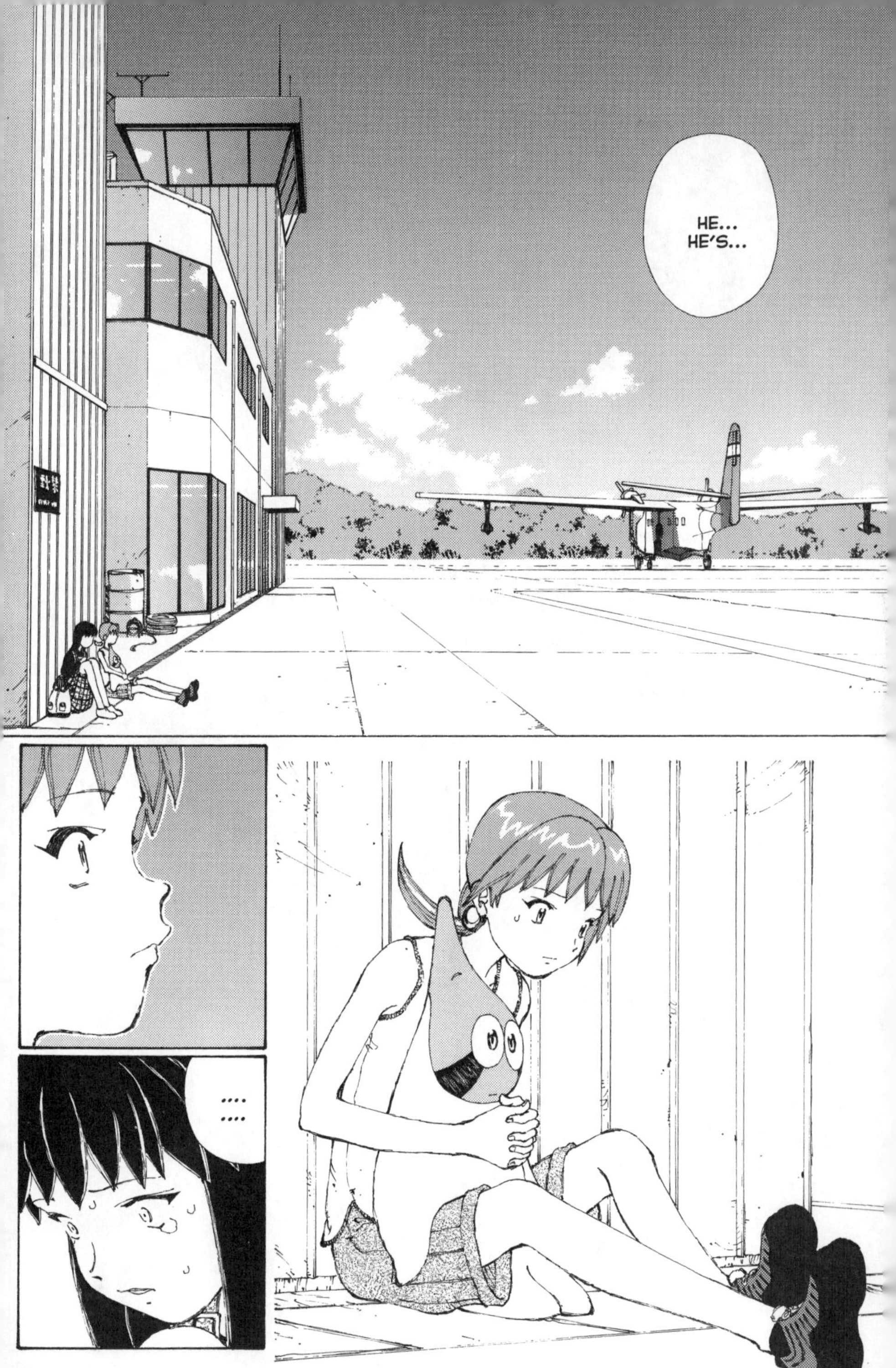
HE...
HE'S...
....
....

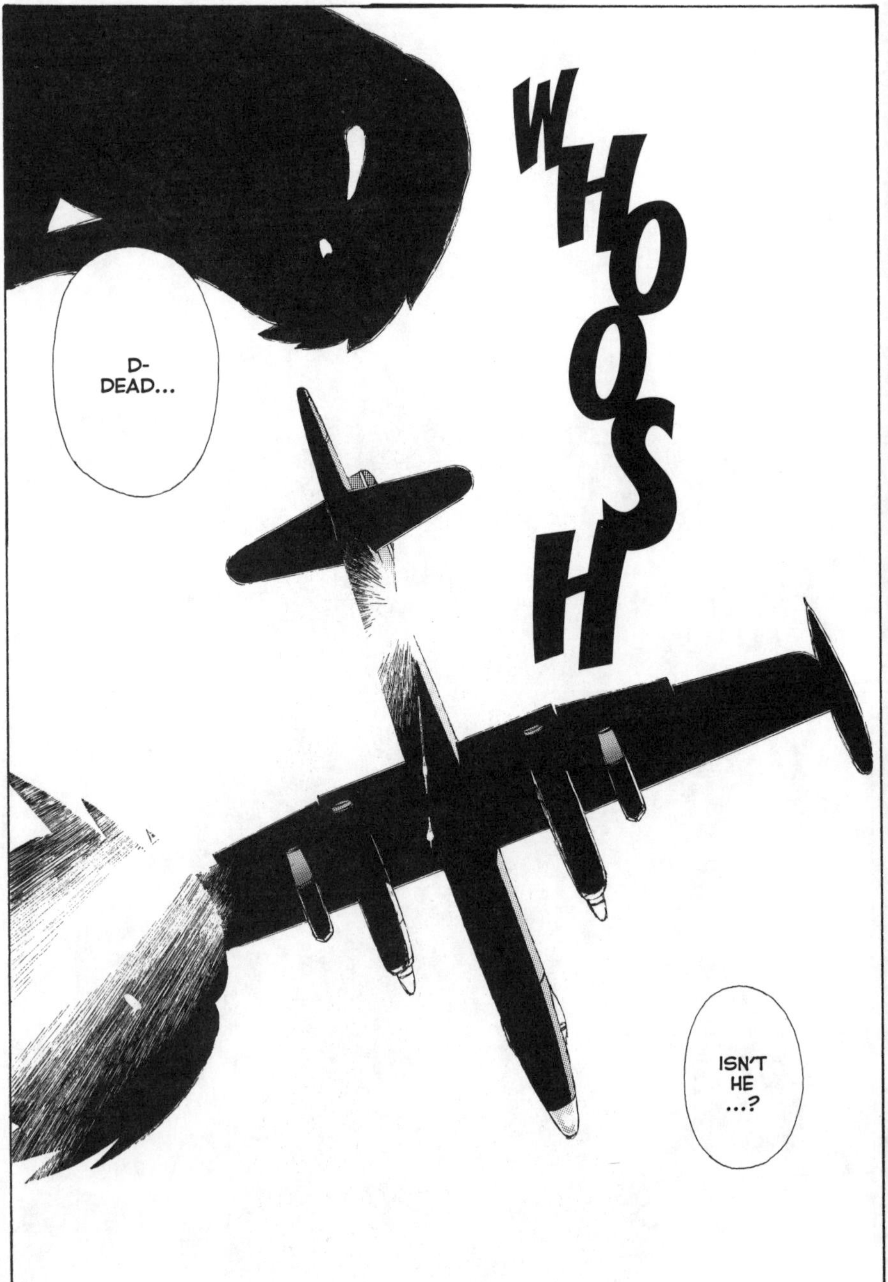
WHOOSH
D-
DEAD...
ISN'T
HE
...?

NIGHT OF EVIL DREAMS

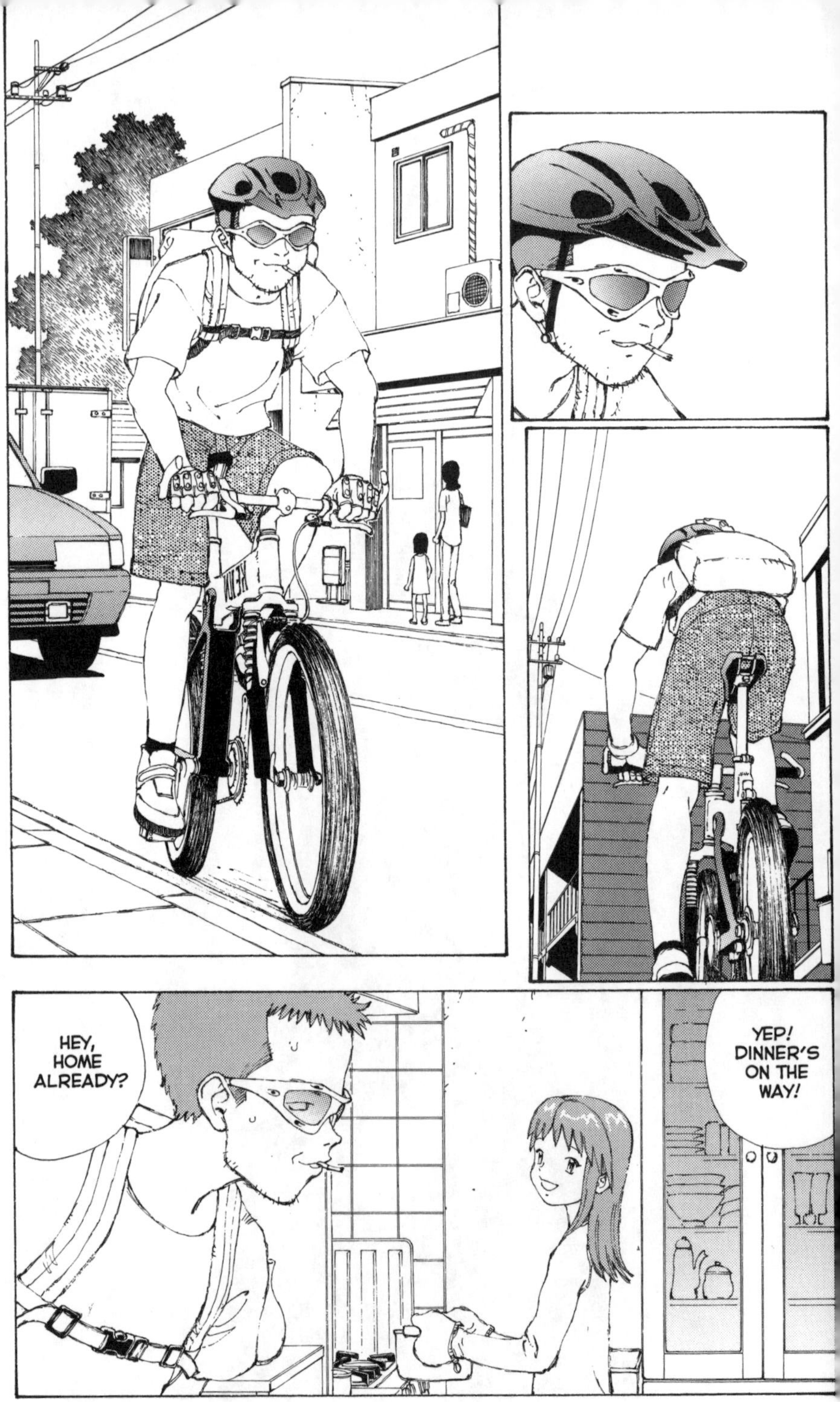
YEP! DINNER'S ON THE WAY!
HEY, HOME ALREADY?

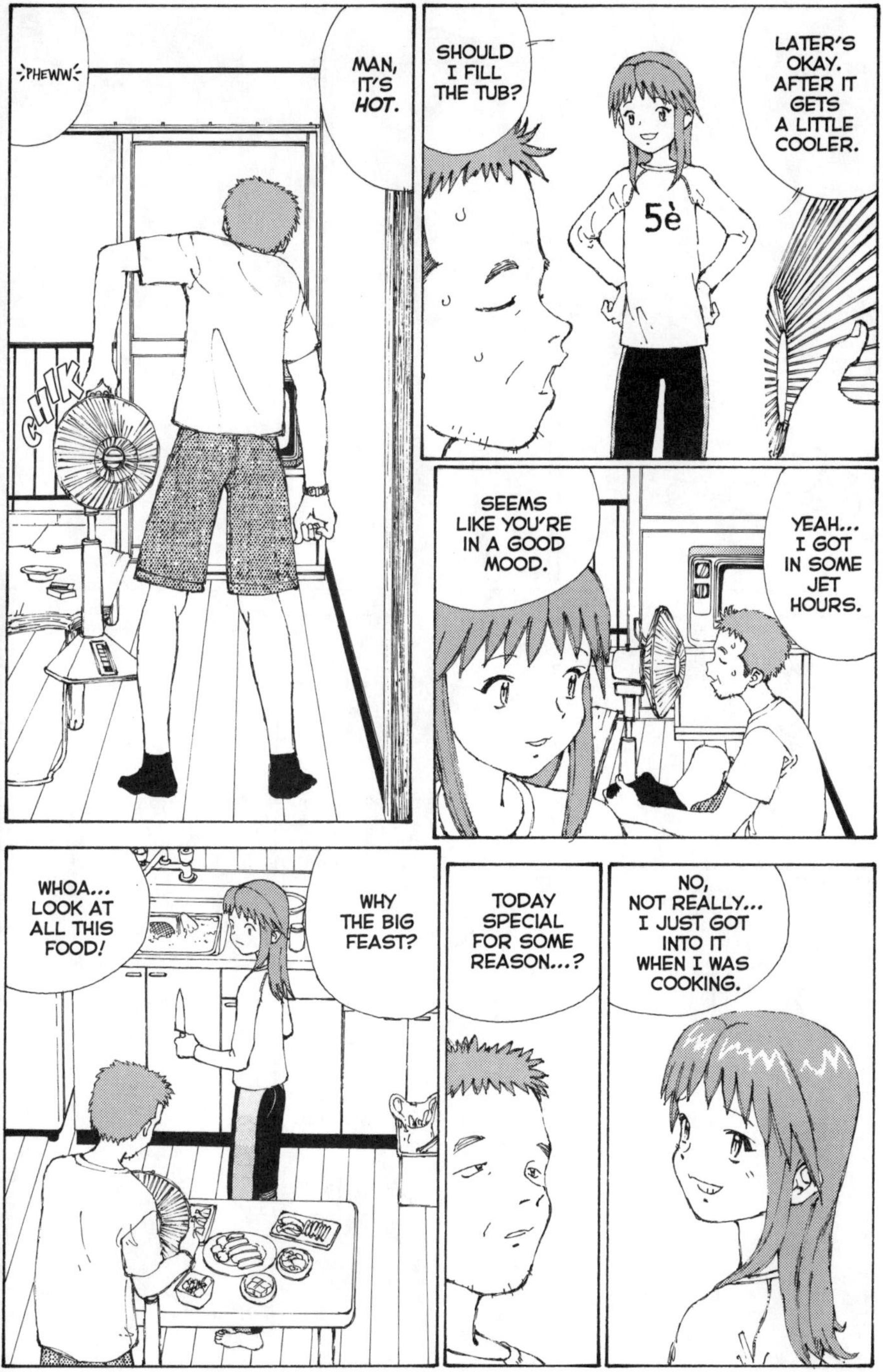
PHEWW
MAN, IT'S *HOT*.
CHIK
SHOULD I FILL THE TUB?
LATER'S OKAY. AFTER IT GETS A LITTLE COOLER.
5è
SEEMS LIKE YOU'RE IN A GOOD MOOD.
YEAH... I GOT IN SOME JET HOURS.
WHOA... LOOK AT ALL THIS FOOD!
WHY THE BIG FEAST?
TODAY SPECIAL FOR SOME REASON...?
NO, NOT REALLY... I JUST GOT INTO IT WHEN I WAS COOKING.

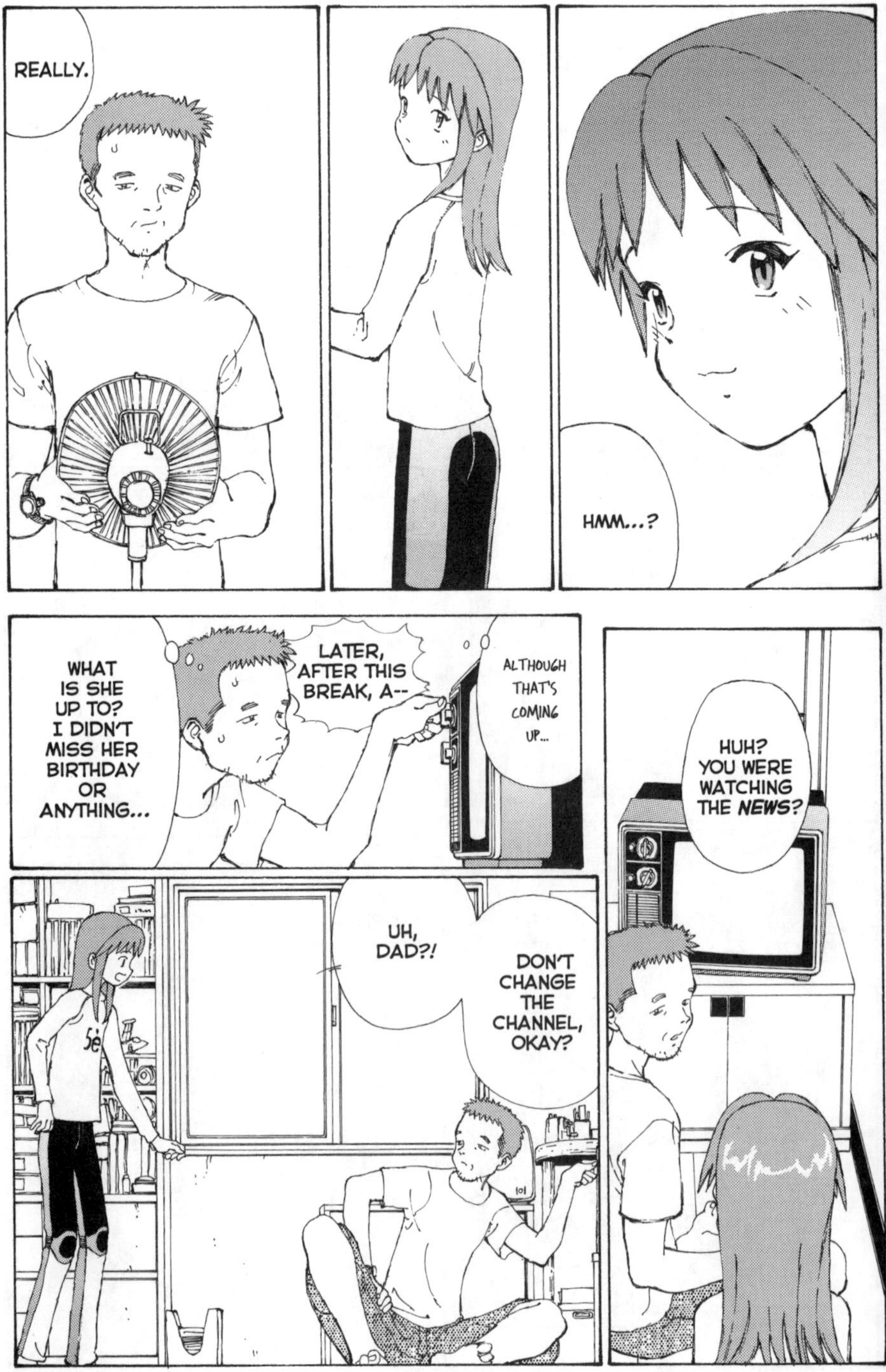
HMM...?
REALLY.
HUH? YOU WERE WATCHING THE *NEWS*?
ALTHOUGH THAT'S COMING UP...
LATER, AFTER THIS BREAK, A--
WHAT IS SHE UP TO? I DIDN'T MISS HER BIRTHDAY OR ANYTHING...
UH, DAD?!
DON'T CHANGE THE CHANNEL, OKAY?

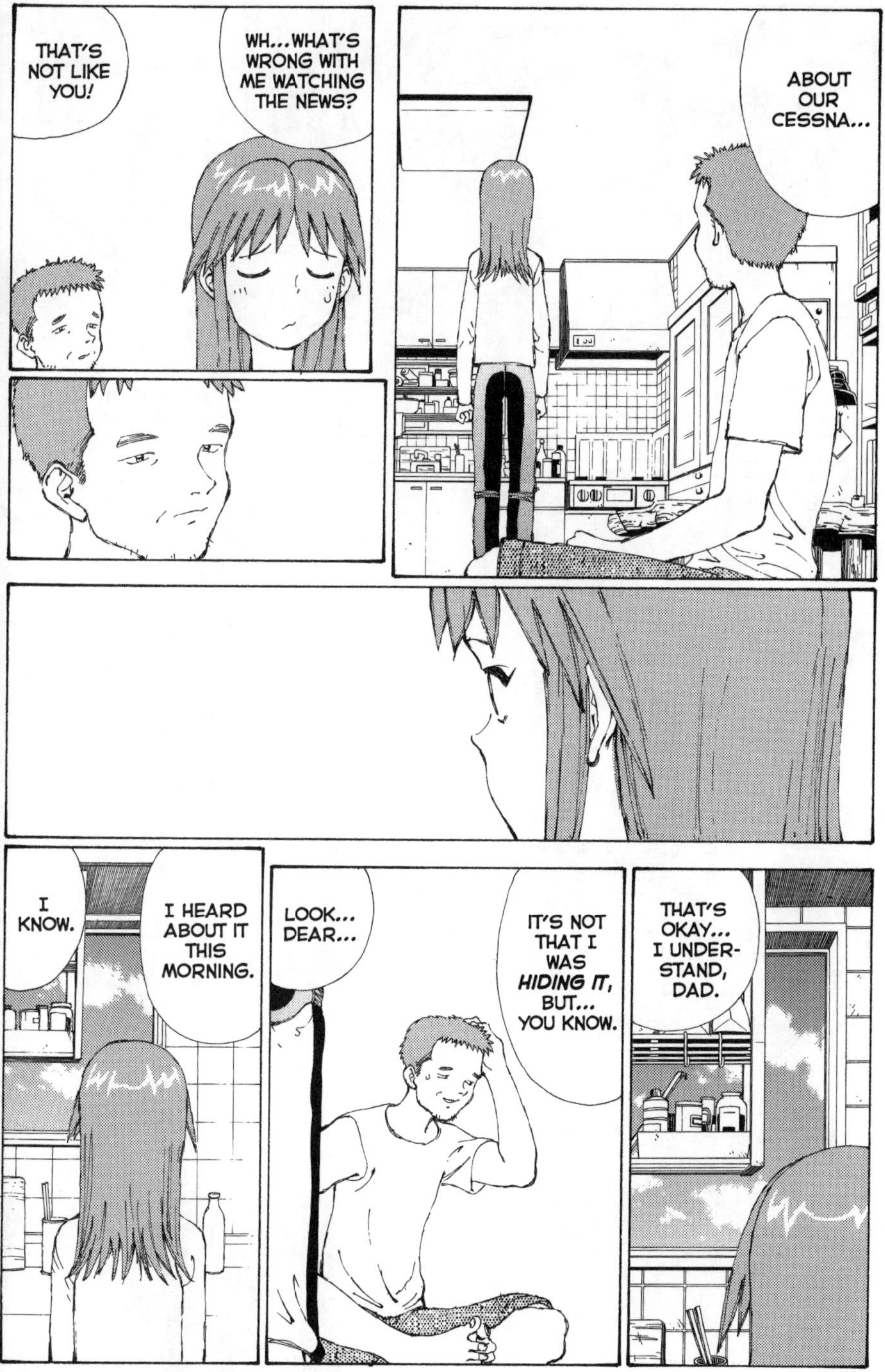
THAT'S NOT LIKE YOU!
WH...WHAT'S WRONG WITH ME WATCHING THE NEWS?
ABOUT OUR CESSNA...
I KNOW.
I HEARD ABOUT IT THIS MORNING.
LOOK... DEAR...
IT'S NOT THAT I WAS *HIDING IT*, BUT... YOU KNOW.
THAT'S OKAY... I UNDERSTAND, DAD.

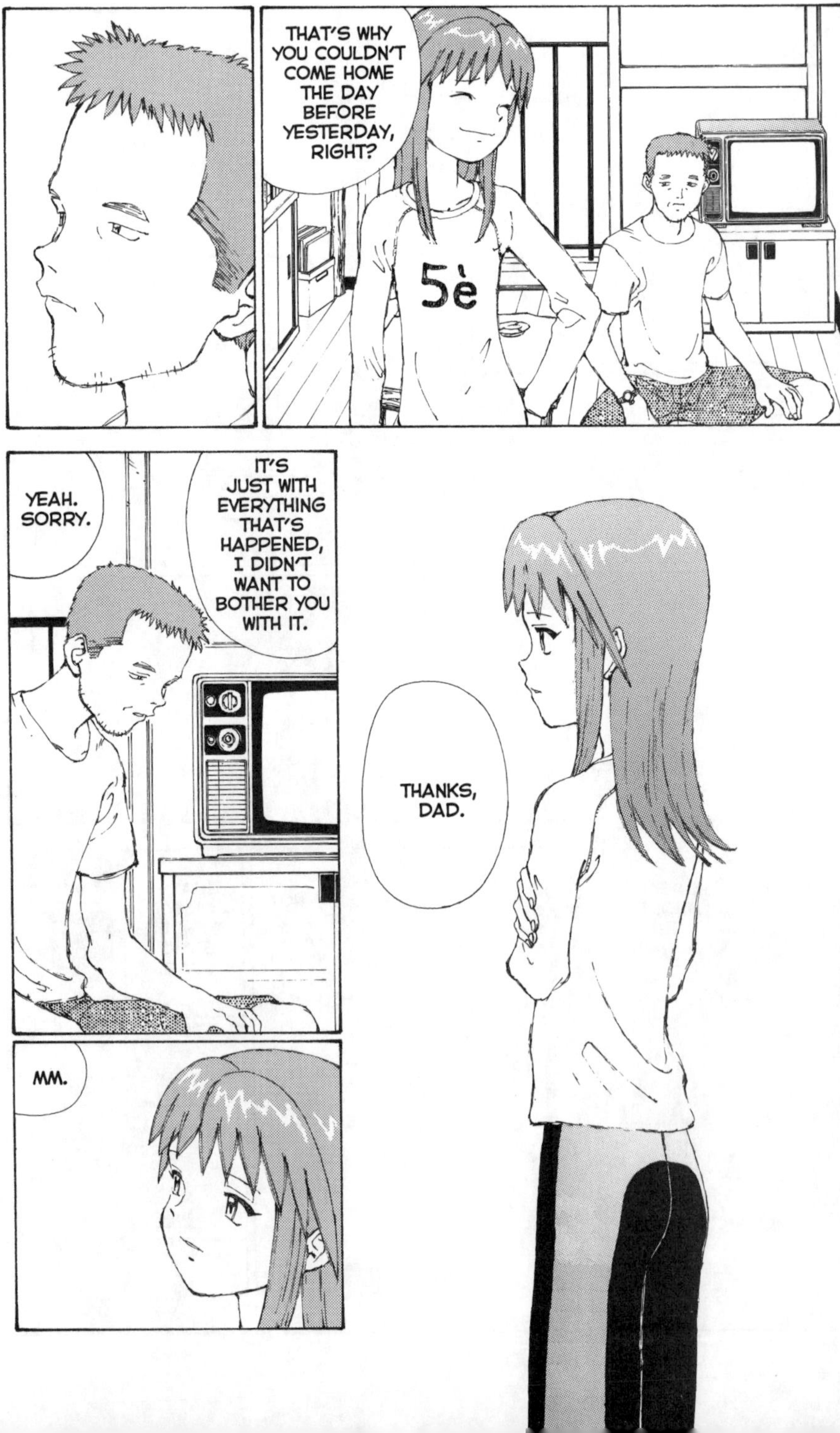
THAT'S WHY YOU COULDN'T COME HOME THE DAY BEFORE YESTERDAY, RIGHT?
THANKS, DAD.
IT'S JUST WITH EVERYTHING THAT'S HAPPENED, I DIDN'T WANT TO BOTHER YOU WITH IT.
YEAH. SORRY.
MM.

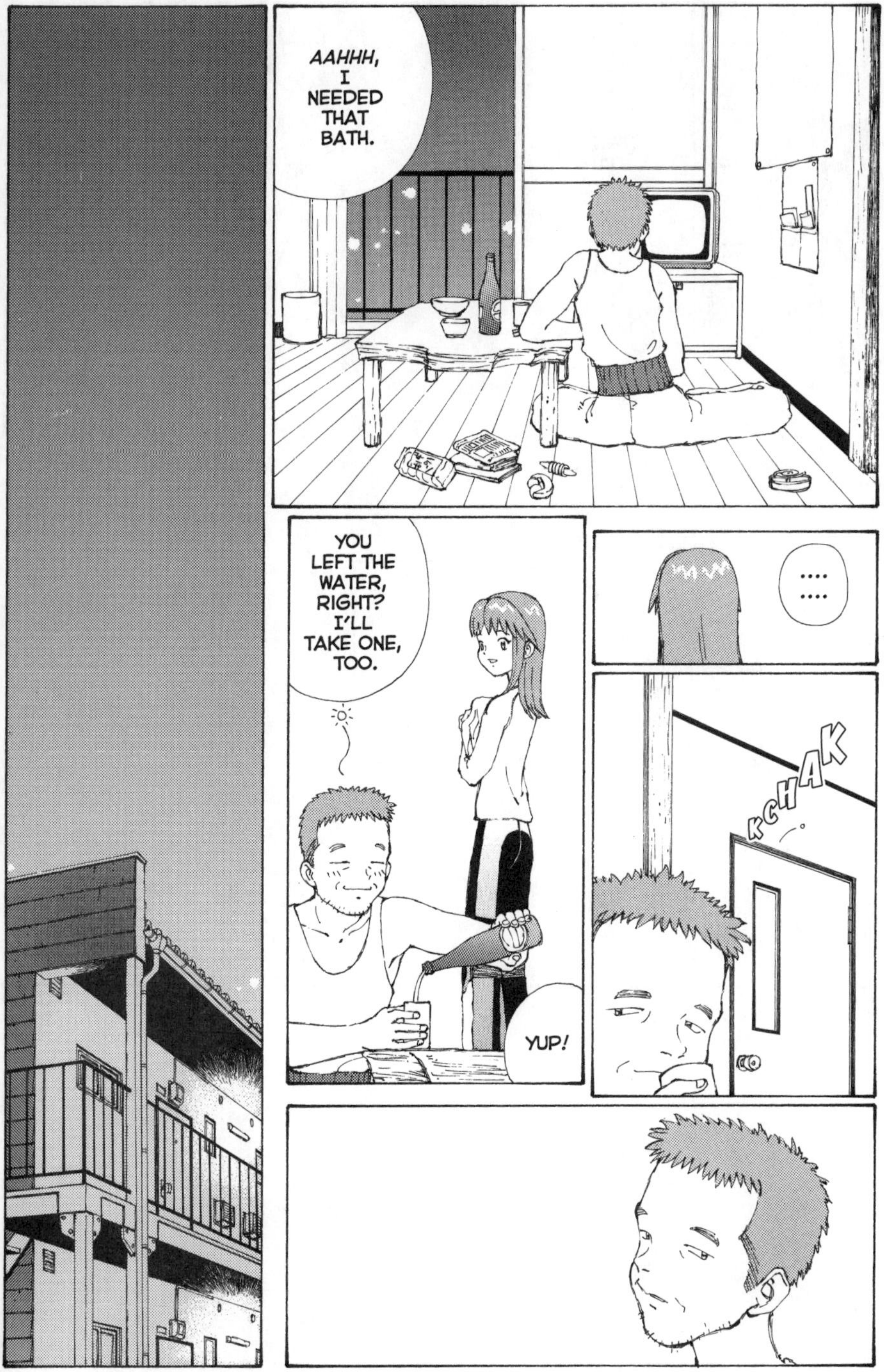
AAHHH, I NEEDED THAT BATH.
YOU LEFT THE WATER, RIGHT? I'LL TAKE ONE, TOO.
YUP!
....
....
KCHAK

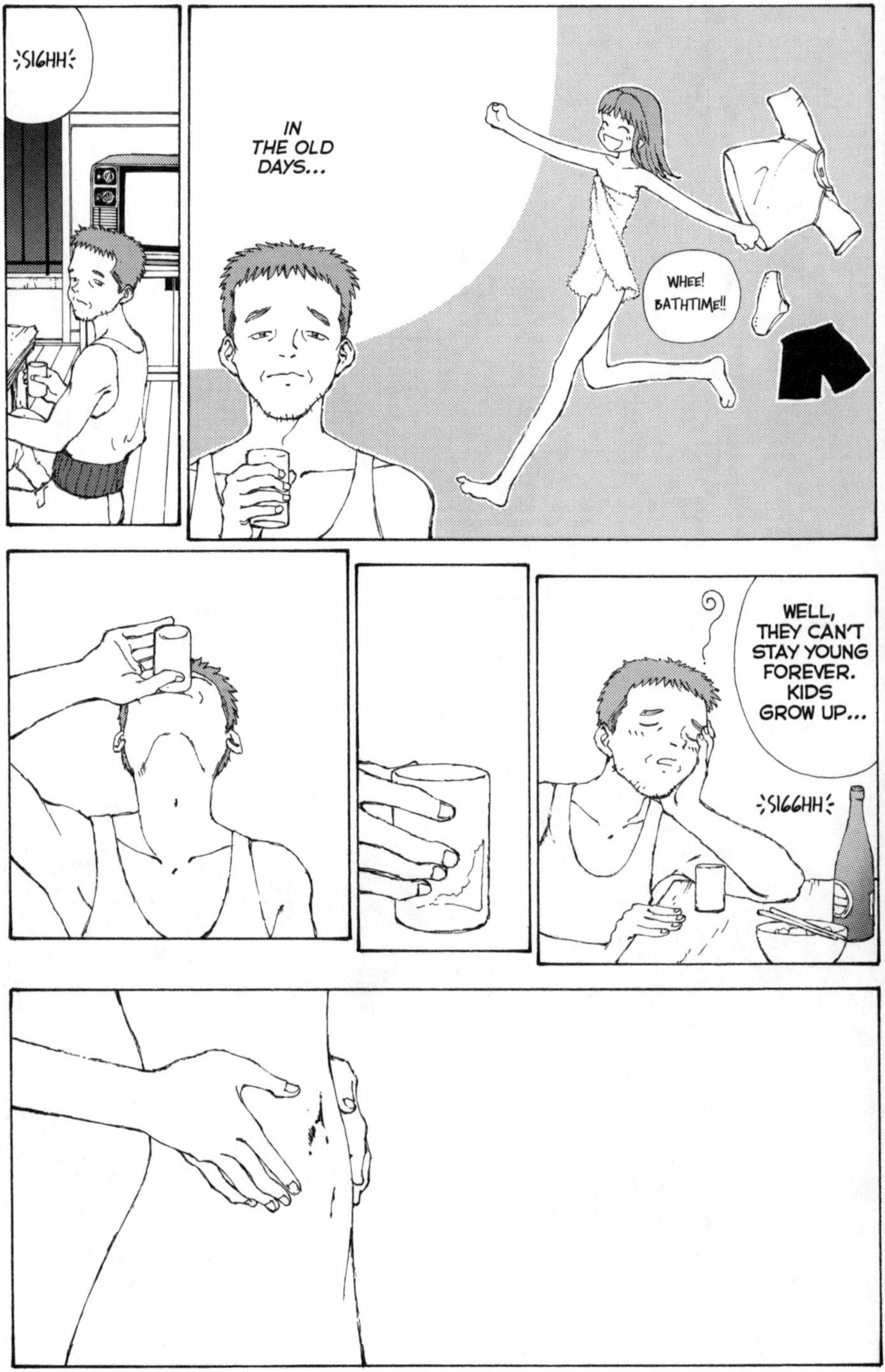
IN THE OLD DAYS...
WHEE! BATHTIME!!
SIGHH
WELL, THEY CAN'T STAY YOUNG FOREVER. KIDS GROW UP...
SIGGHH

HMM...
MAYBE I
BETTER NOT
SOAK IN
THE WATER
TOO LONG.

VREEEEEE

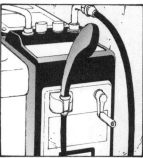

WHEWW...
I'M SO
TIRED...

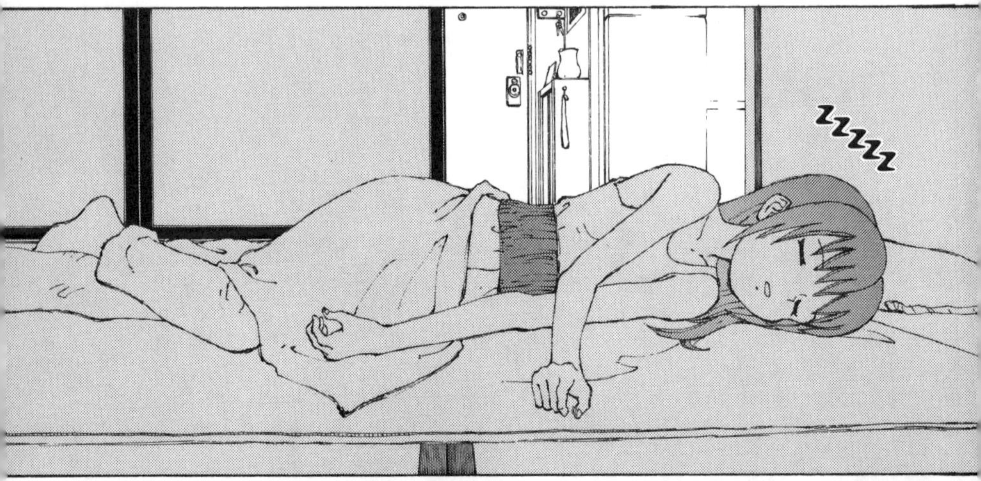
ZZZZZ

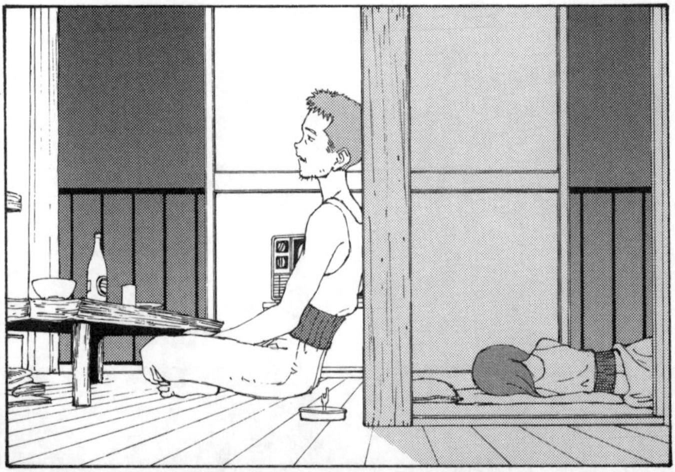

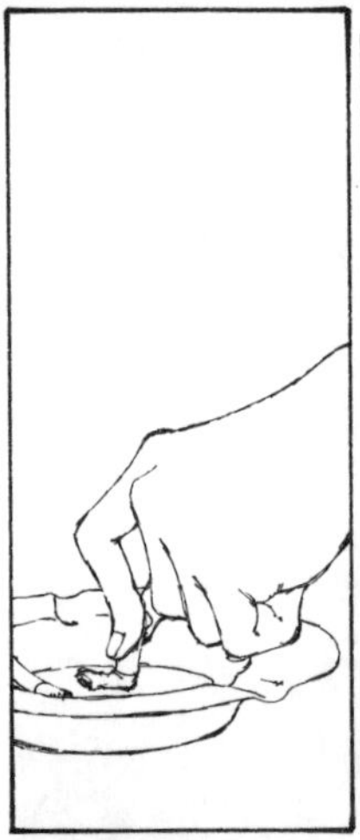

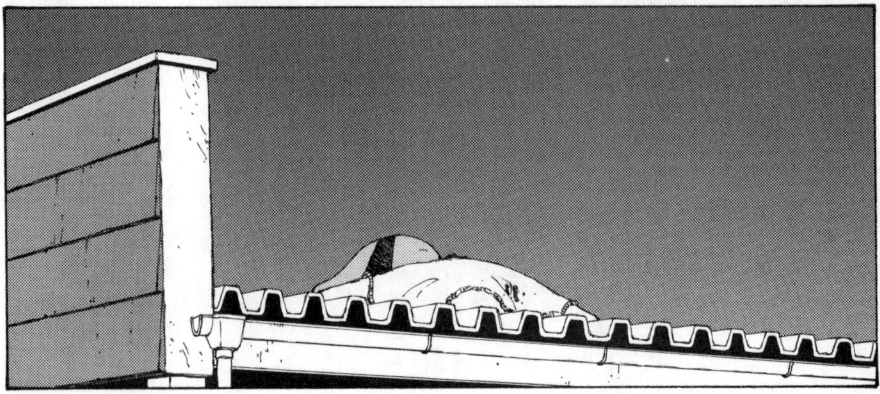

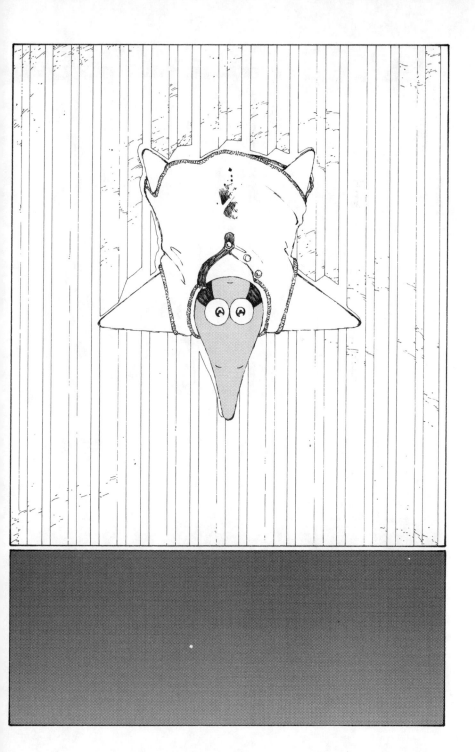

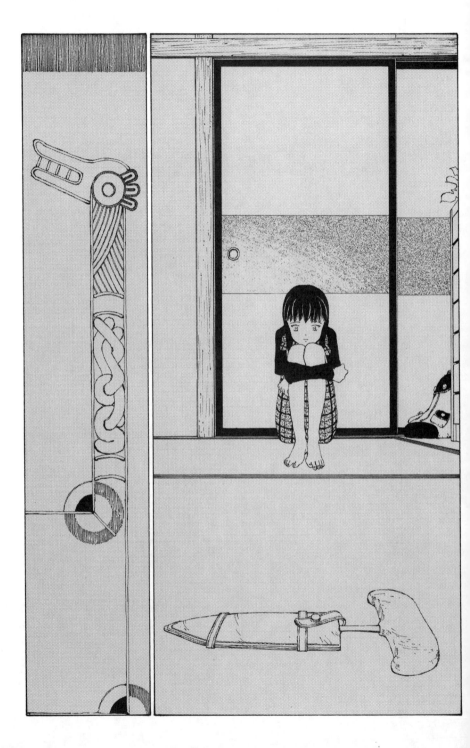

WEEOOO
WEEOOOO
WEEOOOO
?!?
VSHHHHH

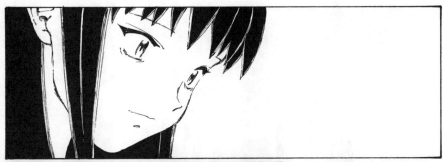

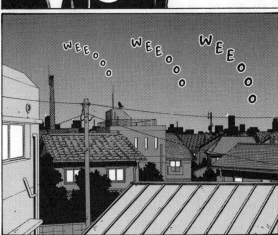

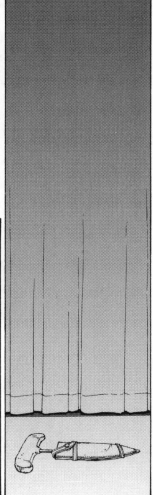

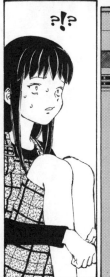

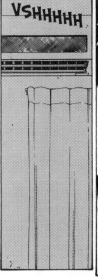

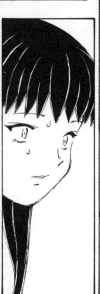

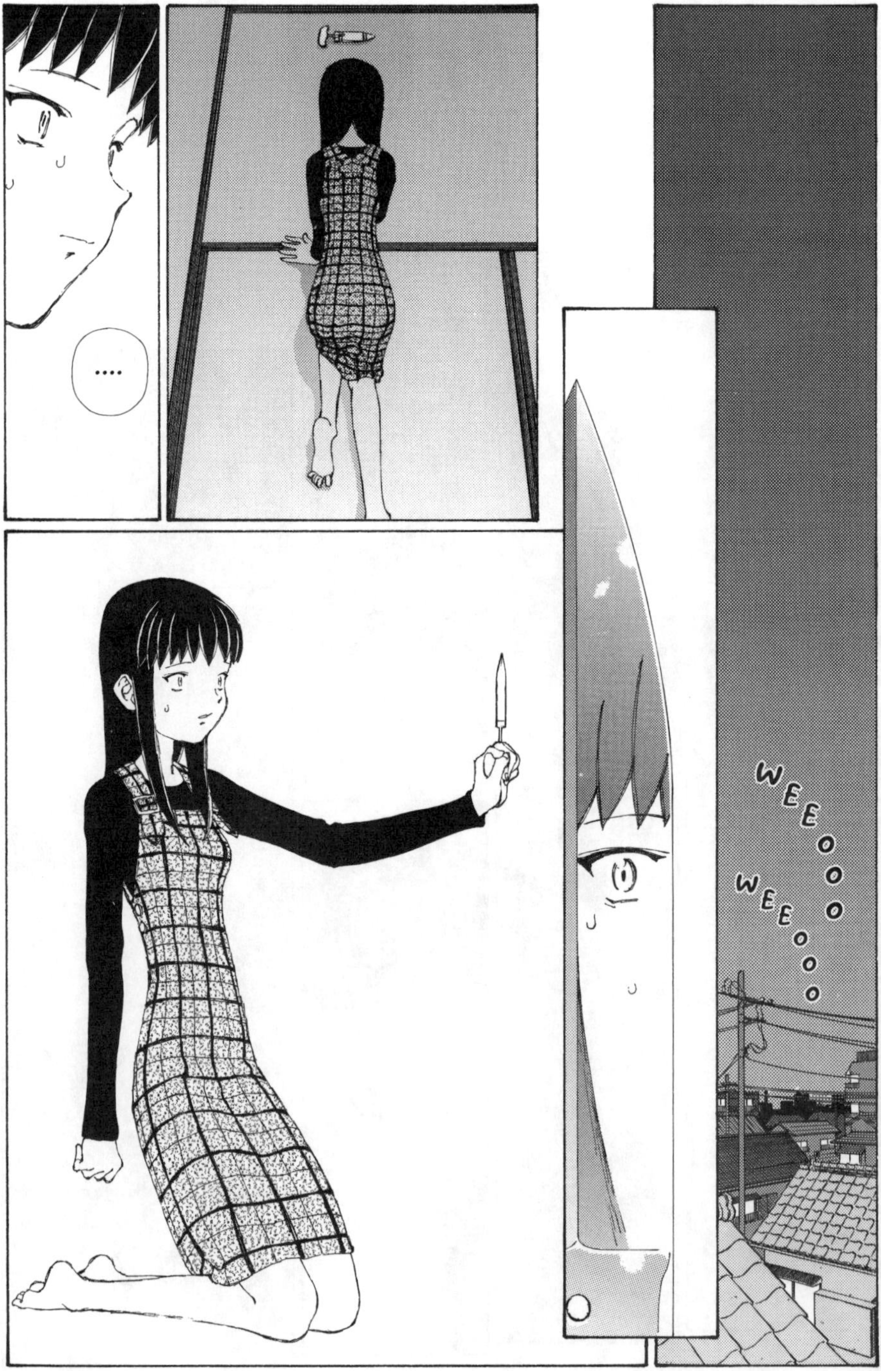
WEEOOO
WEEOOO
....

THE STAR CHAMBER CLUB

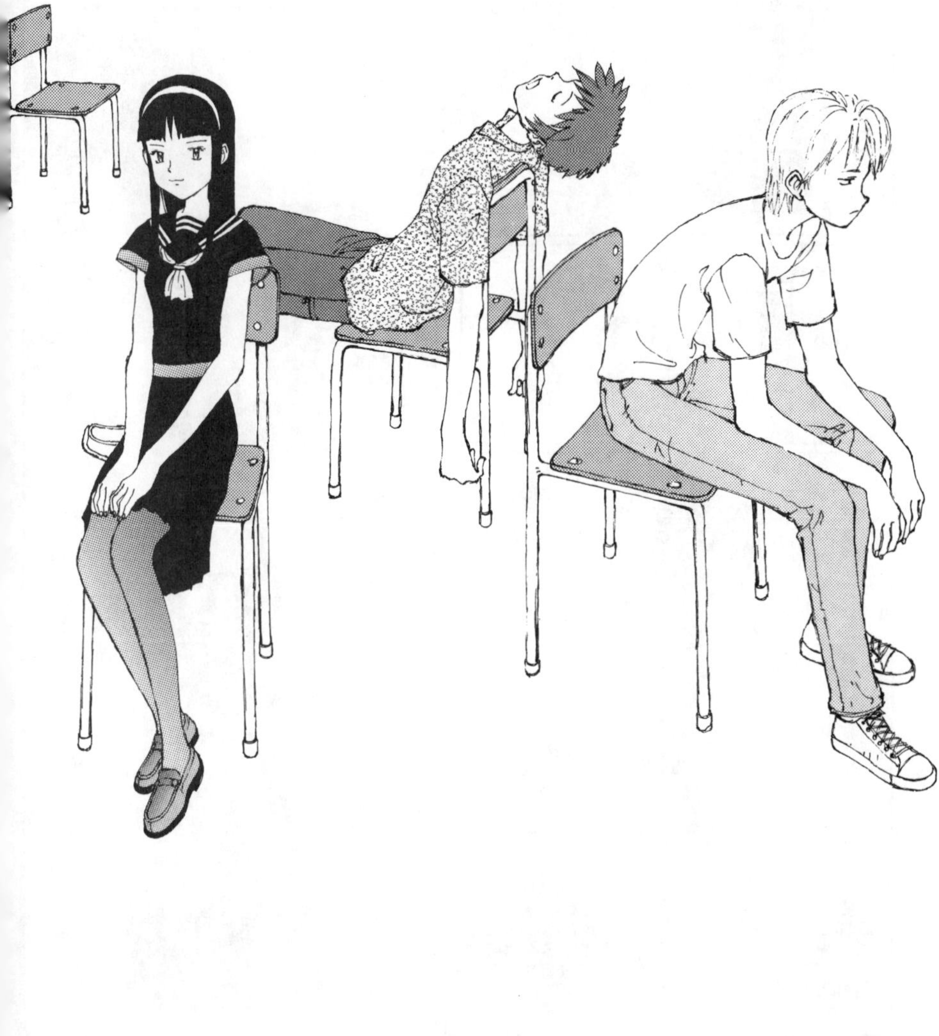

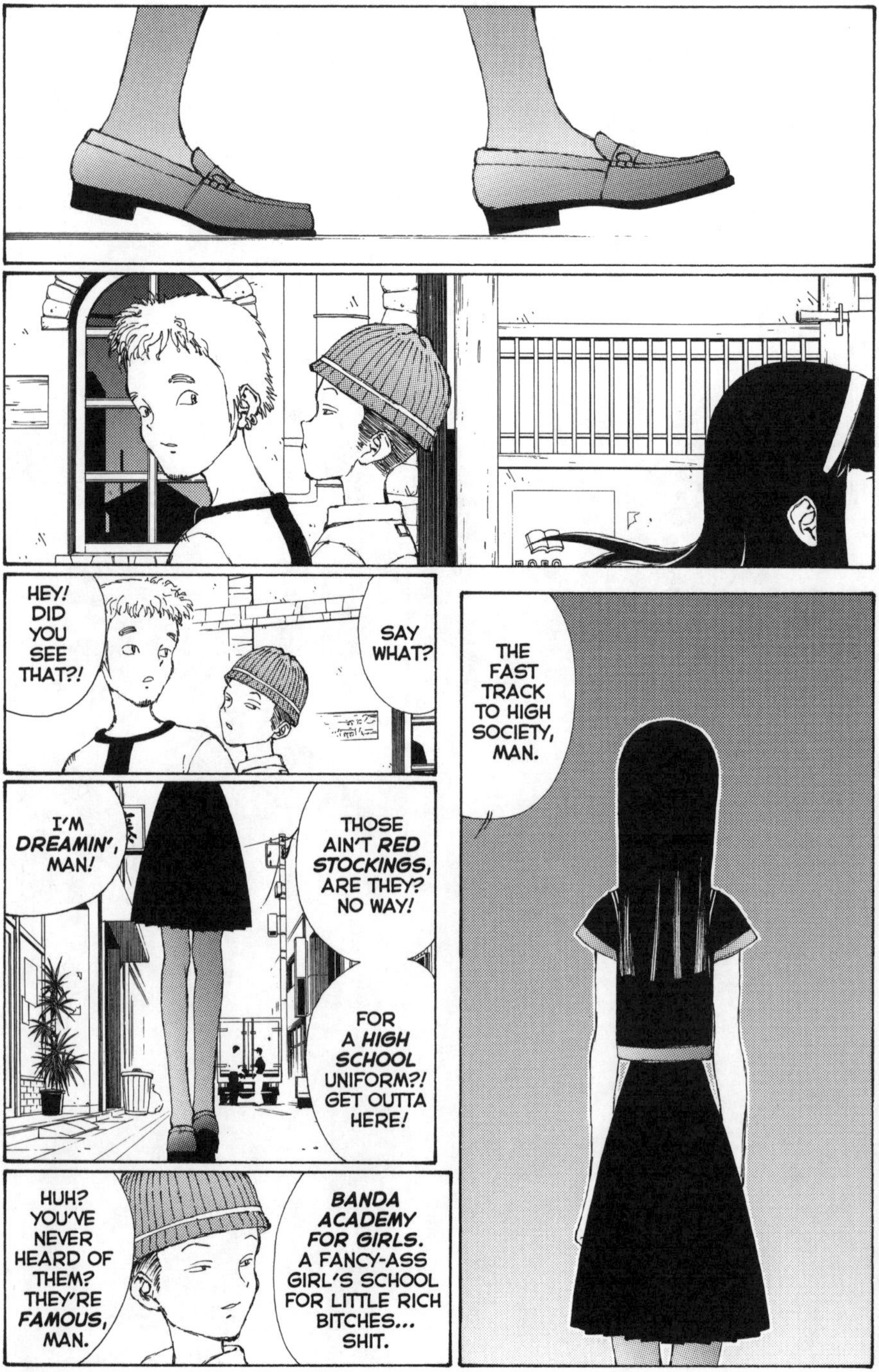
HEY! DID YOU SEE THAT?!
SAY WHAT?
I'M *DREAMIN'*, MAN!
THOSE AIN'T *RED STOCKINGS*, ARE THEY? NO WAY!
FOR A *HIGH SCHOOL* UNIFORM?! GET OUTTA HERE!
HUH? YOU'VE NEVER HEARD OF THEM? THEY'RE *FAMOUS*, MAN.
BANDA ACADEMY FOR GIRLS. A FANCY-ASS GIRL'S SCHOOL FOR LITTLE RICH BITCHES... SHIT.
THE FAST TRACK TO HIGH SOCIETY, MAN.

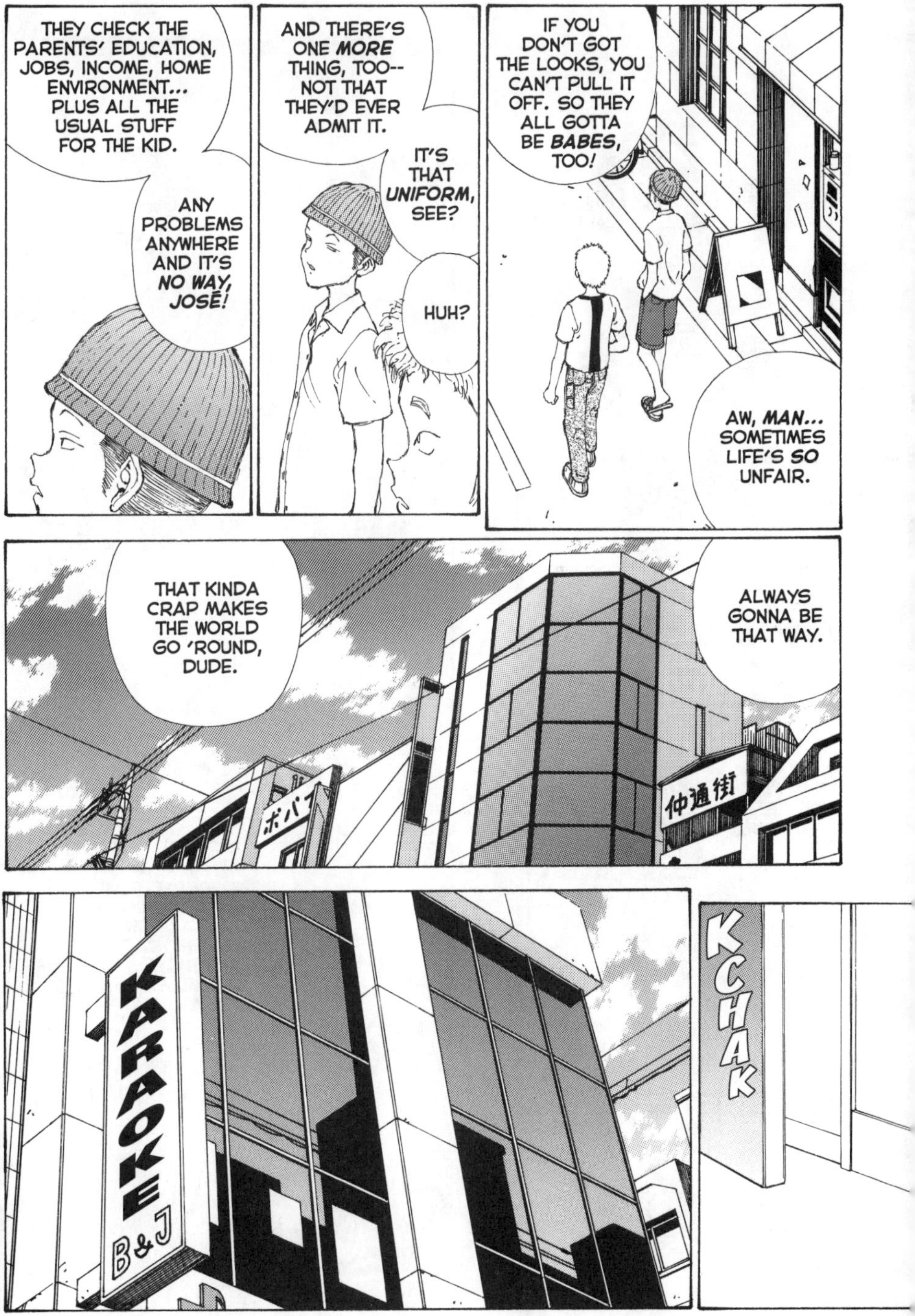
THEY CHECK THE PARENTS' EDUCATION, JOBS, INCOME, HOME ENVIRONMENT... PLUS ALL THE USUAL STUFF FOR THE KID.
ANY PROBLEMS ANYWHERE AND IT'S NO WAY, JOSÉ!
AND THERE'S ONE MORE THING, TOO-- NOT THAT THEY'D EVER ADMIT IT.
IT'S THAT UNIFORM, SEE?
HUH?
IF YOU DON'T GOT THE LOOKS, YOU CAN'T PULL IT OFF. SO THEY ALL GOTTA BE BABES, TOO!
AW, MAN... SOMETIMES LIFE'S SO UNFAIR.
THAT KINDA CRAP MAKES THE WORLD GO 'ROUND, DUDE.
ALWAYS GONNA BE THAT WAY.
仲通街
KARAOKE
B&J
KCHAK

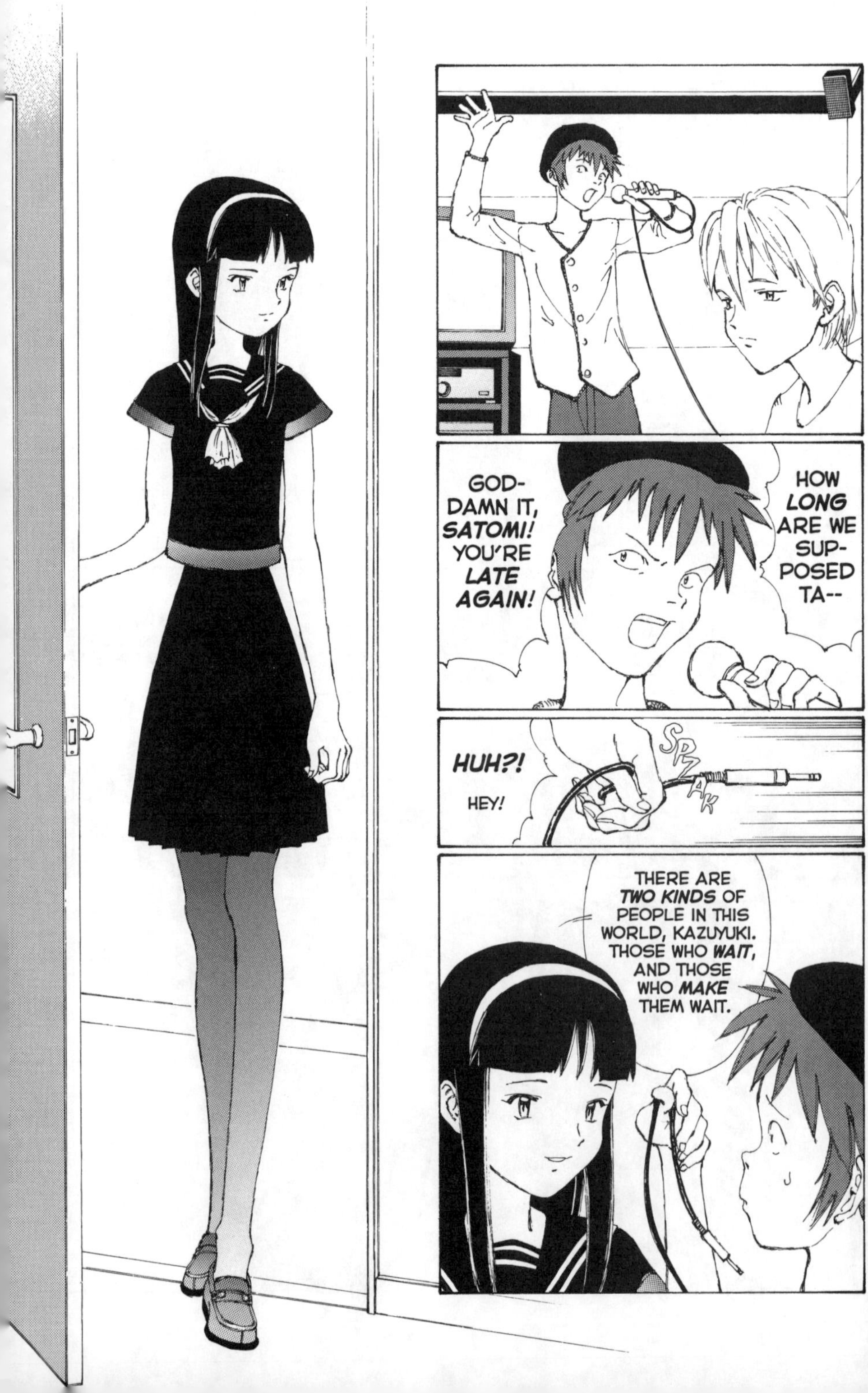
GOD-DAMN IT, SATOMI! YOU'RE LATE AGAIN!
HOW LONG ARE WE SUP-POSED TA--
HUH?!
HEY!
SPZAK
THERE ARE TWO KINDS OF PEOPLE IN THIS WORLD, KAZUYUKI. THOSE WHO WAIT, AND THOSE WHO MAKE THEM WAIT.

AND OF COURSE...

...I AM ONE OF THOSE WHO MAKES PEOPLE *WAIT*.

AFTER ALL, IT'S NO *FUN* WAITING... IS IT? ♥

HEY, NAOZUMI. *SAY* SOMETHING TO HER, WHY DON'T YOU?

AND SLAP HER AROUND A BIT, TOO.

SAY SOMETHING...? ALL RIGHT-- *PERSONALLY*, I DON'T CARE.

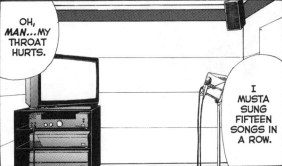

OH, *MAN*...MY THROAT HURTS.

I MUSTA SUNG FIFTEEN SONGS IN A ROW.

LORD NAOZUMI HERE WOULDN'T SING ANYTHING...

AND WHY SHOULD I...?

I'M NOT INTERESTED IN PATHETIC SONGS ABOUT *LOVE*...OR *LUST*...

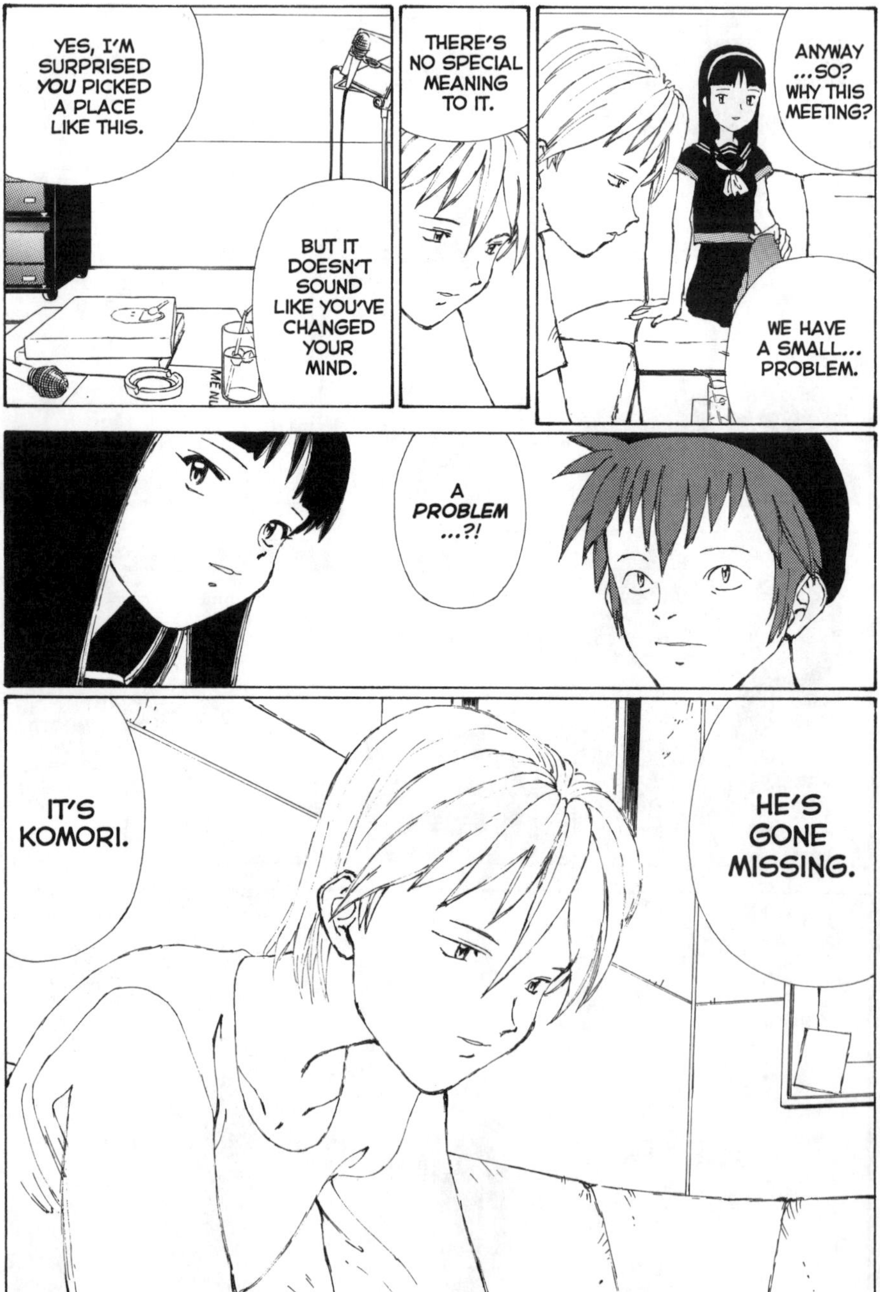
YES, I'M SURPRISED *YOU* PICKED A PLACE LIKE THIS.
BUT IT DOESN'T SOUND LIKE YOU'VE CHANGED YOUR MIND.
MENU
THERE'S NO SPECIAL MEANING TO IT.
ANYWAY ...SO? WHY THIS MEETING?
WE HAVE A SMALL... PROBLEM.
A *PROBLEM* ...?!
IT'S KOMORI.
HE'S GONE MISSING.

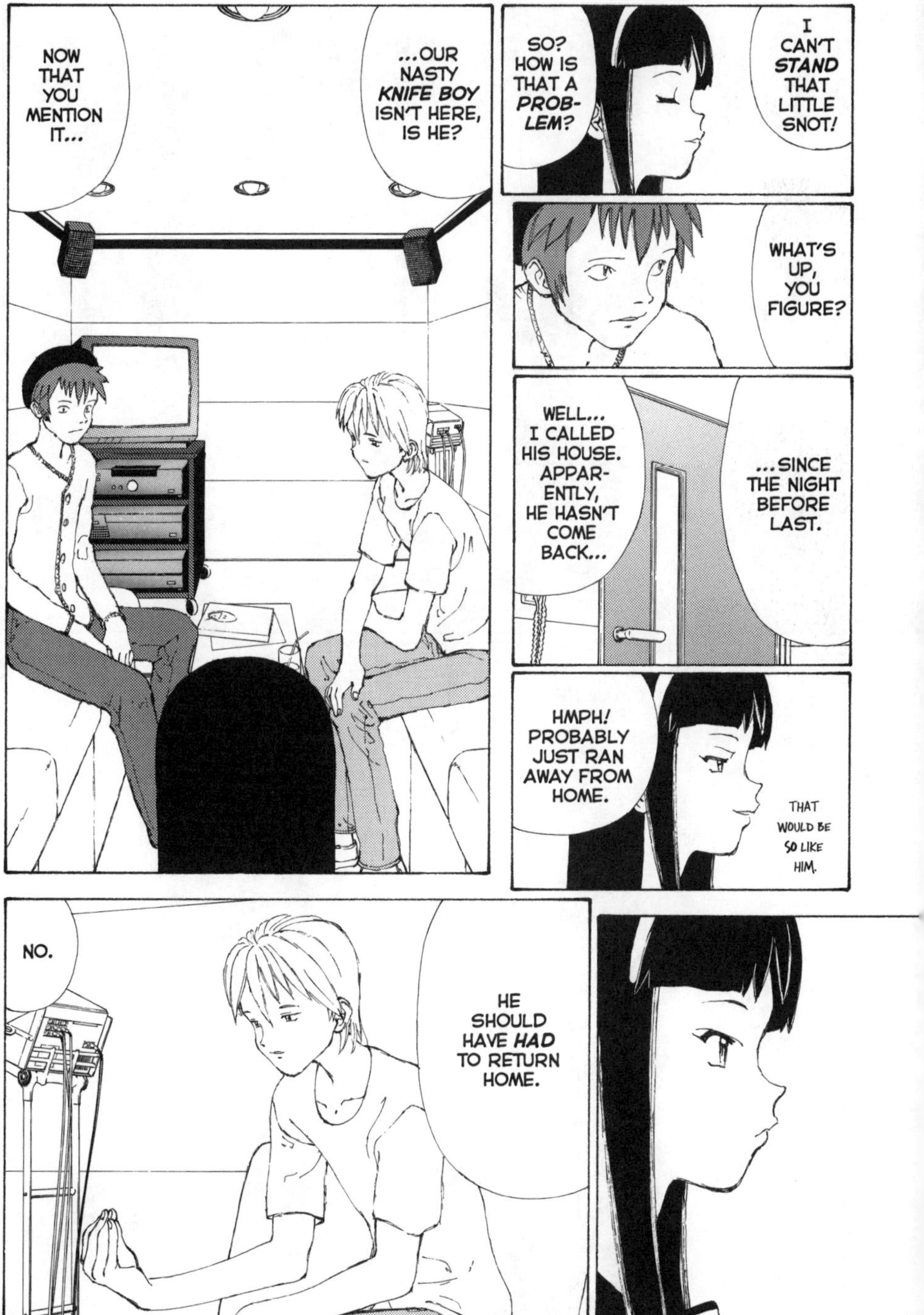
NOW THAT YOU MENTION IT...
...OUR NASTY *KNIFE BOY* ISN'T HERE, IS HE?
SO? HOW IS THAT A *PROBLEM*?
I CAN'T *STAND* THAT LITTLE SNOT!
WHAT'S UP, YOU FIGURE?
WELL... I CALLED HIS HOUSE. APPARENTLY, HE HASN'T COME BACK...
...SINCE THE NIGHT BEFORE LAST.
HMPH! PROBABLY JUST RAN AWAY FROM HOME.
THAT WOULD BE SO LIKE HIM.
NO.
HE SHOULD HAVE *HAD* TO RETURN HOME.

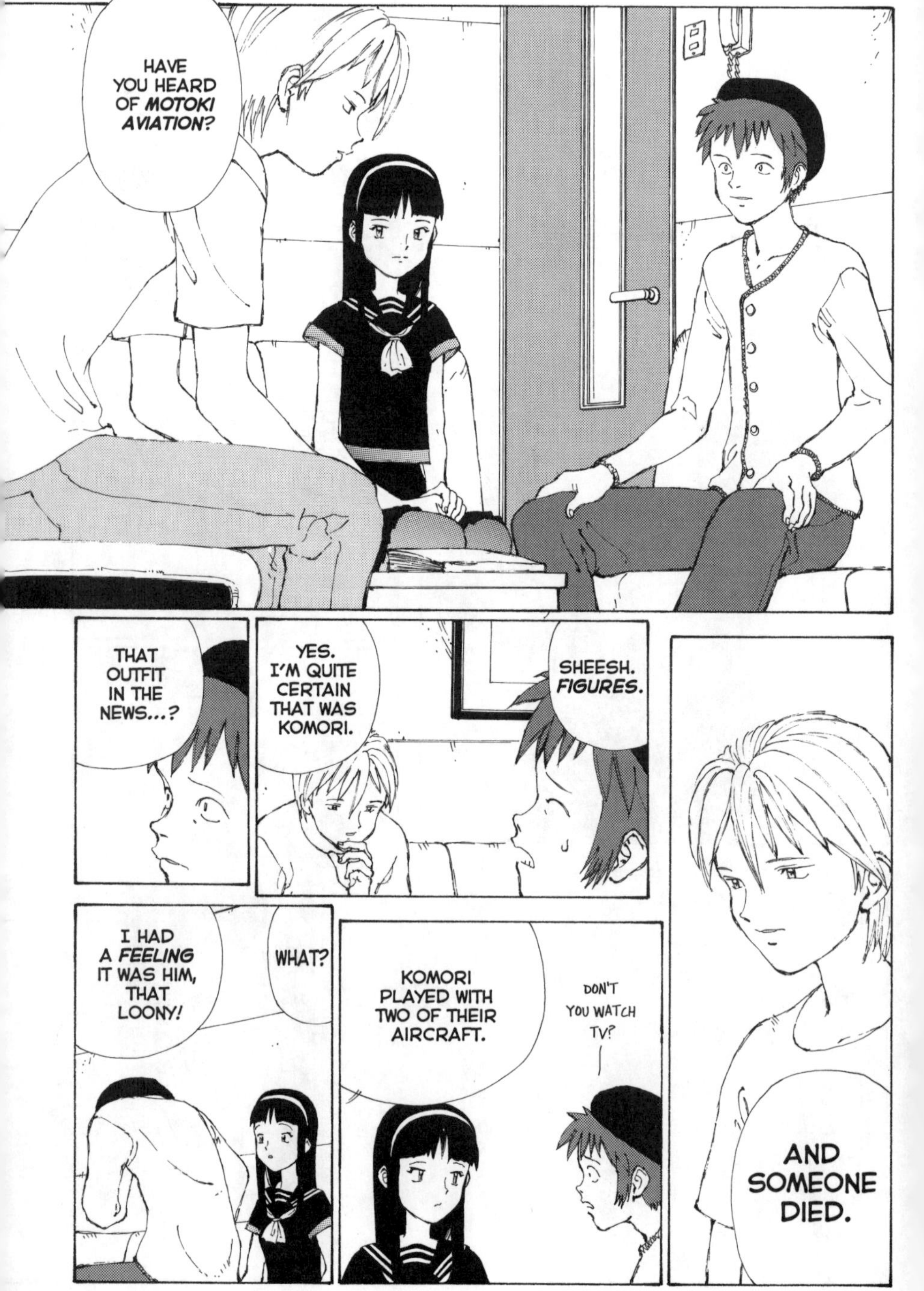
HAVE YOU HEARD OF *MOTOKI AVIATION*?
THAT OUTFIT IN THE NEWS...?
YES. I'M QUITE CERTAIN THAT WAS KOMORI.
SHEESH. *FIGURES*.
I HAD A *FEELING* IT WAS HIM, THAT LOONY*!*
WHAT?
KOMORI PLAYED WITH TWO OF THEIR AIRCRAFT.
DON'T YOU WATCH TV?
AND SOMEONE DIED.

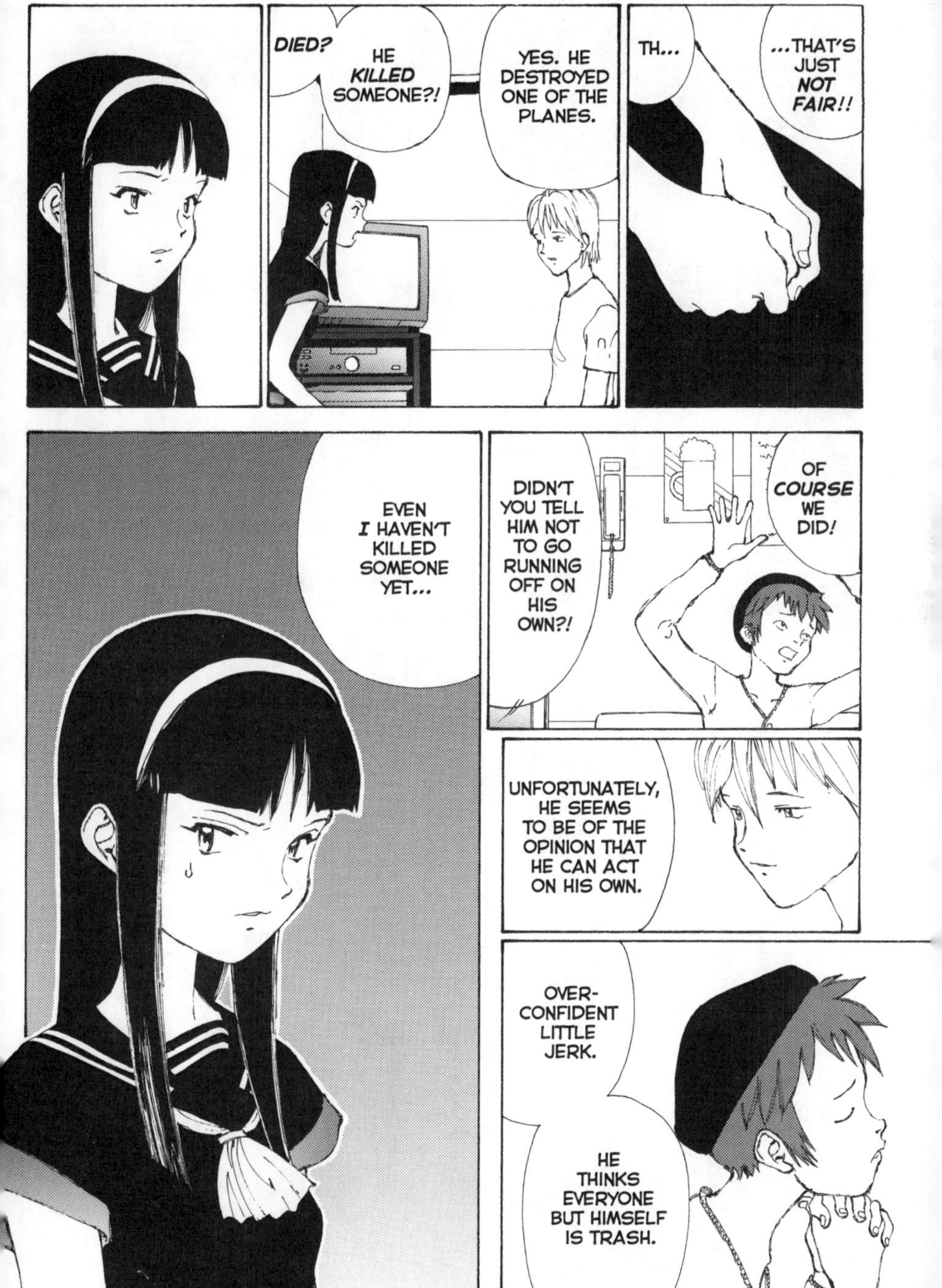
DIED?
HE KILLED SOMEONE?!
YES. HE DESTROYED ONE OF THE PLANES.
TH...
...THAT'S JUST NOT FAIR!!
EVEN I HAVEN'T KILLED SOMEONE YET...
DIDN'T YOU TELL HIM NOT TO GO RUNNING OFF ON HIS OWN?!
OF COURSE WE DID!
UNFORTUNATELY, HE SEEMS TO BE OF THE OPINION THAT HE CAN ACT ON HIS OWN.
OVER-CONFIDENT LITTLE JERK.
HE THINKS EVERYONE BUT HIMSELF IS TRASH.

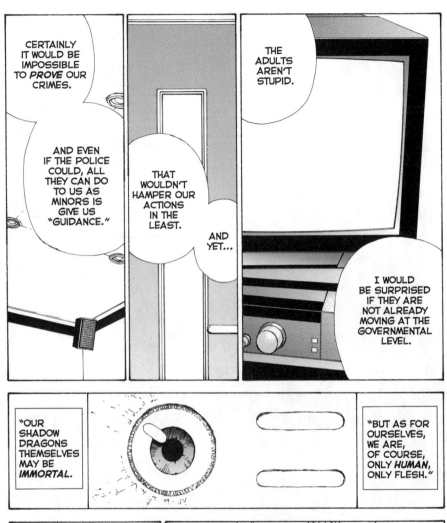

CERTAINLY IT WOULD BE IMPOSSIBLE TO *PROVE* OUR CRIMES.

AND EVEN IF THE POLICE COULD, ALL THEY CAN DO TO US AS MINORS IS GIVE US "GUIDANCE."

THAT WOULDN'T HAMPER OUR ACTIONS IN THE LEAST.

AND YET...

THE ADULTS AREN'T STUPID.

I WOULD BE SURPRISED IF THEY ARE NOT ALREADY MOVING AT THE GOVERNMENTAL LEVEL.

"OUR SHADOW DRAGONS THEMSELVES MAY BE *IMMORTAL*.

"BUT AS FOR OURSELVES, WE ARE, OF COURSE, ONLY *HUMAN*, ONLY FLESH."

WE HAD BETTER BE CAREFUL.

SO...YOU THINK THE POLICE--OR SOMEONE LIKE THAT--HAS KOMORI?

I DON'T KNOW. I DON'T KNOW AT ALL.

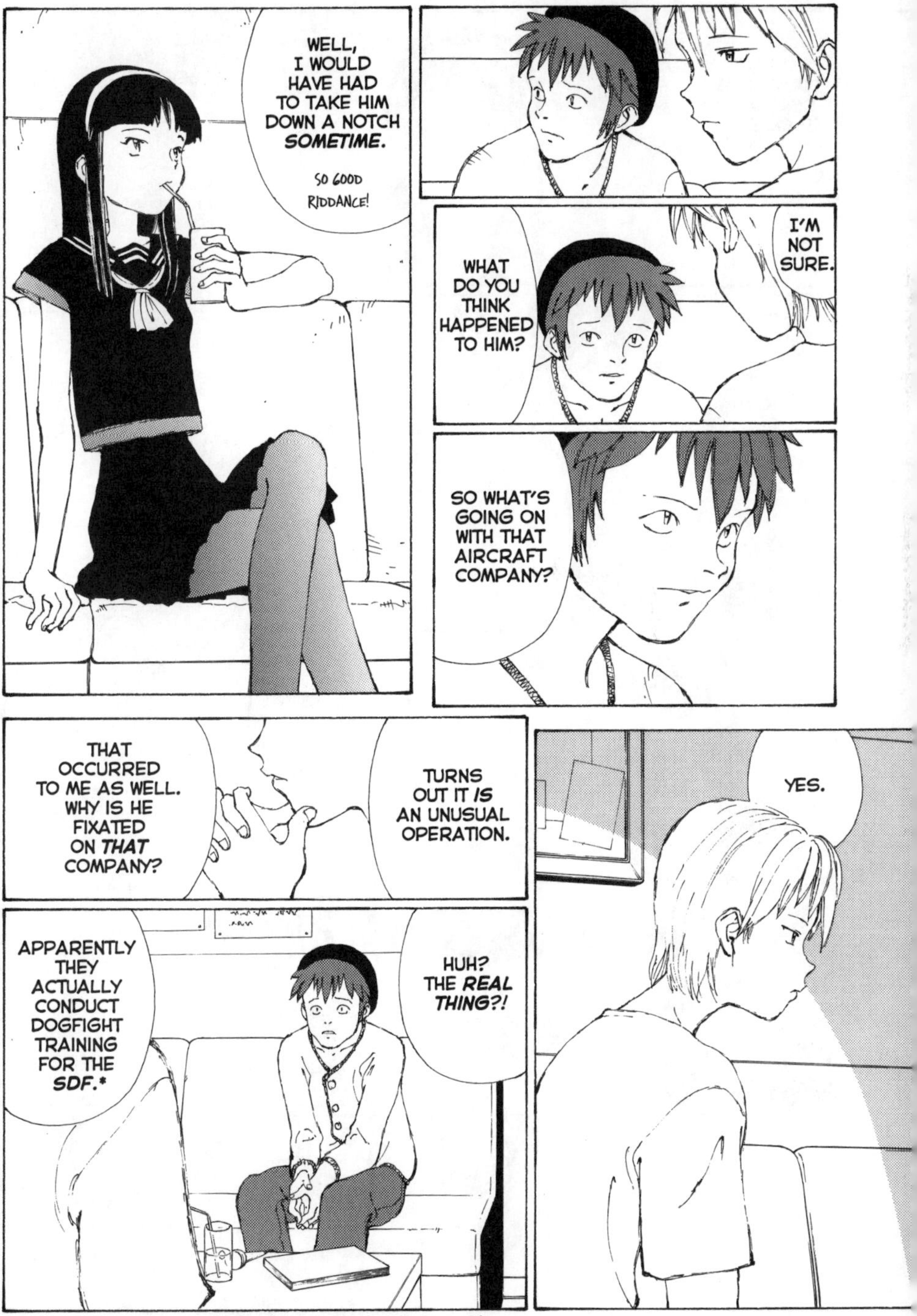
WELL, I WOULD HAVE HAD TO TAKE HIM DOWN A NOTCH SOMETIME.
SO GOOD RIDDANCE!
WHAT DO YOU THINK HAPPENED TO HIM?
I'M NOT SURE.
SO WHAT'S GOING ON WITH THAT AIRCRAFT COMPANY?
THAT OCCURRED TO ME AS WELL. WHY IS HE FIXATED ON THAT COMPANY?
TURNS OUT IT IS AN UNUSUAL OPERATION.
APPARENTLY THEY ACTUALLY CONDUCT DOGFIGHT TRAINING FOR THE SDF.*
HUH? THE REAL THING?!
YES.

*THE JAPANESE MILITARY (SELF DEFENSE FORCE)

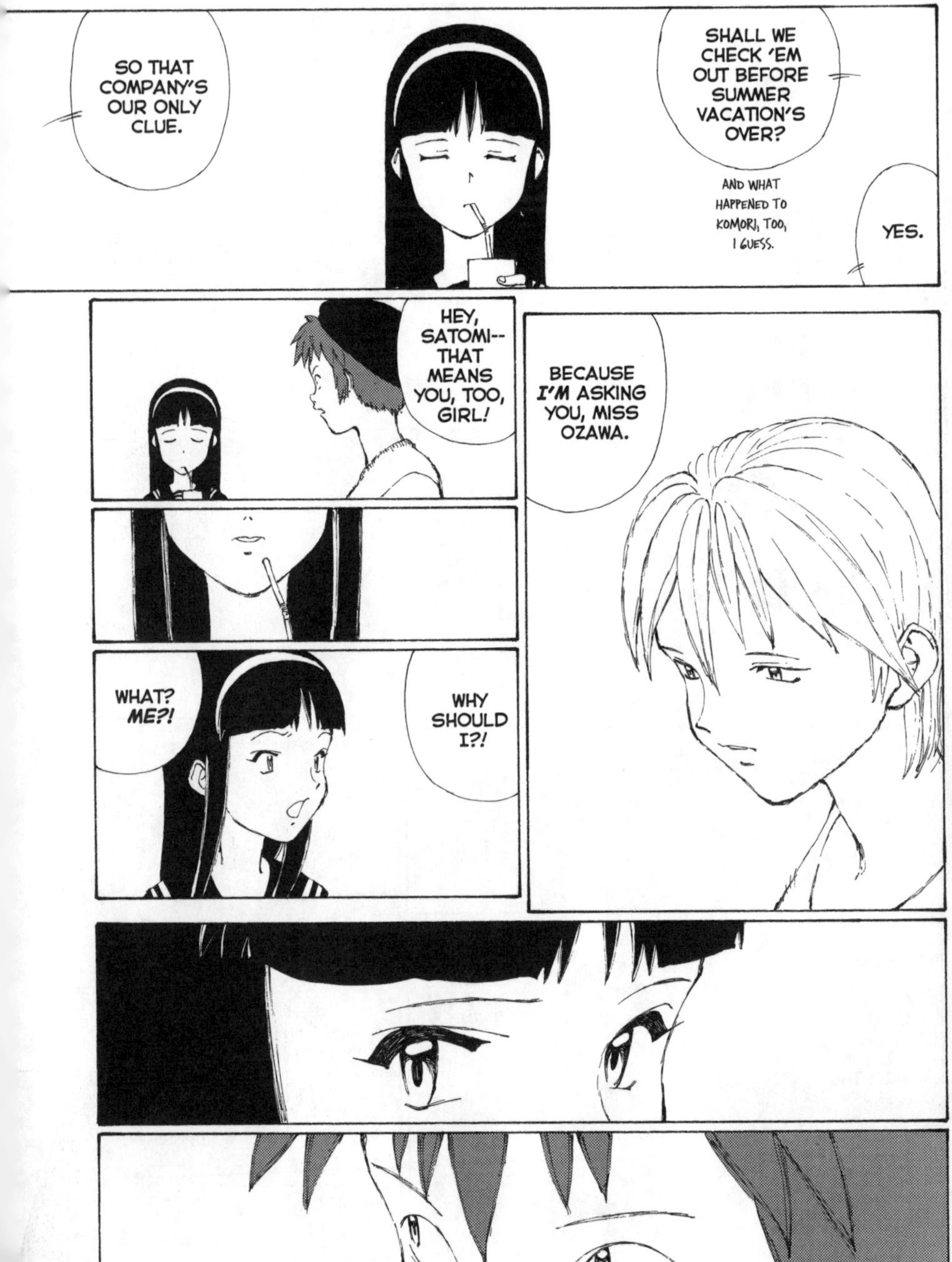
SO THAT COMPANY'S OUR ONLY CLUE.
SHALL WE CHECK 'EM OUT BEFORE SUMMER VACATION'S OVER?
AND WHAT HAPPENED TO KOMORI, TOO, I GUESS.
YES.
HEY, SATOMI-- THAT MEANS YOU, TOO, GIRL!
WHAT? ME?!
WHY SHOULD I?!
BECAUSE I'M ASKING YOU, MISS OZAWA.

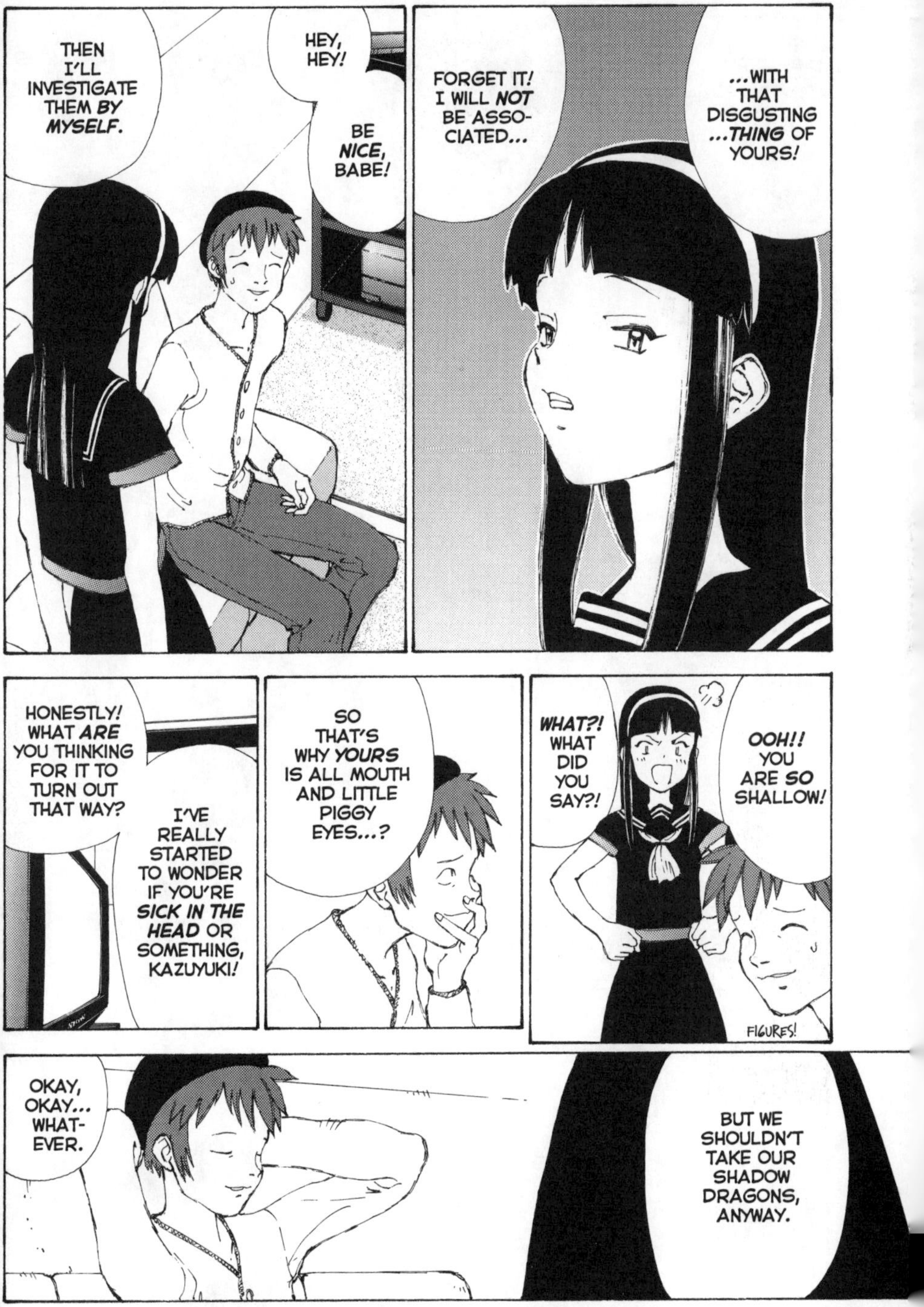
THEN I'LL INVESTIGATE THEM *BY MYSELF*.
HEY, HEY!
BE *NICE*, BABE!
FORGET IT! I WILL *NOT* BE ASSO-CIATED...
...WITH THAT DISGUSTING ...*THING* OF YOURS!
HONESTLY! WHAT *ARE* YOU THINKING FOR IT TO TURN OUT THAT WAY?
I'VE REALLY STARTED TO WONDER IF YOU'RE *SICK IN THE HEAD* OR SOMETHING, KAZUYUKI!
SO THAT'S WHY *YOURS* IS ALL MOUTH AND LITTLE PIGGY EYES...?
WHAT?! WHAT DID YOU SAY?!
OOH!! YOU ARE *SO* SHALLOW!
FIGURES!
OKAY, OKAY... WHAT-EVER.
BUT WE SHOULDN'T TAKE OUR SHADOW DRAGONS, ANYWAY.

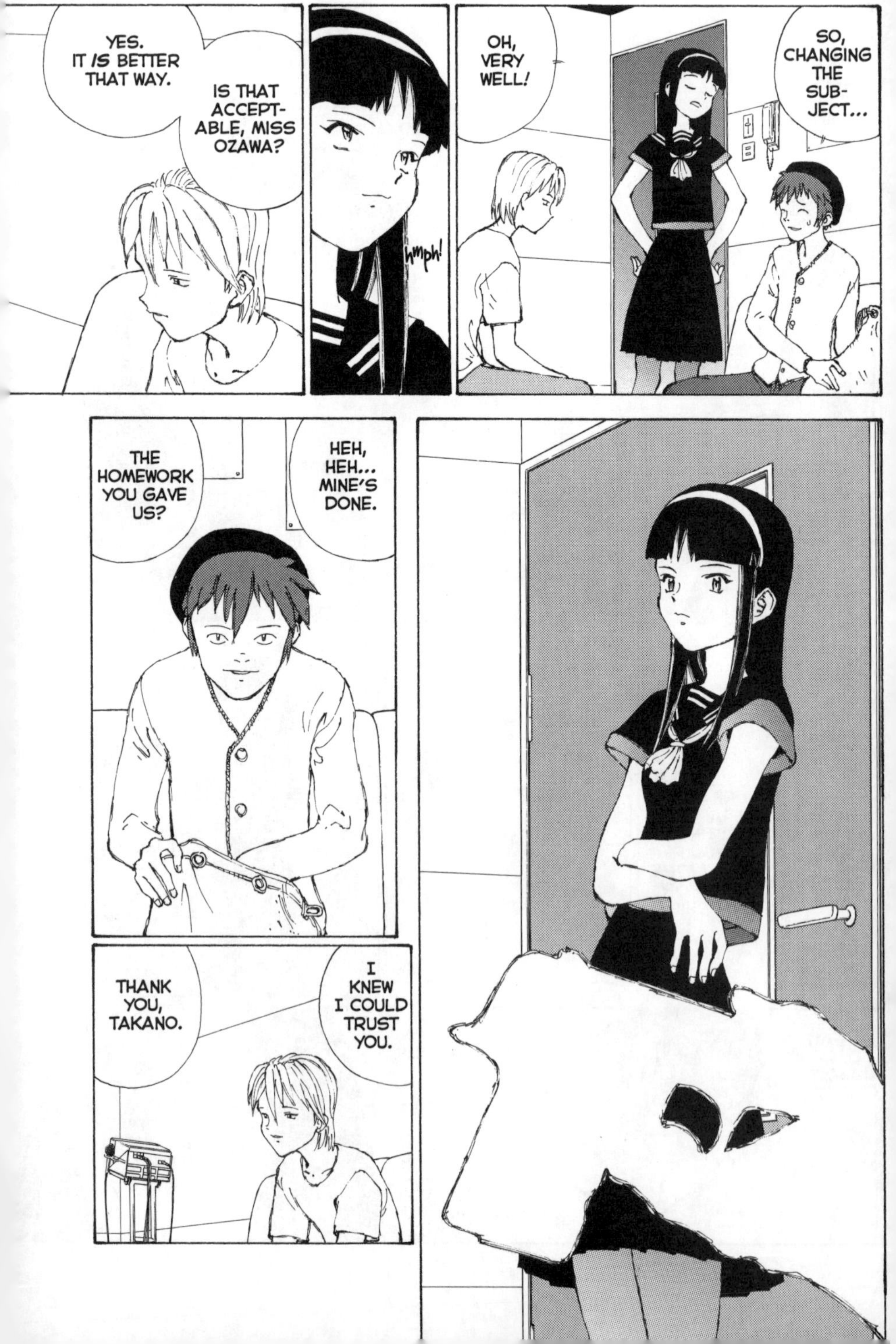
YES. IT IS BETTER THAT WAY.
IS THAT ACCEPTABLE, MISS OZAWA?
hmph!
OH, VERY WELL!
SO, CHANGING THE SUBJECT...
THE HOMEWORK YOU GAVE US?
HEH, HEH... MINE'S DONE.
THANK YOU, TAKANO.
I KNEW I COULD TRUST YOU.

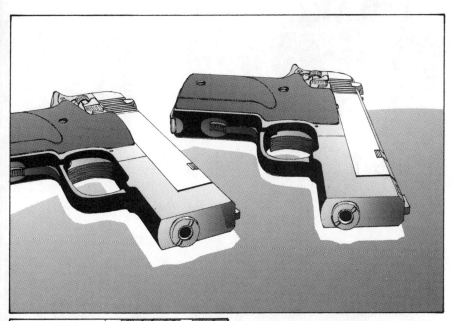

I FIGURED THE PRINCESS HERE WOULD HATE THE IDEA, SO I JUST DID THREE OF THEM.
AND WHILE I WAS AT IT, I TRIED WORKING UP THESE.
DID YOU TEST-FIRE THEM?
I DID INDEED. THEY WORK LIKE A CHARM.
AT LEAST LEARN HOW THEY WORK, OKAY, SATOMI?
heh, heh!

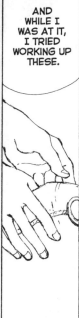

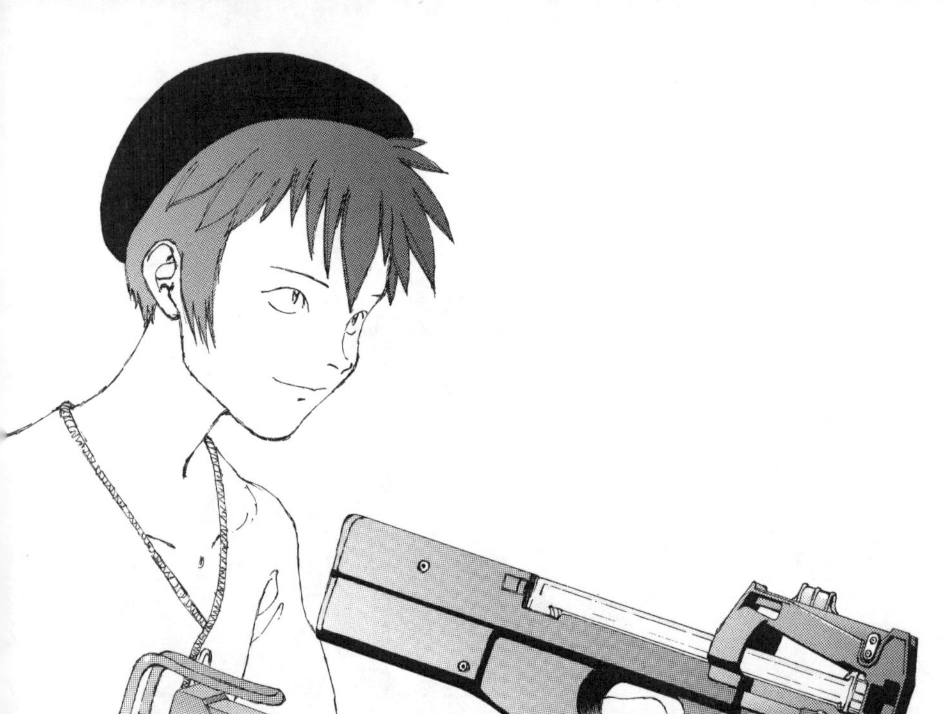

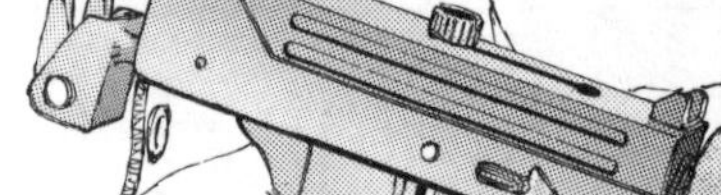
DO THEY WORK?
YUP!

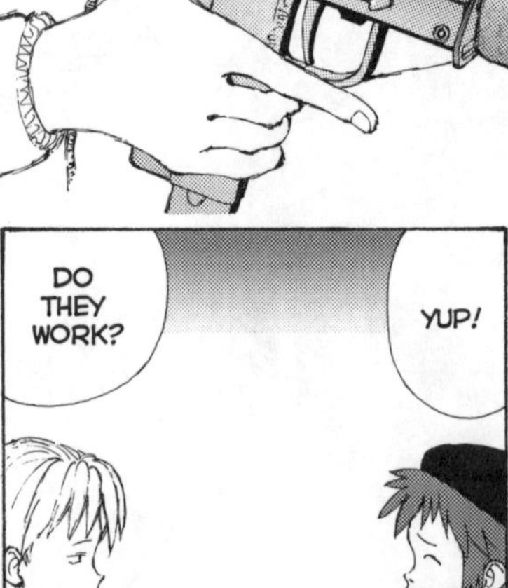
WELL, IF POSSIBLE, I WANT TO DO IT ALL WITHOUT RESORTING TO THESE.

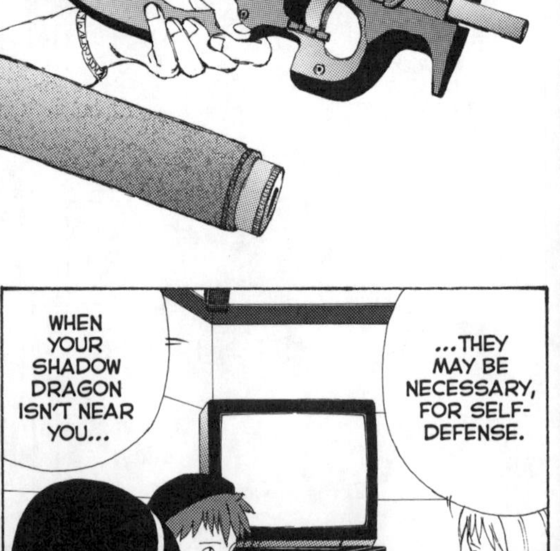
WHEN YOUR SHADOW DRAGON ISN'T NEAR YOU...
...THEY MAY BE NECESSARY, FOR SELF-DEFENSE.

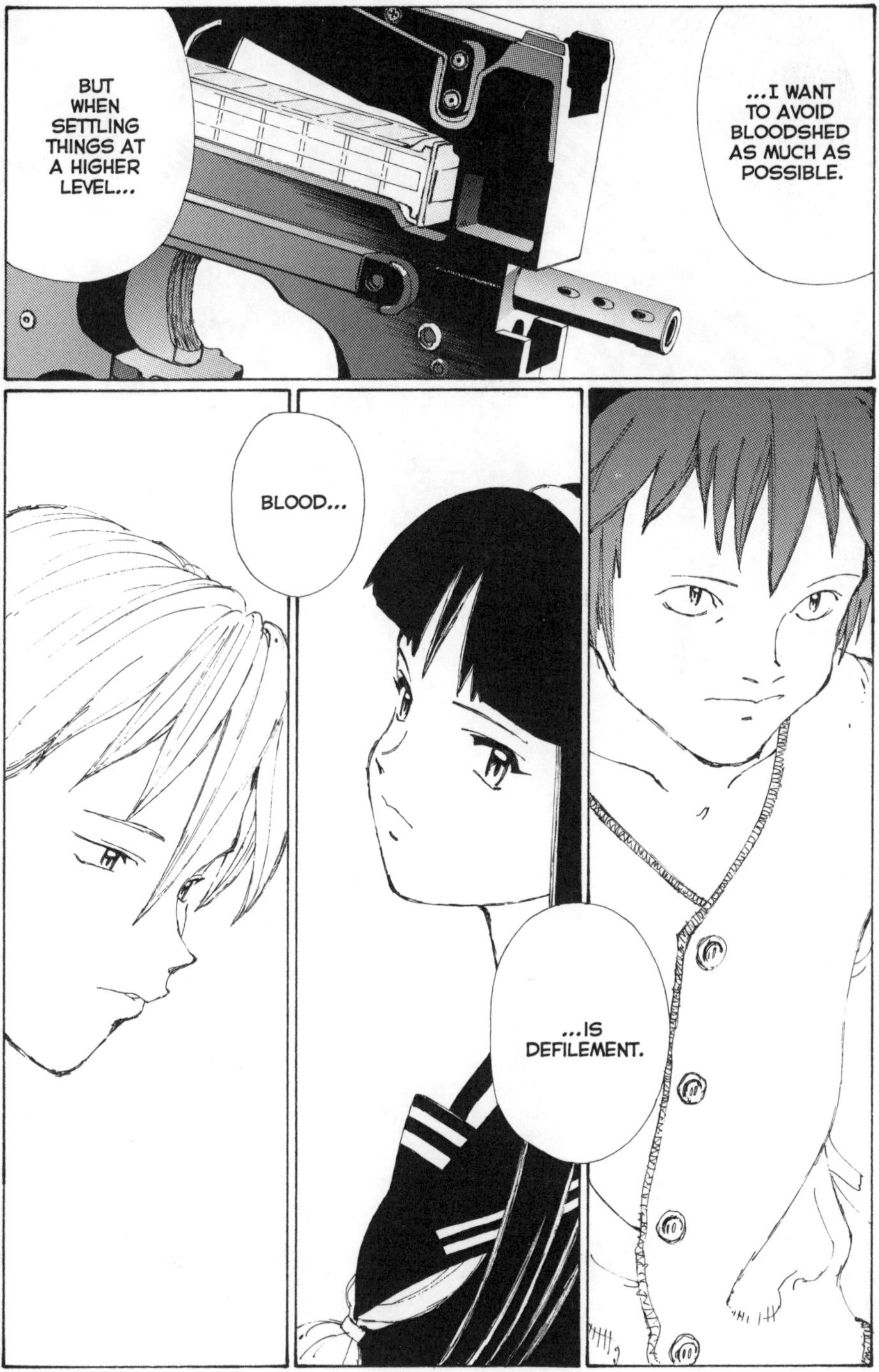
BUT WHEN SETTLING THINGS AT A HIGHER LEVEL...
...I WANT TO AVOID BLOODSHED AS MUCH AS POSSIBLE.
BLOOD...
...IS DEFILEMENT.

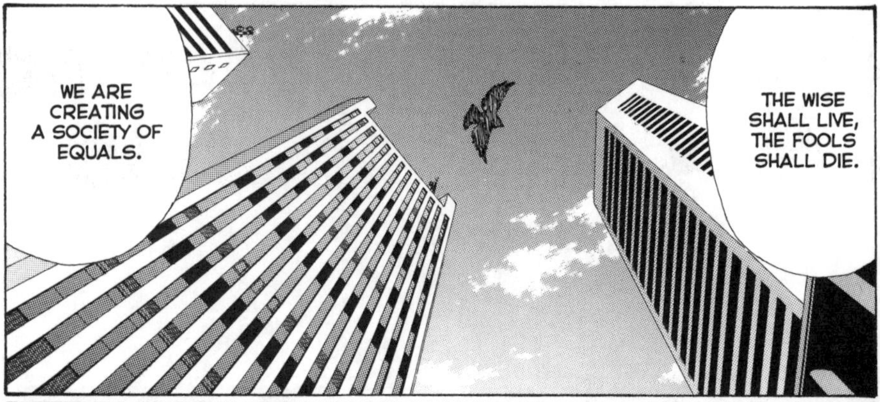
THE WISE SHALL LIVE, THE FOOLS SHALL DIE.
WE ARE CREATING A SOCIETY OF EQUALS.

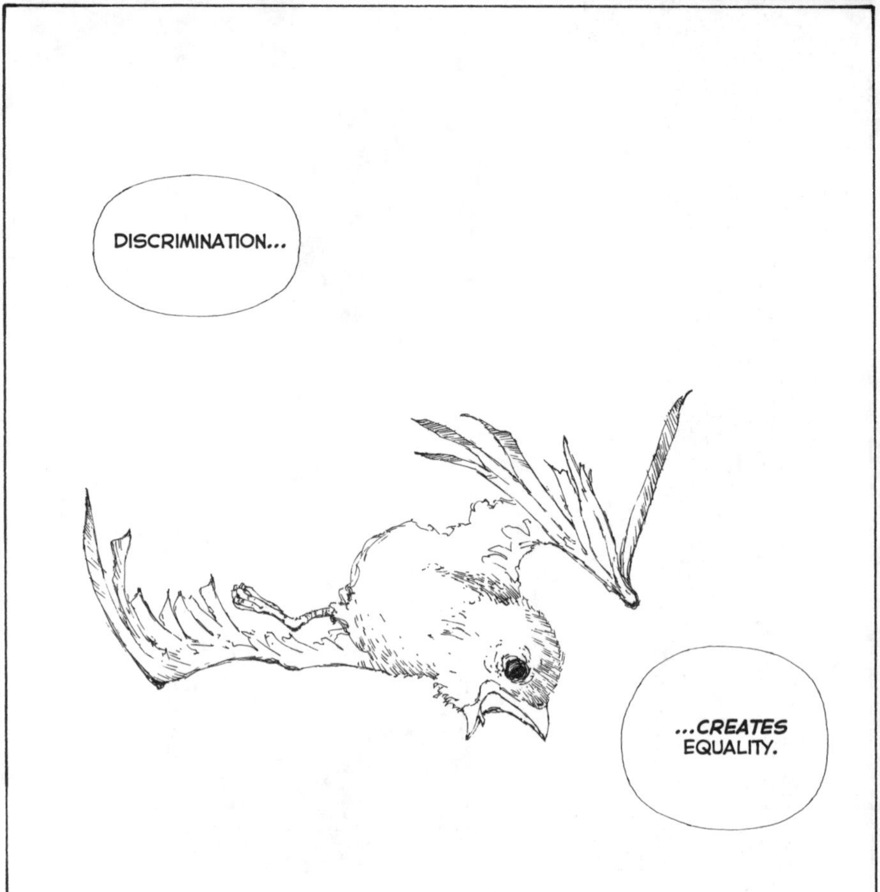
DISCRIMINATION...
...CREATES EQUALITY.

STAR CHAMBER II: THE SPECIAL RESEARCH COUNCIL ON MILITARY BALLOONS

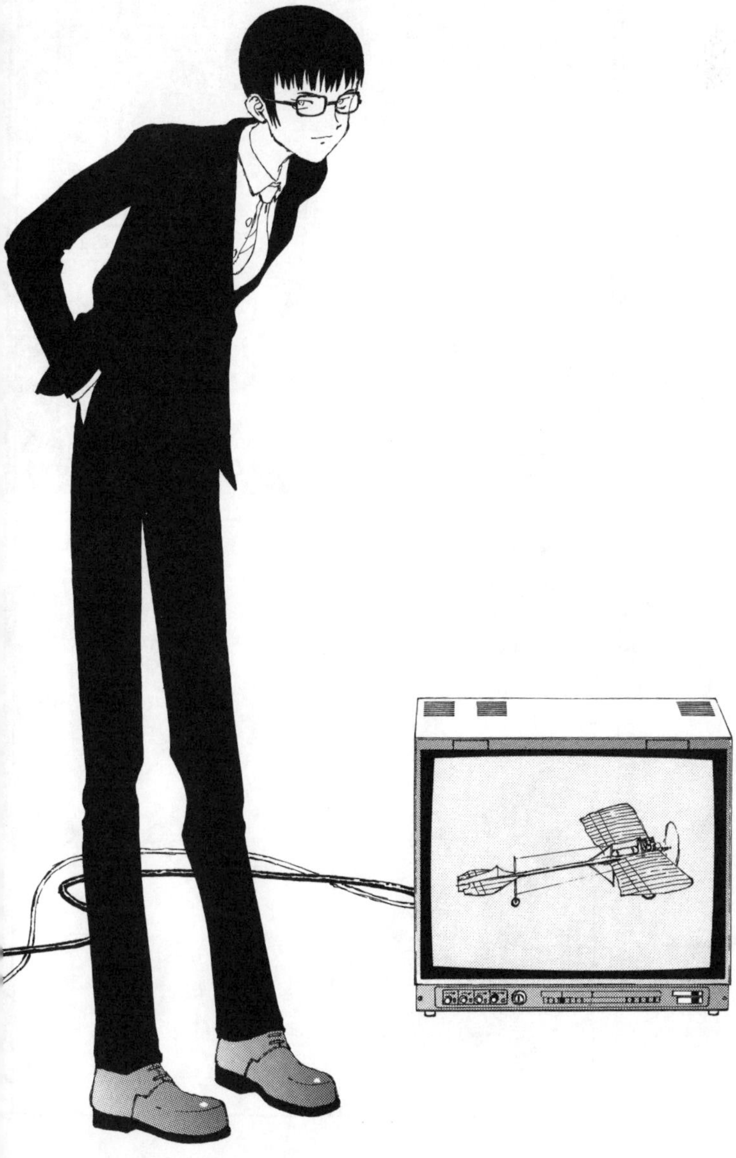

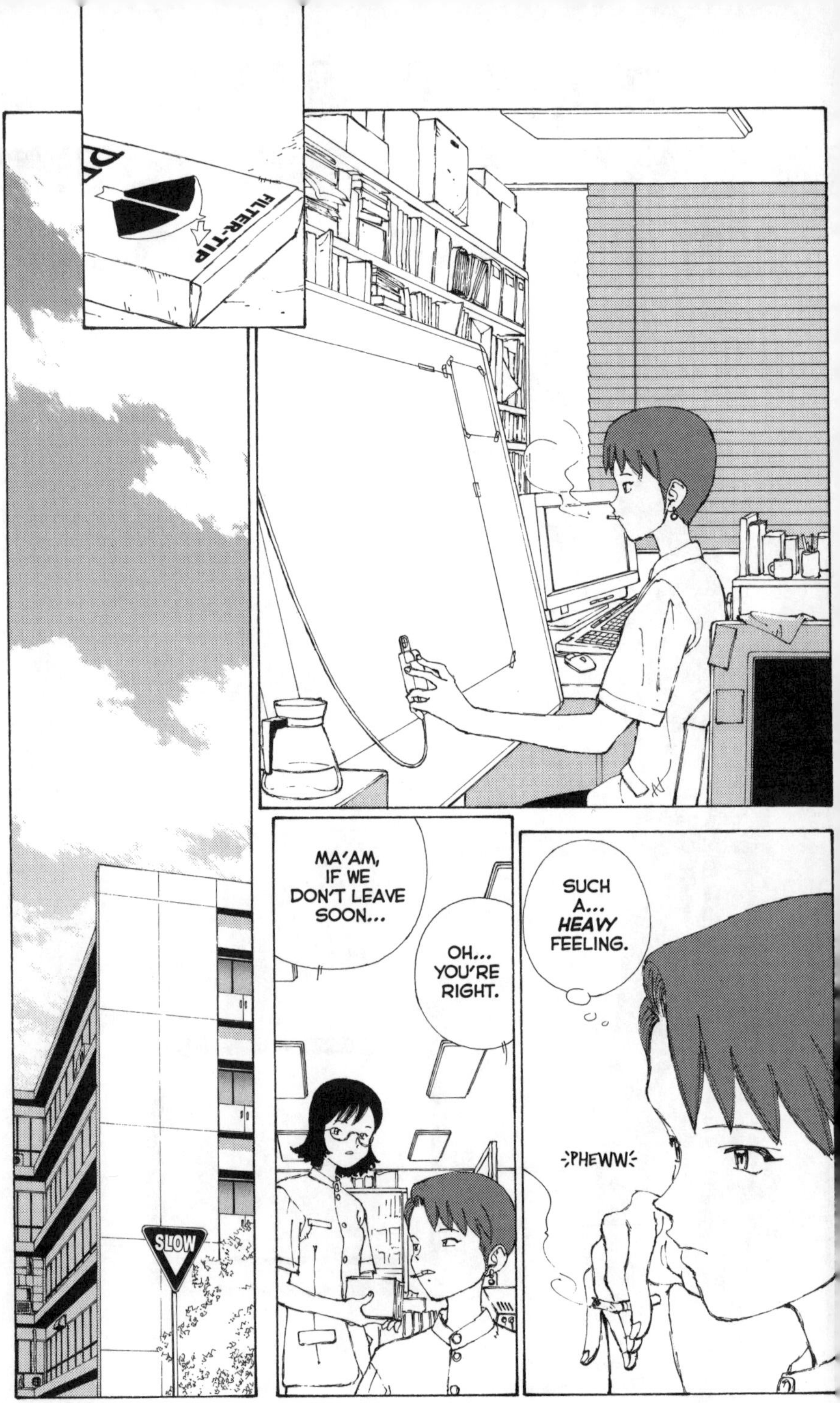
FILTER-TIP
SUCH A... HEAVY FEELING.
PHEWW
MA'AM, IF WE DON'T LEAVE SOON...
OH... YOU'RE RIGHT.
SLOW

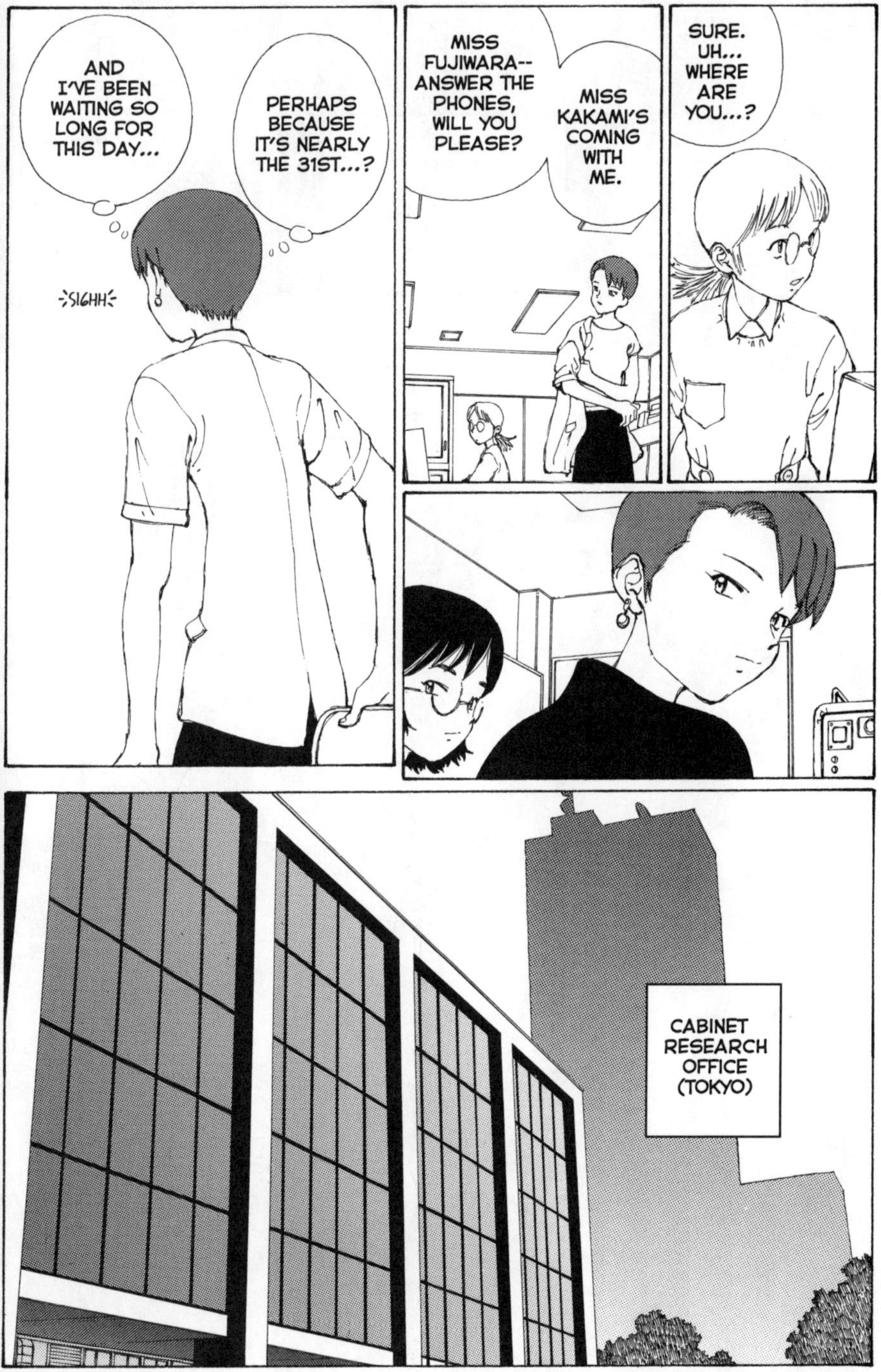
AND I'VE BEEN WAITING SO LONG FOR THIS DAY...
PERHAPS BECAUSE IT'S NEARLY THE 31ST...?
SIGHH
MISS FUJIWARA-- ANSWER THE PHONES, WILL YOU PLEASE?
MISS KAKAMI'S COMING WITH ME.
SURE. UH... WHERE ARE YOU...?
CABINET RESEARCH OFFICE (TOKYO)

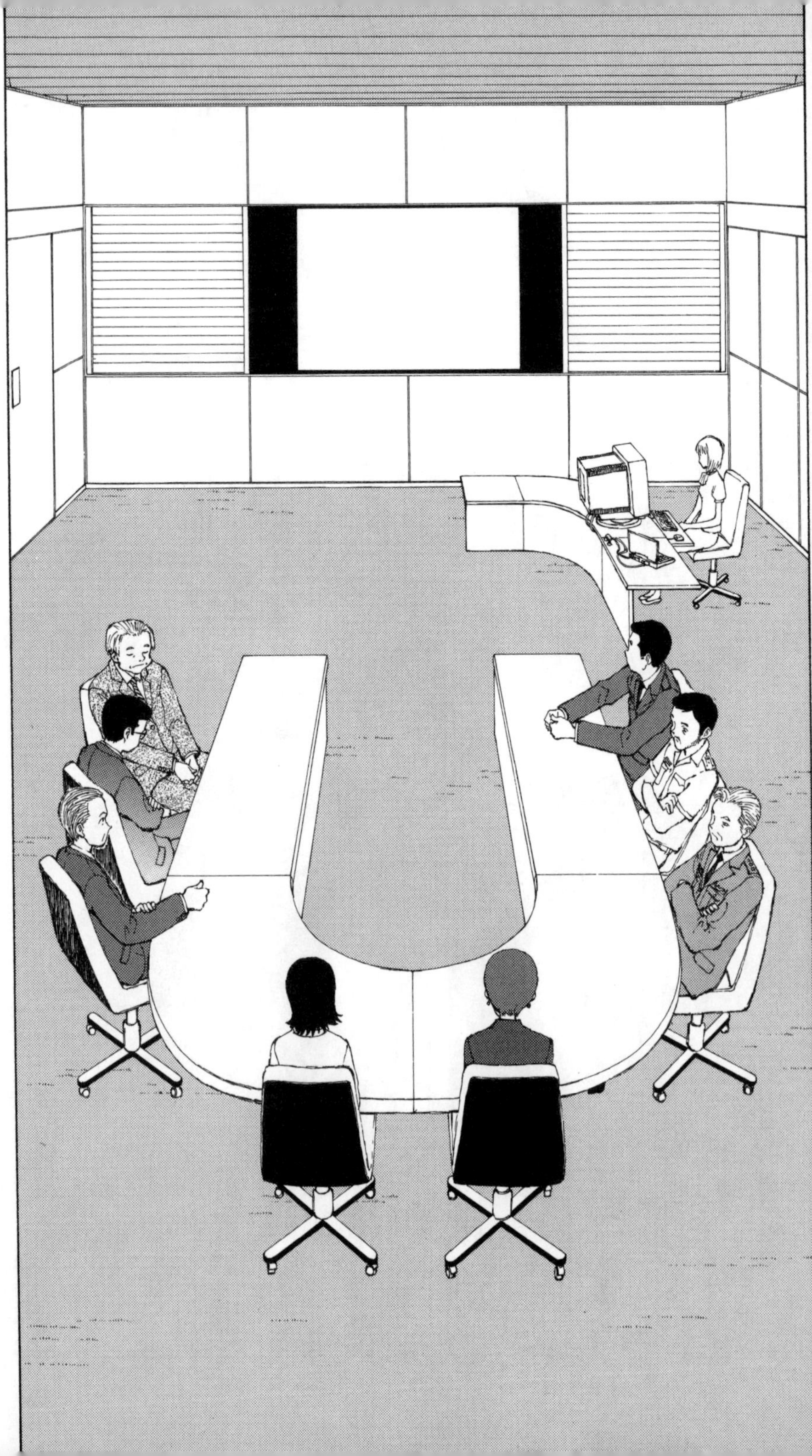

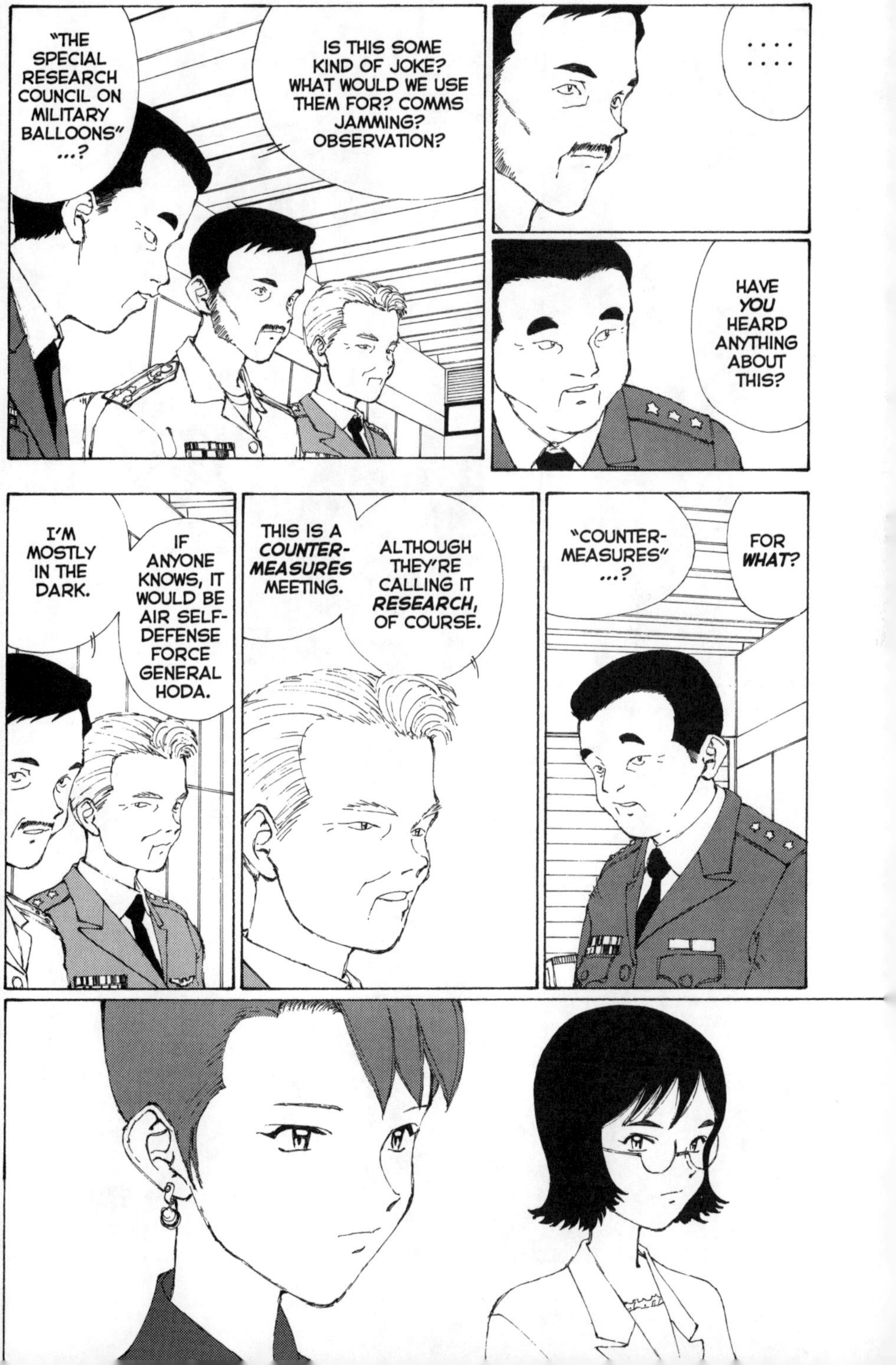
"THE SPECIAL RESEARCH COUNCIL ON MILITARY BALLOONS" ...?
IS THIS SOME KIND OF JOKE? WHAT WOULD WE USE THEM FOR? COMMS JAMMING? OBSERVATION?
....
HAVE *YOU* HEARD ANYTHING ABOUT THIS?
I'M MOSTLY IN THE DARK.
IF ANYONE KNOWS, IT WOULD BE AIR SELF-DEFENSE FORCE GENERAL HODA.
THIS IS A *COUNTERMEASURES* MEETING.
ALTHOUGH THEY'RE CALLING IT *RESEARCH*, OF COURSE.
"COUNTER-MEASURES" ...?
FOR *WHAT*?

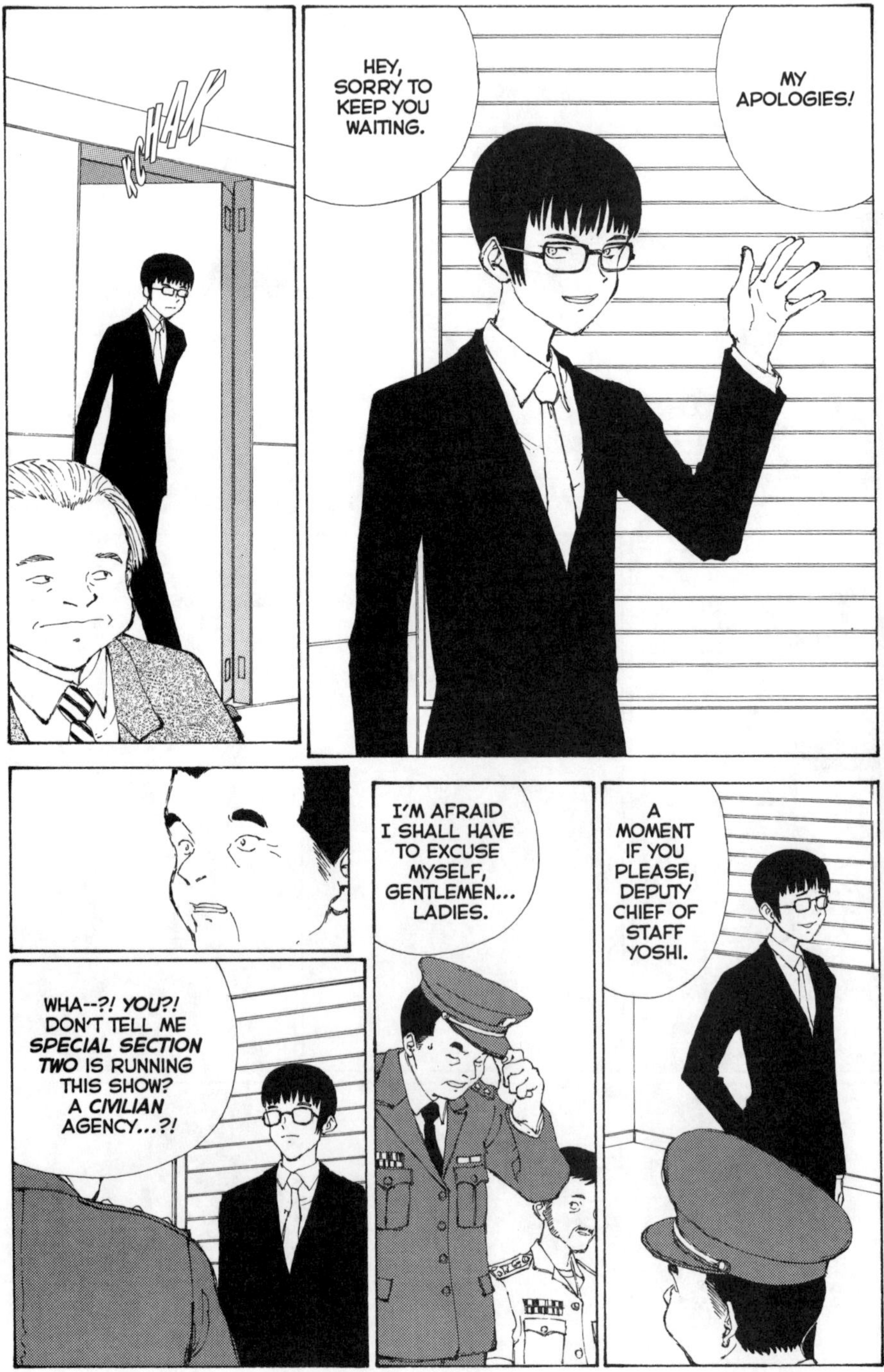
MY APOLOGIES!
HEY, SORRY TO KEEP YOU WAITING.
KCHAK
A MOMENT IF YOU PLEASE, DEPUTY CHIEF OF STAFF YOSHI.
I'M AFRAID I SHALL HAVE TO EXCUSE MYSELF, GENTLEMEN... LADIES.
WHA--?! *YOU?!* DON'T TELL ME ***SPECIAL SECTION TWO*** IS RUNNING THIS SHOW? A ***CIVILIAN*** AGENCY...?!

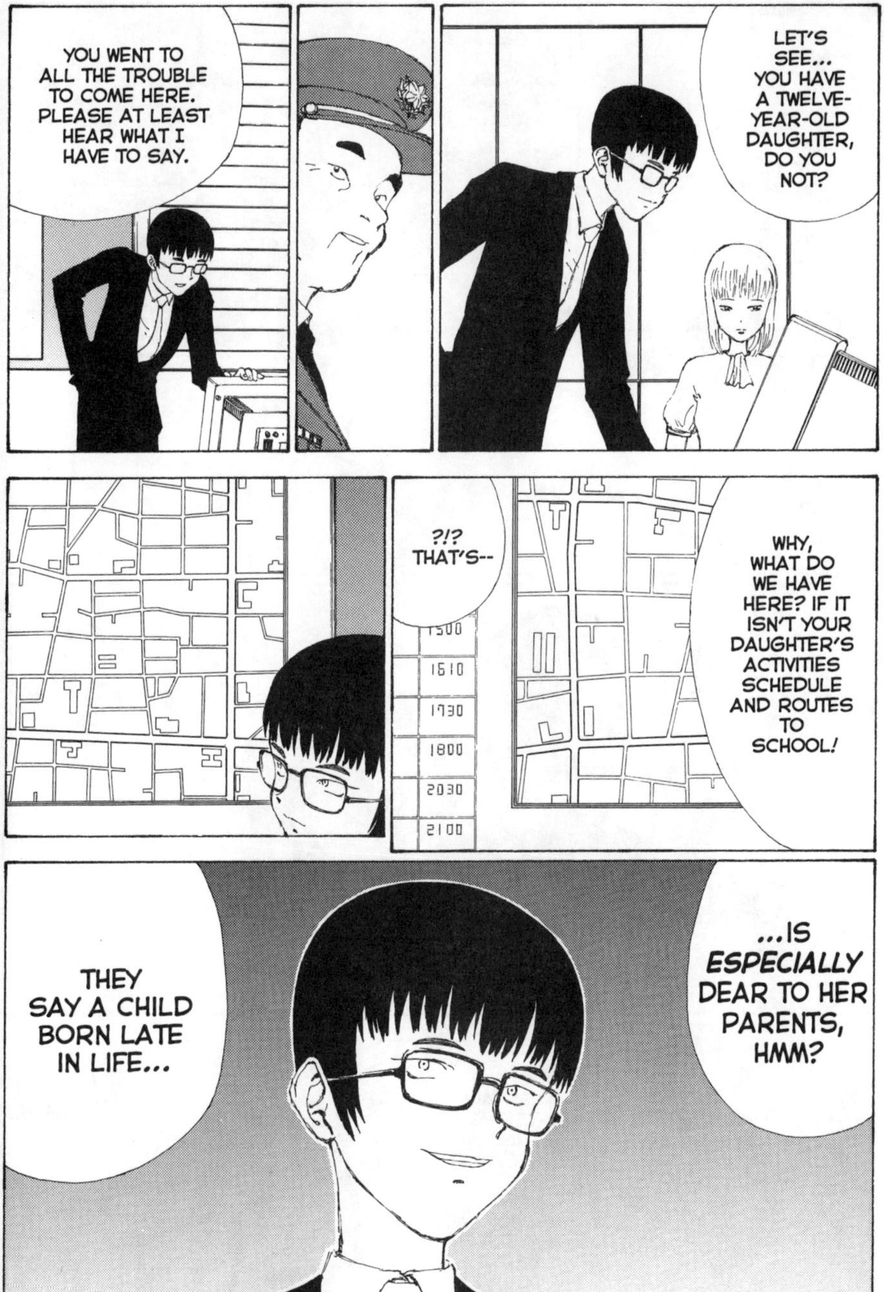
YOU WENT TO ALL THE TROUBLE TO COME HERE. PLEASE AT LEAST HEAR WHAT I HAVE TO SAY.
LET'S SEE... YOU HAVE A TWELVE-YEAR-OLD DAUGHTER, DO YOU NOT?
?!? THAT'S--
1500
1610
1730
1800
2030
2100
WHY, WHAT DO WE HAVE HERE? IF IT ISN'T YOUR DAUGHTER'S ACTIVITIES SCHEDULE AND ROUTES TO SCHOOL!
THEY SAY A CHILD BORN LATE IN LIFE...
...IS *ESPECIALLY* DEAR TO HER PARENTS, HMM?

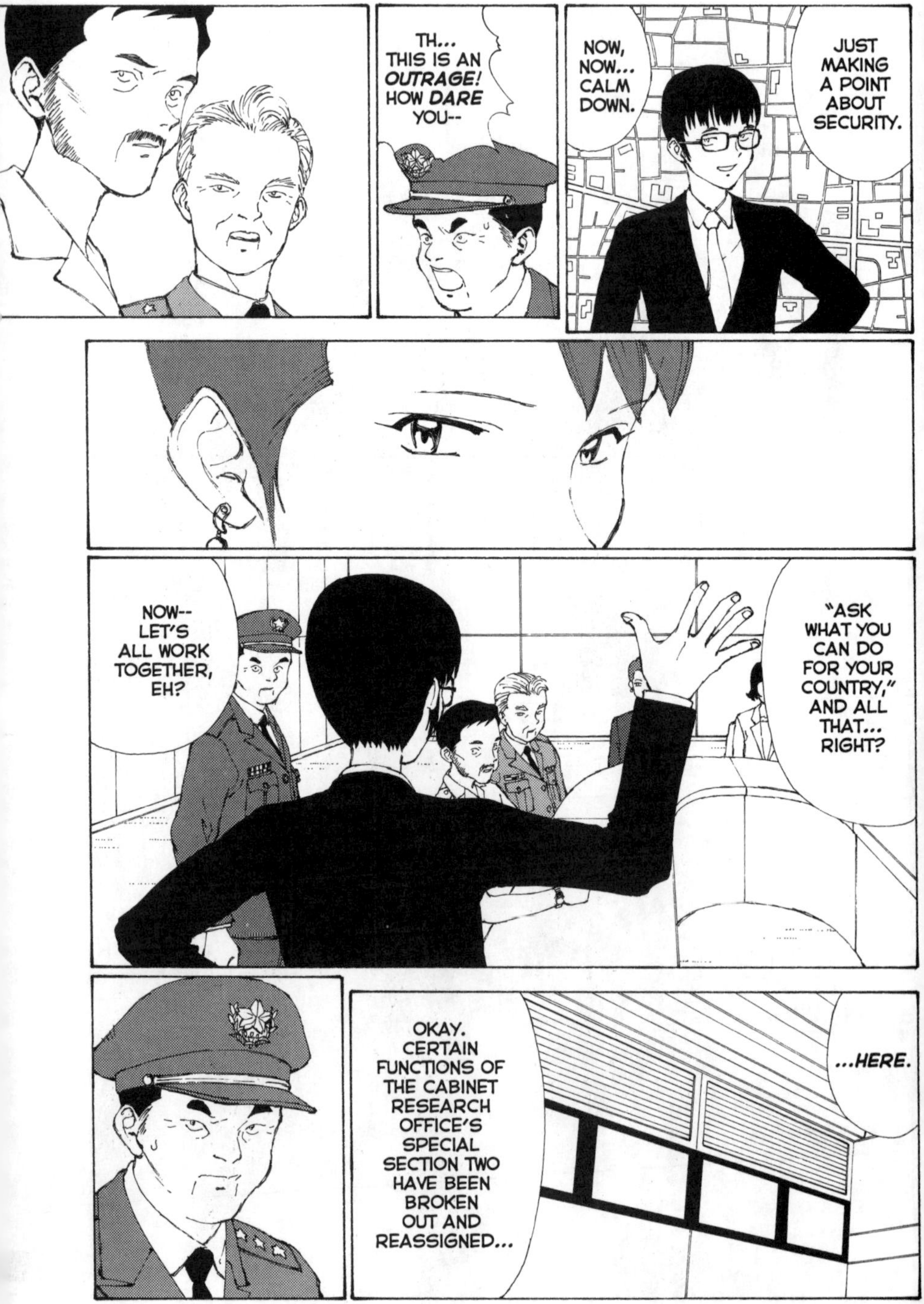
TH... THIS IS AN *OUTRAGE!* HOW *DARE* YOU--
NOW, NOW... CALM DOWN.
JUST MAKING A POINT ABOUT SECURITY.
NOW-- LET'S ALL WORK TOGETHER, EH?
"ASK WHAT YOU CAN DO FOR YOUR COUNTRY," AND ALL THAT... RIGHT?
OKAY. CERTAIN FUNCTIONS OF THE CABINET RESEARCH OFFICE'S SPECIAL SECTION TWO HAVE BEEN BROKEN OUT AND REASSIGNED...
...HERE.

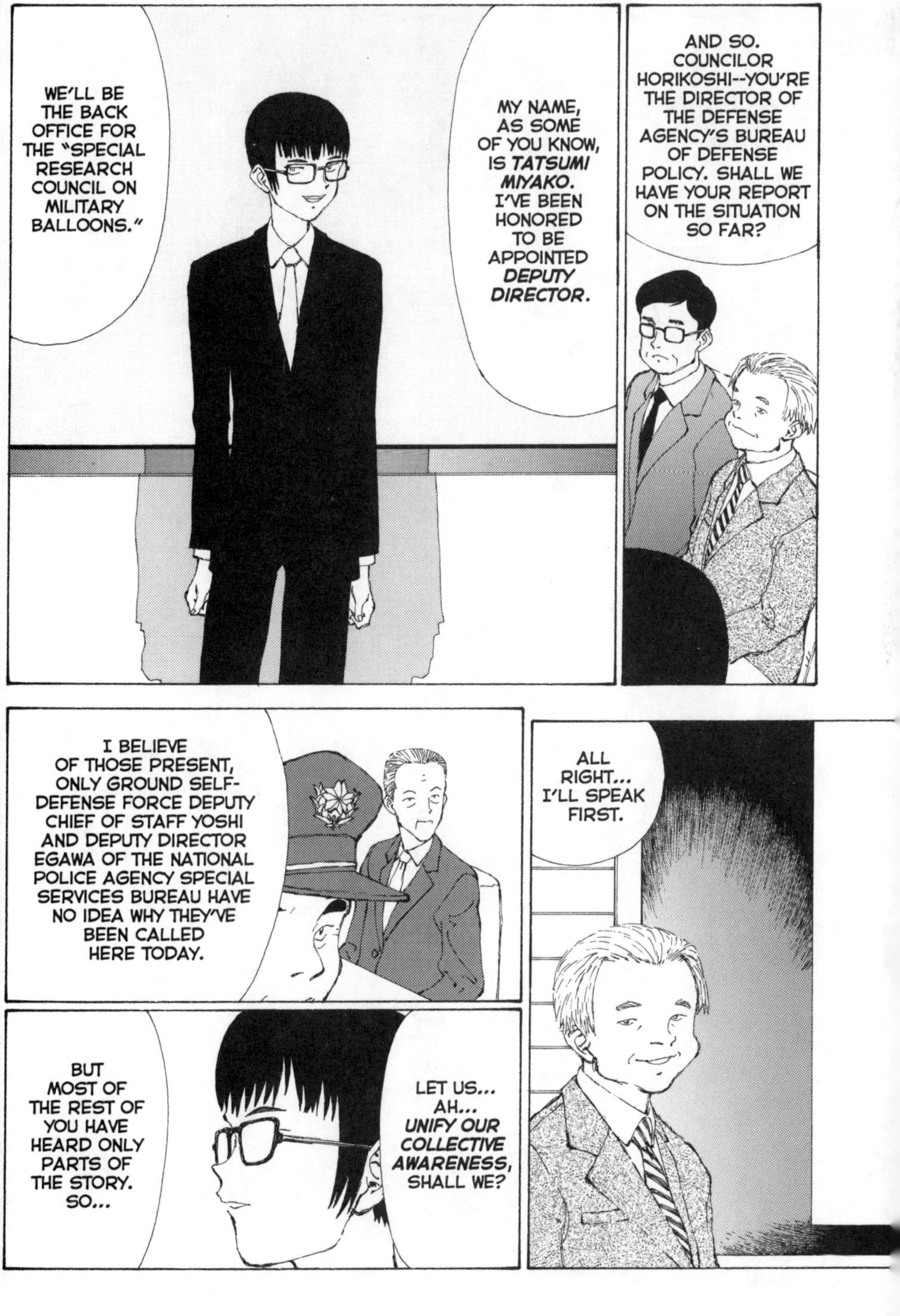
WE'LL BE THE BACK OFFICE FOR THE "SPECIAL RESEARCH COUNCIL ON MILITARY BALLOONS."
MY NAME, AS SOME OF YOU KNOW, IS *TATSUMI MIYAKO*. I'VE BEEN HONORED TO BE APPOINTED *DEPUTY DIRECTOR*.
AND SO. COUNCILOR HORIKOSHI--YOU'RE THE DIRECTOR OF THE DEFENSE AGENCY'S BUREAU OF DEFENSE POLICY. SHALL WE HAVE YOUR REPORT ON THE SITUATION SO FAR?
I BELIEVE OF THOSE PRESENT, ONLY GROUND SELF-DEFENSE FORCE DEPUTY CHIEF OF STAFF YOSHI AND DEPUTY DIRECTOR EGAWA OF THE NATIONAL POLICE AGENCY SPECIAL SERVICES BUREAU HAVE NO IDEA WHY THEY'VE BEEN CALLED HERE TODAY.
BUT MOST OF THE REST OF YOU HAVE HEARD ONLY PARTS OF THE STORY. SO...
LET US... AH... *UNIFY OUR COLLECTIVE AWARENESS*, SHALL WE?
ALL RIGHT... I'LL SPEAK FIRST.

AUGUST 3RD, THIS YEAR. ONE OF OUR, uh...*AWACS* RADAR AIRCRAFT LOITERING NEAR THE OGASAWARA ISLANDS PICKED UP AN UNIDENTIFIED AIRCRAFT.

SPEED, APPROXIMATELY THREE HUNDRED KNOTS...uh...THAT'S ABOUT THREE HUNDRED FIFTY MILES AN HOUR. COURSE... BEARING DUE NORTH, STRAIGHT TOWARD TOKYO.

THERE WAS NO *IFF* RESPONSE, NO MATCHING FLIGHT PLAN ON FILE.

WE IMMEDIATELY SCRAMBLED TWO *F-15S* FIGHTERS FROM HYAKURI AIR BASE.

THEY MADE VISUAL CONTACT... AND, uh...

...IMMEDIATELY TURNED ON THEIR GUN CAMERAS.

THIS IS WHAT THEY SAW--AN UNIDENTIFIED FLYING OBJECT APPROXIMATELY SIXTY-FIVE FEET IN LENGTH.

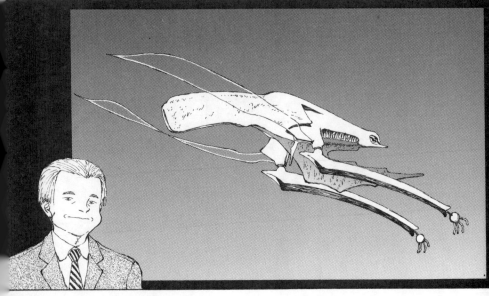

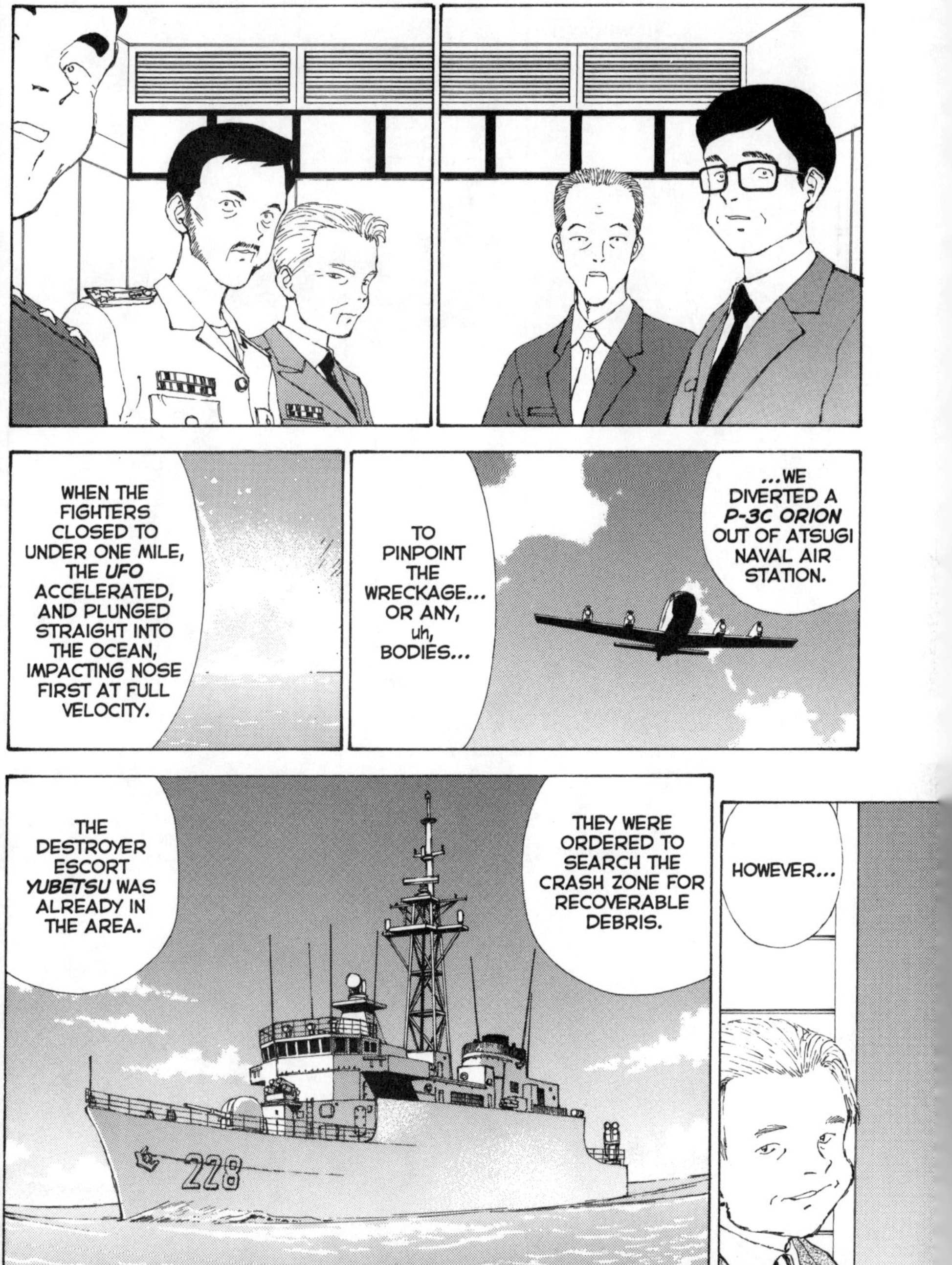
WHEN THE FIGHTERS CLOSED TO UNDER ONE MILE, THE *UFO* ACCELERATED, AND PLUNGED STRAIGHT INTO THE OCEAN, IMPACTING NOSE FIRST AT FULL VELOCITY.
TO PINPOINT THE WRECKAGE... OR ANY, uh, BODIES...
...WE DIVERTED A *P-3C ORION* OUT OF ATSUGI NAVAL AIR STATION.
THE DESTROYER ESCORT *YUBETSU* WAS ALREADY IN THE AREA.
228
THEY WERE ORDERED TO SEARCH THE CRASH ZONE FOR RECOVERABLE DEBRIS.
HOWEVER...

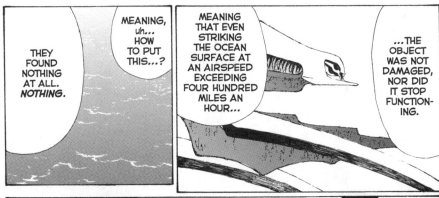

THEY FOUND NOTHING AT ALL. *NOTHING.*

MEANING, uh... HOW TO PUT THIS...?

MEANING THAT EVEN STRIKING THE OCEAN SURFACE AT AN AIRSPEED EXCEEDING FOUR HUNDRED MILES AN HOUR...

...THE OBJECT WAS NOT DAMAGED, NOR DID IT STOP FUNCTIONING.

WHAT?! RIDICULOUS!

IMPOSSIBLE!

I ADMIT IT'S SHOCKING, BUT... IT'S TRUE.

AT THIS POINT, THE *P-3C* INITIATED AN *ASW* SWEEP USING SONOBUOYS AND *MAD.*

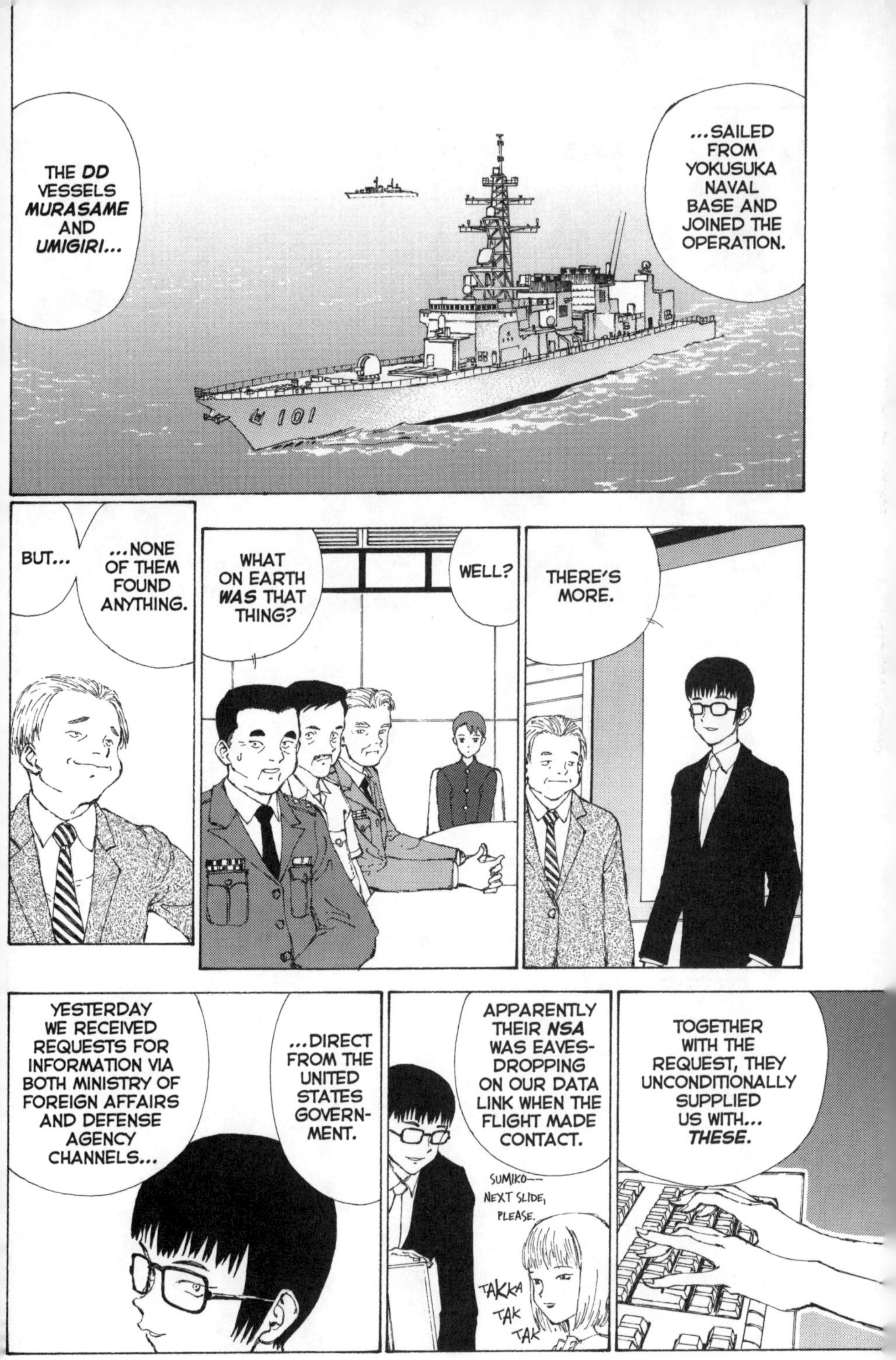
THE DD VESSELS MURASAME AND UMIGIRI...
...SAILED FROM YOKUSUKA NAVAL BASE AND JOINED THE OPERATION.
BUT...
...NONE OF THEM FOUND ANYTHING.
WHAT ON EARTH WAS THAT THING?
WELL?
THERE'S MORE.
YESTERDAY WE RECEIVED REQUESTS FOR INFORMATION VIA BOTH MINISTRY OF FOREIGN AFFAIRS AND DEFENSE AGENCY CHANNELS...
...DIRECT FROM THE UNITED STATES GOVERN-MENT.
APPARENTLY THEIR NSA WAS EAVES-DROPPING ON OUR DATA LINK WHEN THE FLIGHT MADE CONTACT.
SUMIKO--- NEXT SLIDE, PLEASE.
TAKKA TAK TAK
TOGETHER WITH THE REQUEST, THEY UNCONDITIONALLY SUPPLIED US WITH... THESE.

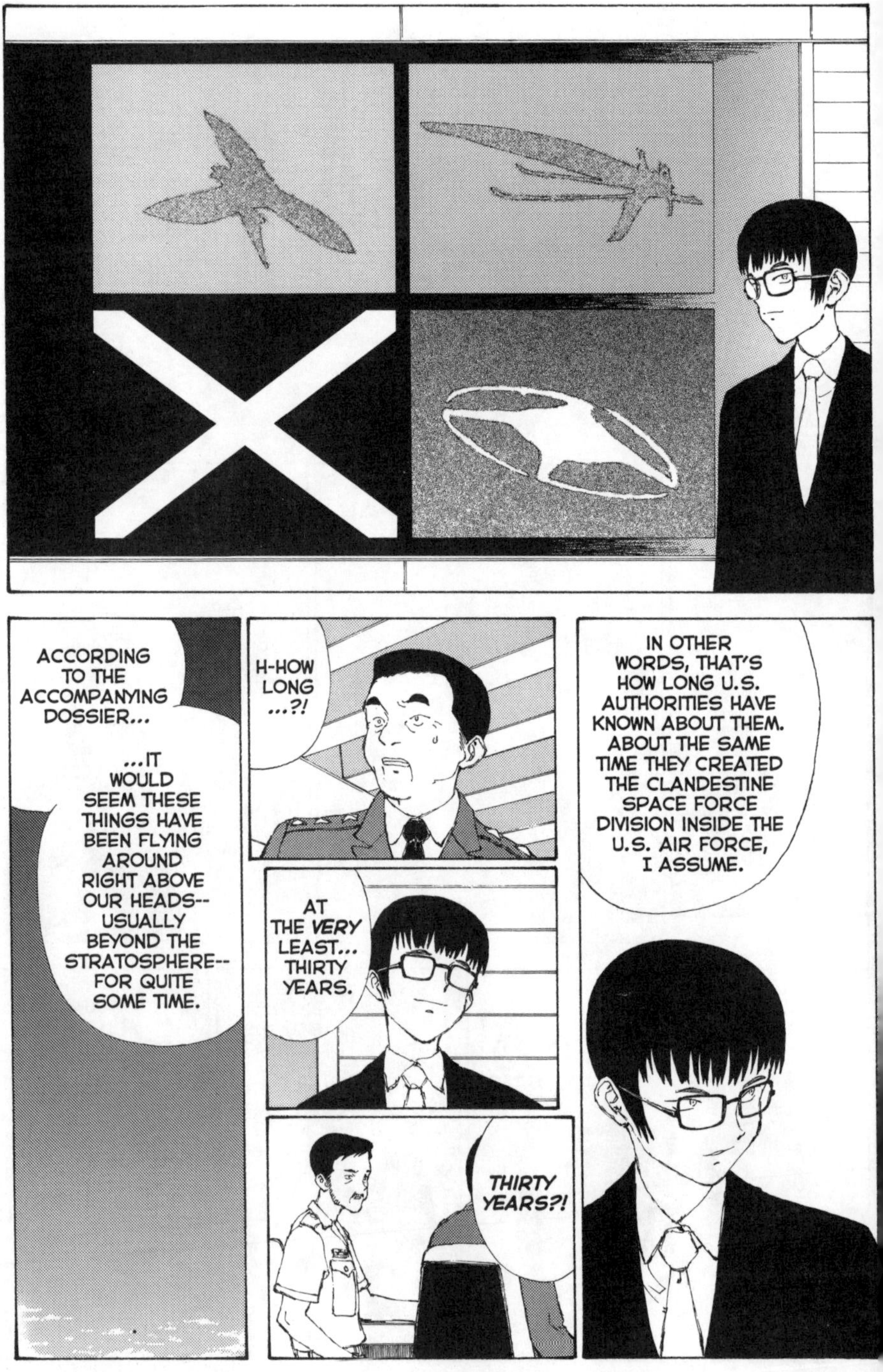
ACCORDING TO THE ACCOMPANYING DOSSIER...
...IT WOULD SEEM THESE THINGS HAVE BEEN FLYING AROUND RIGHT ABOVE OUR HEADS--USUALLY BEYOND THE STRATOSPHERE--FOR QUITE SOME TIME.
H-HOW LONG ...?!
AT THE *VERY* LEAST... THIRTY YEARS.
THIRTY YEARS?!
IN OTHER WORDS, THAT'S HOW LONG U.S. AUTHORITIES HAVE KNOWN ABOUT THEM. ABOUT THE SAME TIME THEY CREATED THE CLANDESTINE SPACE FORCE DIVISION INSIDE THE U.S. AIR FORCE, I ASSUME.

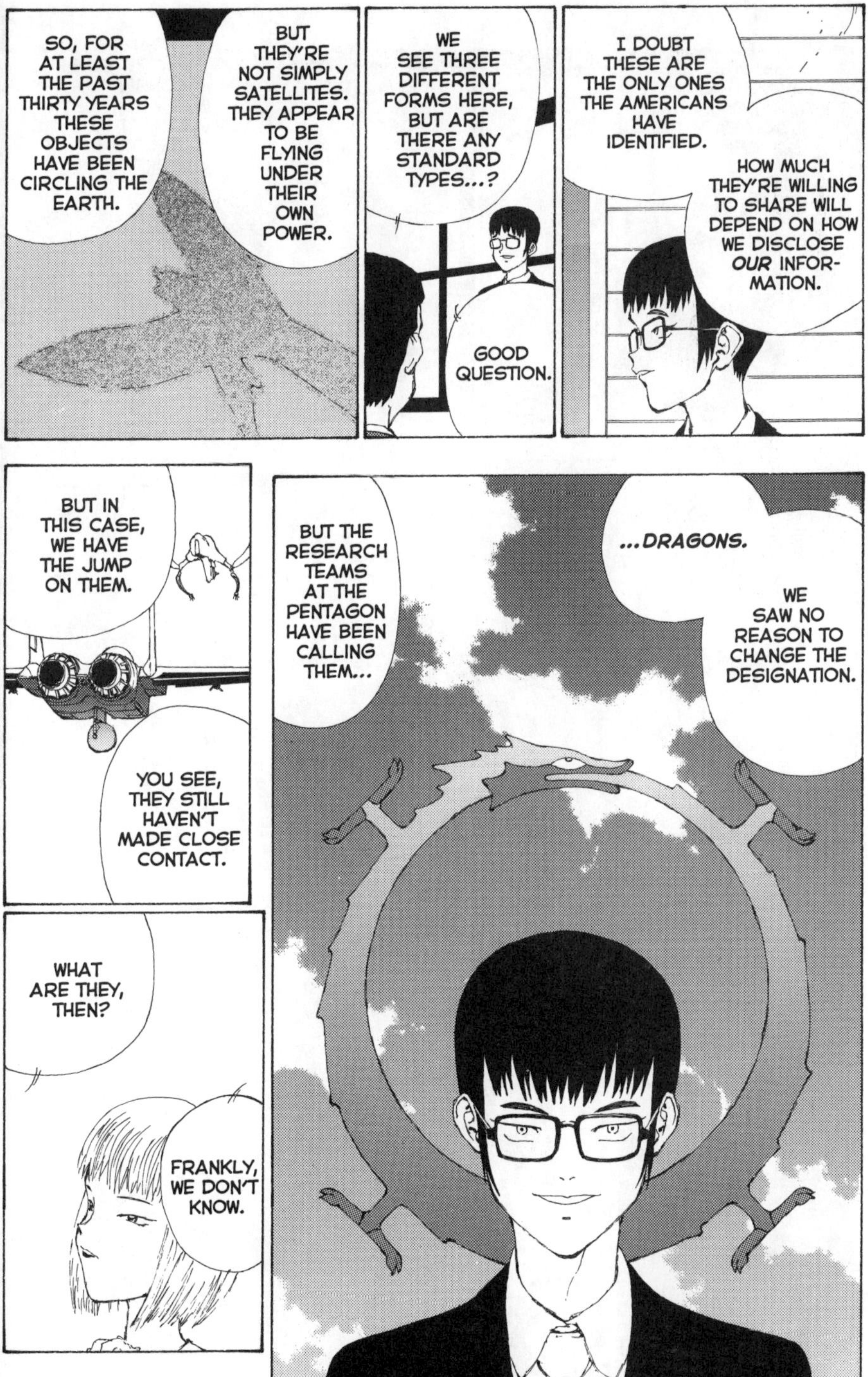
SO, FOR AT LEAST THE PAST THIRTY YEARS THESE OBJECTS HAVE BEEN CIRCLING THE EARTH.
BUT THEY'RE NOT SIMPLY SATELLITES. THEY APPEAR TO BE FLYING UNDER THEIR OWN POWER.
WE SEE THREE DIFFERENT FORMS HERE, BUT ARE THERE ANY STANDARD TYPES...?
GOOD QUESTION.
I DOUBT THESE ARE THE ONLY ONES THE AMERICANS HAVE IDENTIFIED.
HOW MUCH THEY'RE WILLING TO SHARE WILL DEPEND ON HOW WE DISCLOSE *OUR* INFORMATION.
BUT IN THIS CASE, WE HAVE THE JUMP ON THEM.
YOU SEE, THEY STILL HAVEN'T MADE CLOSE CONTACT.
WHAT ARE THEY, THEN?
FRANKLY, WE DON'T KNOW.
BUT THE RESEARCH TEAMS AT THE PENTAGON HAVE BEEN CALLING THEM...
...DRAGONS.
WE SAW NO REASON TO CHANGE THE DESIGNATION.

SO ARE THESE, UH... OBJECTS THAT COME FROM... ER...*OUTER SPACE?*

DON'T WORRY-- YOU CAN CALL THEM *ALIENS.*

AT THIS STAGE, OF COURSE WE MUSTN'T RULE OUT *ANY* POSSIBILITY.

APPARENTLY THERE'S SOME CONSENSUS IN THE PENTAGON THAT THEY PRE-DATE RECORDED HISTORY.

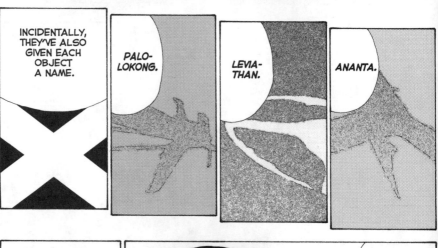

INCIDENTALLY, THEY'VE ALSO GIVEN EACH OBJECT A NAME.

PALO- LOKONG.

LEVIA- THAN.

ANANTA.

ALL TAKEN FROM THE DRAGONS AND SNAKES OF MYTH AND LEGEND.

CONSEQUENTLY, WE'VE NAMED OUR OBJECT SIMILARLY, AFTER A DRAGON FROM JAPANESE MYTH.

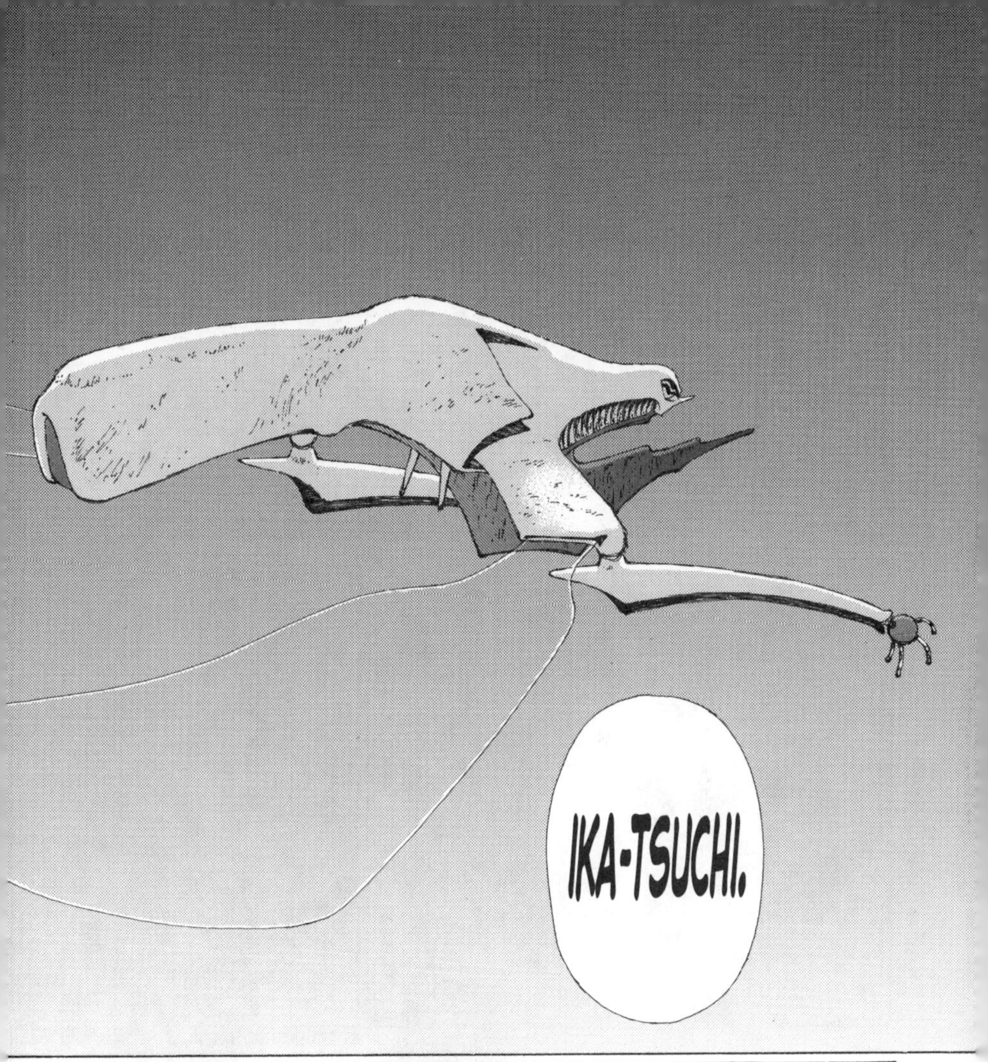
IKA-TSUCHI.
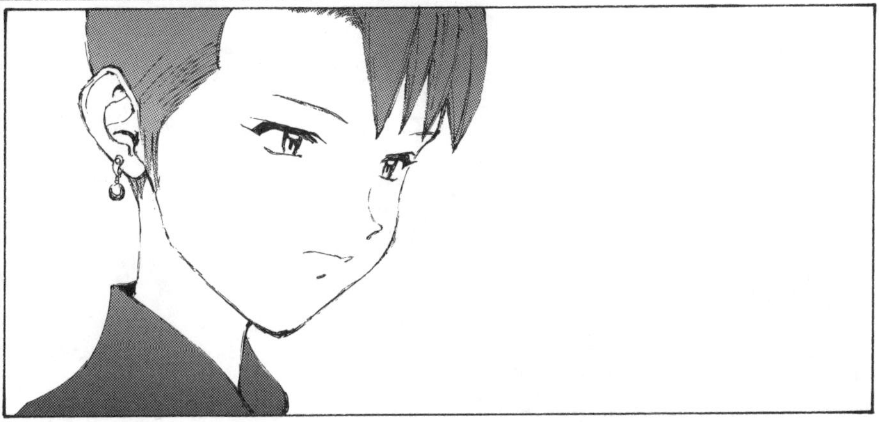

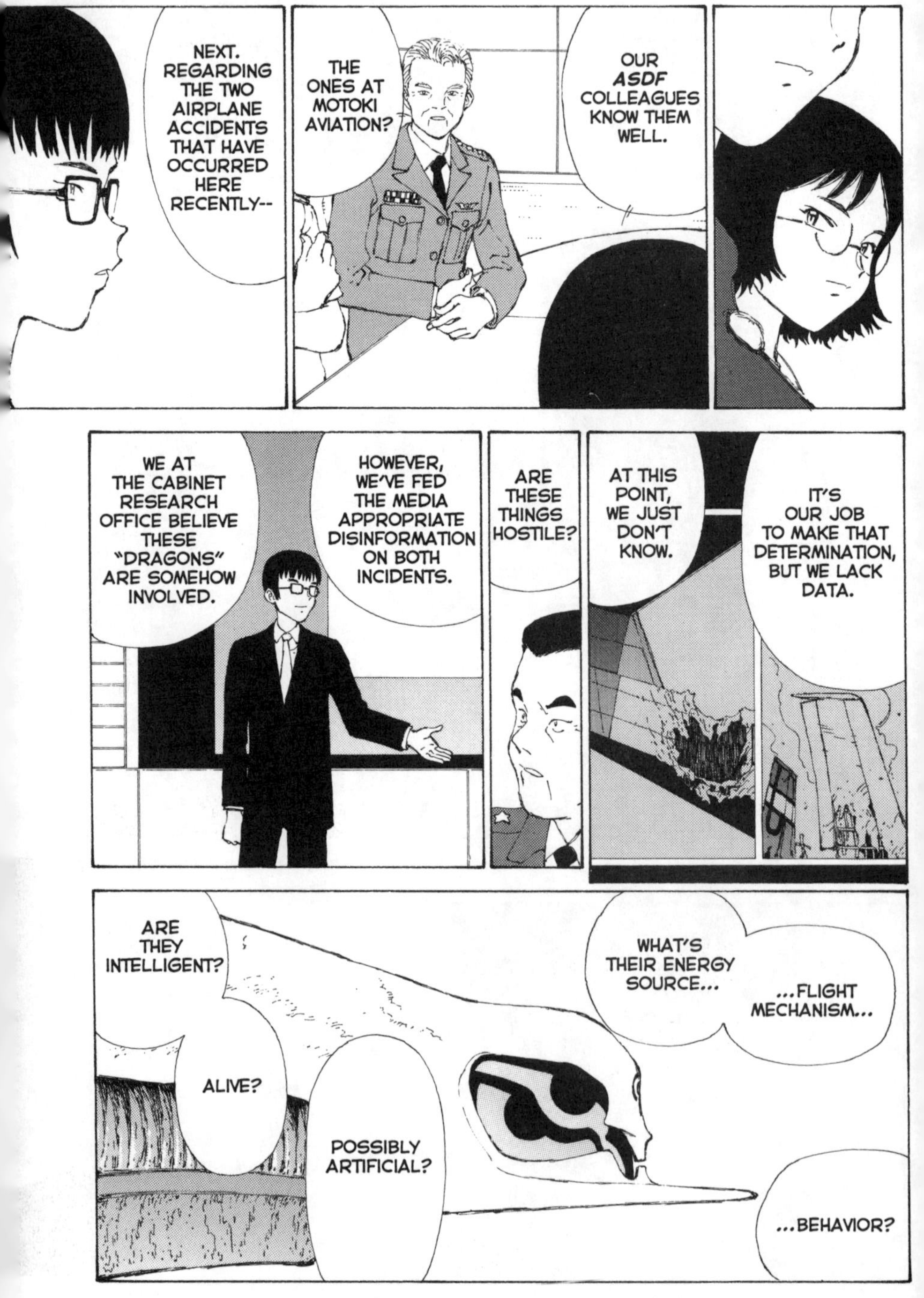
NEXT. REGARDING THE TWO AIRPLANE ACCIDENTS THAT HAVE OCCURRED HERE RECENTLY--
THE ONES AT MOTOKI AVIATION?
OUR *ASDF* COLLEAGUES KNOW THEM WELL.
WE AT THE CABINET RESEARCH OFFICE BELIEVE THESE "DRAGONS" ARE SOMEHOW INVOLVED.
HOWEVER, WE'VE FED THE MEDIA APPROPRIATE DISINFORMATION ON BOTH INCIDENTS.
ARE THESE THINGS HOSTILE?
AT THIS POINT, WE JUST DON'T KNOW.
IT'S OUR JOB TO MAKE THAT DETERMINATION, BUT WE LACK DATA.
ARE THEY INTELLIGENT?
ALIVE?
POSSIBLY ARTIFICIAL?
WHAT'S THEIR ENERGY SOURCE...
...FLIGHT MECHANISM...
...BEHAVIOR?

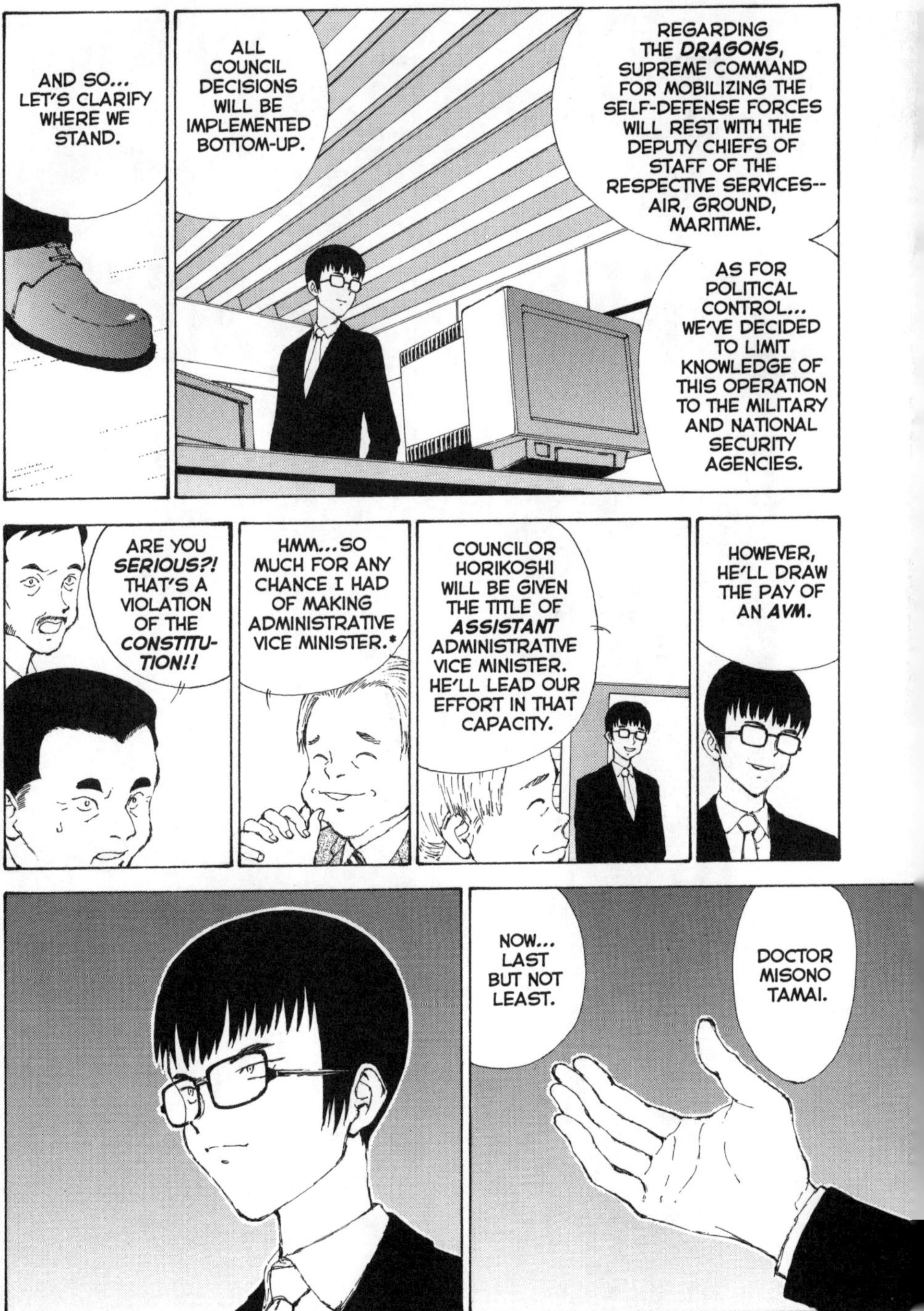
AND SO... LET'S CLARIFY WHERE WE STAND.
ALL COUNCIL DECISIONS WILL BE IMPLEMENTED BOTTOM-UP.
REGARDING THE DRAGONS, SUPREME COMMAND FOR MOBILIZING THE SELF-DEFENSE FORCES WILL REST WITH THE DEPUTY CHIEFS OF STAFF OF THE RESPECTIVE SERVICES--AIR, GROUND, MARITIME.
AS FOR POLITICAL CONTROL... WE'VE DECIDED TO LIMIT KNOWLEDGE OF THIS OPERATION TO THE MILITARY AND NATIONAL SECURITY AGENCIES.
ARE YOU SERIOUS?! THAT'S A VIOLATION OF THE CONSTITUTION!!
HMM...SO MUCH FOR ANY CHANCE I HAD OF MAKING ADMINISTRATIVE VICE MINISTER.*
COUNCILOR HORIKOSHI WILL BE GIVEN THE TITLE OF ASSISTANT ADMINISTRATIVE VICE MINISTER. HE'LL LEAD OUR EFFORT IN THAT CAPACITY.
HOWEVER, HE'LL DRAW THE PAY OF AN AVM.
NOW... LAST BUT NOT LEAST.
DOCTOR MISONO TAMAI.

* Highest professional bureaucratic post in the Defense Agency. The posts above AVM are all political appointees.

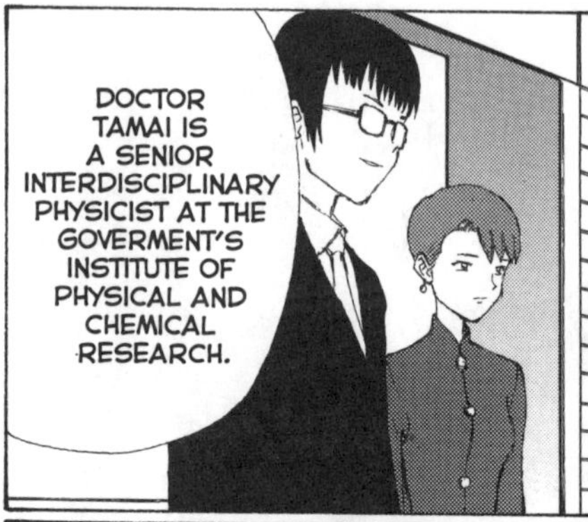
DOCTOR TAMAI IS A SENIOR INTERDISCIPLINARY PHYSICIST AT THE GOVERMENT'S INSTITUTE OF PHYSICAL AND CHEMICAL RESEARCH.
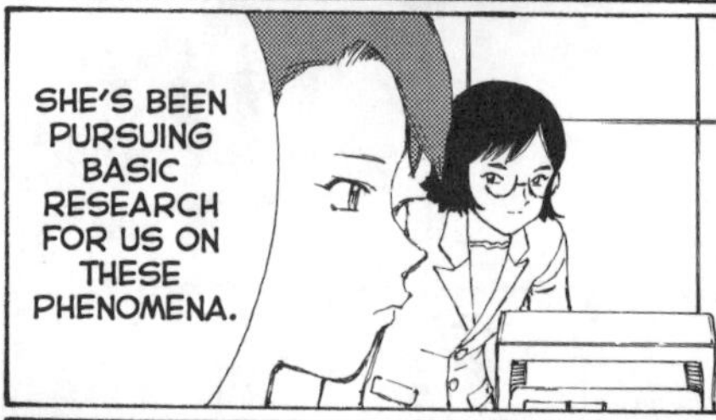
SHE'S BEEN PURSUING BASIC RESEARCH FOR US ON THESE PHENOMENA.
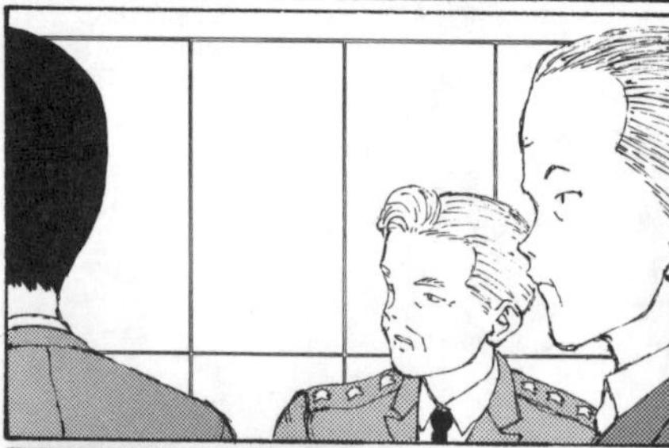
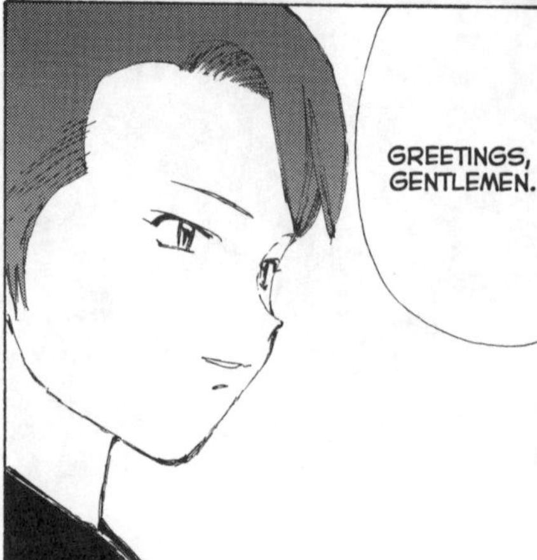
GREETINGS, GENTLEMEN.
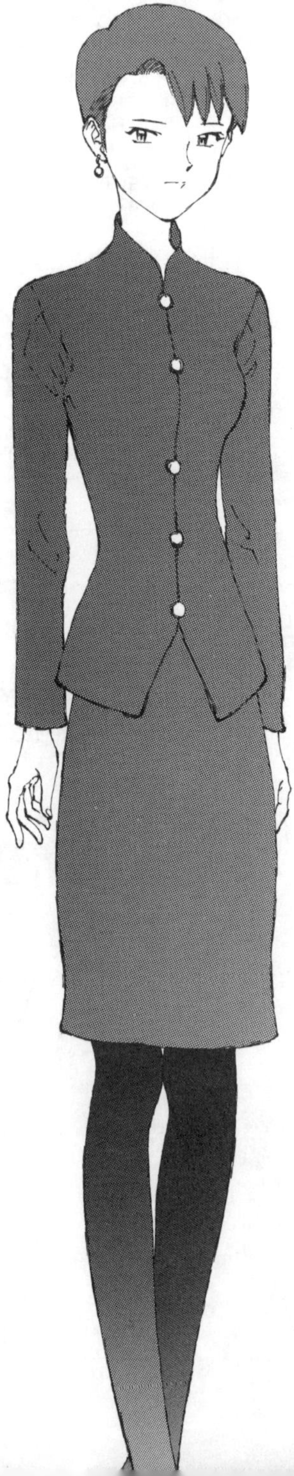

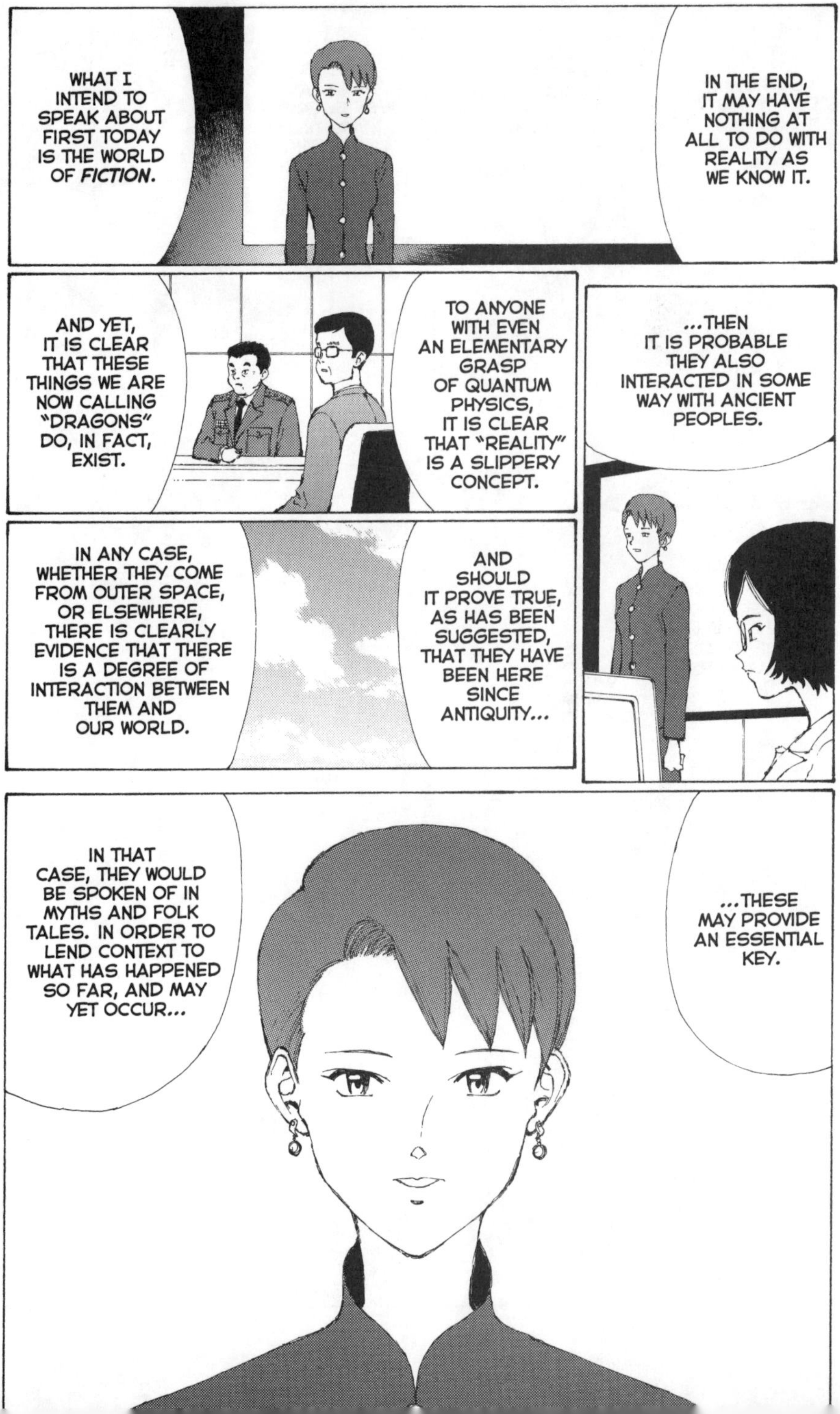
WHAT I INTEND TO SPEAK ABOUT FIRST TODAY IS THE WORLD OF *FICTION*.
IN THE END, IT MAY HAVE NOTHING AT ALL TO DO WITH REALITY AS WE KNOW IT.
AND YET, IT IS CLEAR THAT THESE THINGS WE ARE NOW CALLING "DRAGONS" DO, IN FACT, EXIST.
TO ANYONE WITH EVEN AN ELEMENTARY GRASP OF QUANTUM PHYSICS, IT IS CLEAR THAT "REALITY" IS A SLIPPERY CONCEPT.
IN ANY CASE, WHETHER THEY COME FROM OUTER SPACE, OR ELSEWHERE, THERE IS CLEARLY EVIDENCE THAT THERE IS A DEGREE OF INTERACTION BETWEEN THEM AND OUR WORLD.
AND SHOULD IT PROVE TRUE, AS HAS BEEN SUGGESTED, THAT THEY HAVE BEEN HERE SINCE ANTIQUITY...
...THEN IT IS PROBABLE THEY ALSO INTERACTED IN SOME WAY WITH ANCIENT PEOPLES.
IN THAT CASE, THEY WOULD BE SPOKEN OF IN MYTHS AND FOLK TALES. IN ORDER TO LEND CONTEXT TO WHAT HAS HAPPENED SO FAR, AND MAY YET OCCUR...
...THESE MAY PROVIDE AN ESSENTIAL KEY.

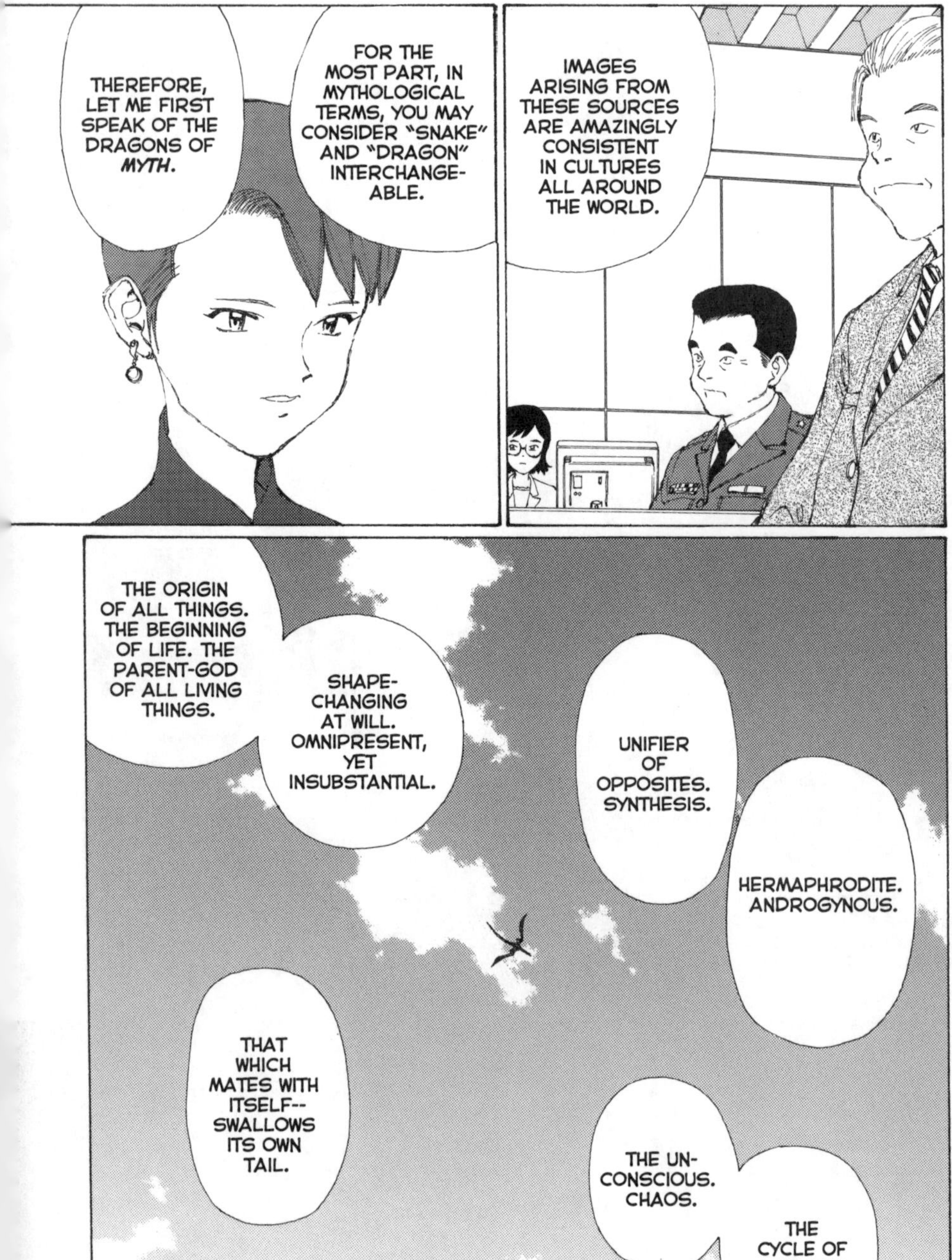
IMAGES ARISING FROM THESE SOURCES ARE AMAZINGLY CONSISTENT IN CULTURES ALL AROUND THE WORLD.
FOR THE MOST PART, IN MYTHOLOGICAL TERMS, YOU MAY CONSIDER "SNAKE" AND "DRAGON" INTERCHANGE-ABLE.
THEREFORE, LET ME FIRST SPEAK OF THE DRAGONS OF *MYTH*.
THE ORIGIN OF ALL THINGS. THE BEGINNING OF LIFE. THE PARENT-GOD OF ALL LIVING THINGS.
SHAPE-CHANGING AT WILL. OMNIPRESENT, YET INSUBSTANTIAL.
UNIFIER OF OPPOSITES. SYNTHESIS.
HERMAPHRODITE. ANDROGYNOUS.
THAT WHICH MATES WITH ITSELF-- SWALLOWS ITS OWN TAIL.
THE UN-CONSCIOUS. CHAOS.
THE CYCLE OF LIFE AND DEATH.

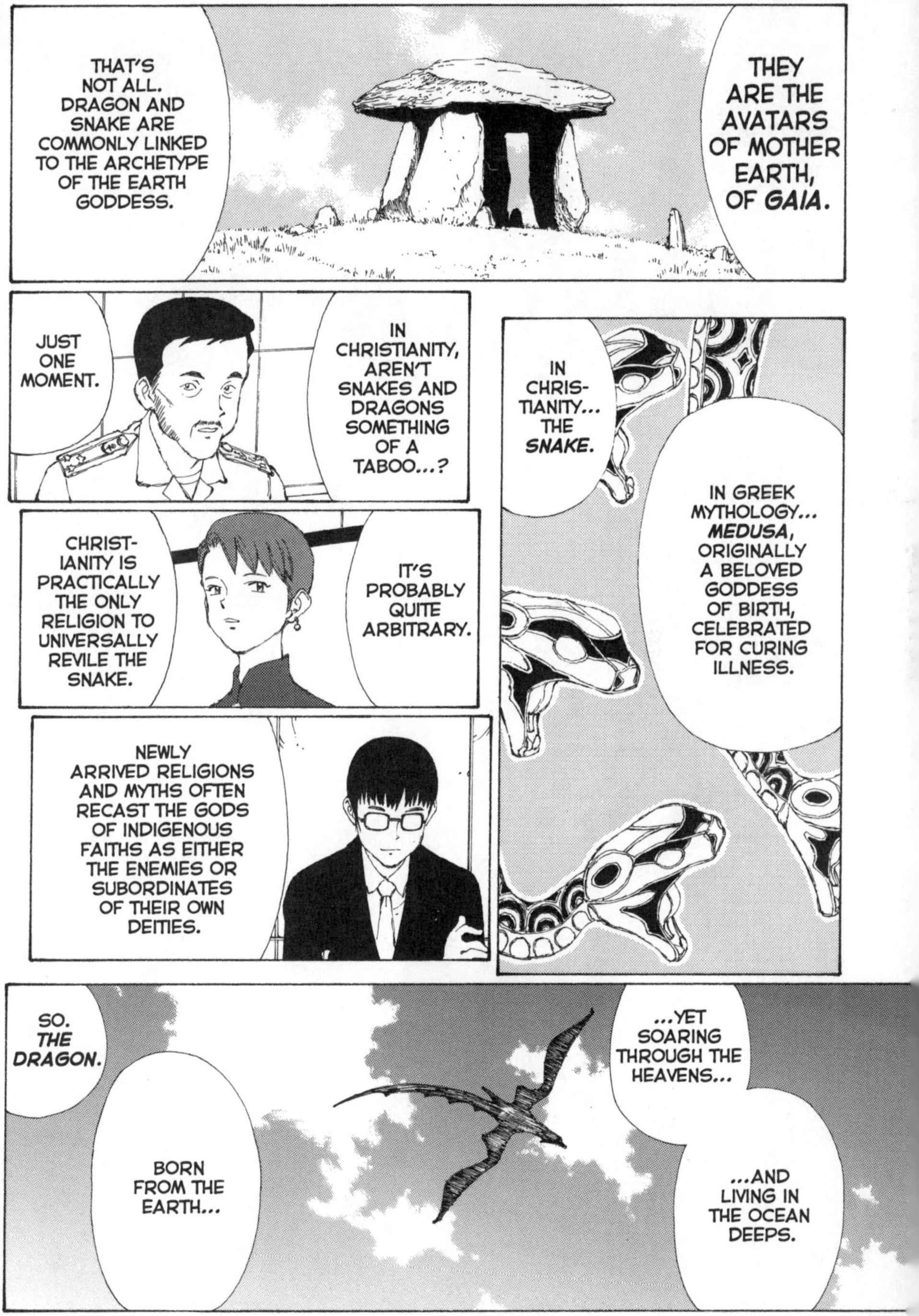
THAT'S NOT ALL. DRAGON AND SNAKE ARE COMMONLY LINKED TO THE ARCHETYPE OF THE EARTH GODDESS.
THEY ARE THE AVATARS OF MOTHER EARTH, OF *GAIA*.
JUST ONE MOMENT.
IN CHRISTIANITY, AREN'T SNAKES AND DRAGONS SOMETHING OF A TABOO...?
CHRIST-IANITY IS PRACTICALLY THE ONLY RELIGION TO UNIVERSALLY REVILE THE SNAKE.
IT'S PROBABLY QUITE ARBITRARY.
NEWLY ARRIVED RELIGIONS AND MYTHS OFTEN RECAST THE GODS OF INDIGENOUS FAITHS AS EITHER THE ENEMIES OR SUBORDINATES OF THEIR OWN DEITIES.
IN CHRIS-TIANITY... THE *SNAKE*.
IN GREEK MYTHOLOGY... *MEDUSA*, ORIGINALLY A BELOVED GODDESS OF BIRTH, CELEBRATED FOR CURING ILLNESS.
SO. *THE DRAGON*.
BORN FROM THE EARTH...
...YET SOARING THROUGH THE HEAVENS...
...AND LIVING IN THE OCEAN DEEPS.

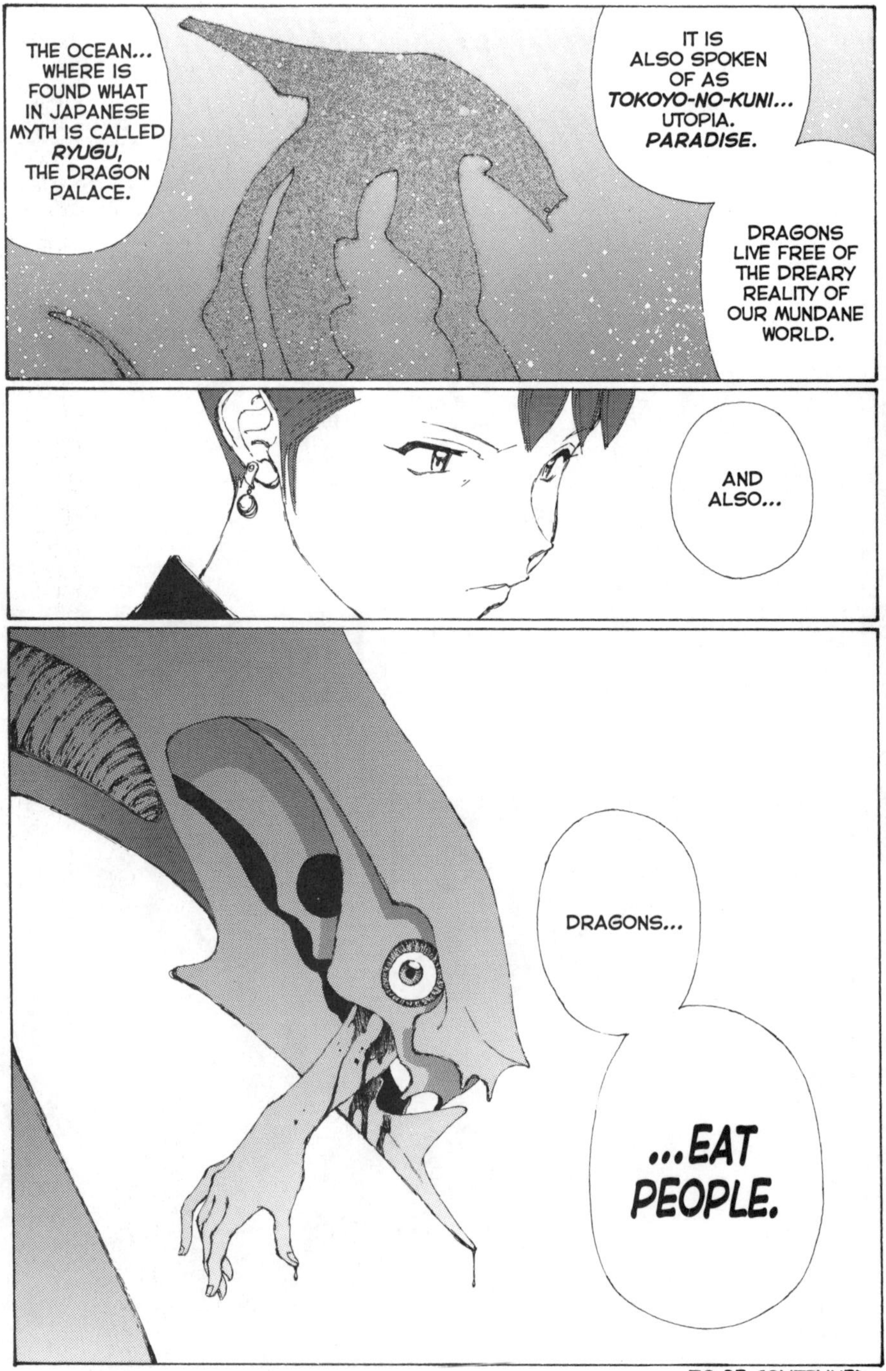
THE OCEAN... WHERE IS FOUND WHAT IN JAPANESE MYTH IS CALLED *RYUGU*, THE DRAGON PALACE.
IT IS ALSO SPOKEN OF AS *TOKOYO-NO-KUNI...* UTOPIA. ***PARADISE.***
DRAGONS LIVE FREE OF THE DREARY REALITY OF OUR MUNDANE WORLD.
AND ALSO...
DRAGONS...
...EAT PEOPLE.

TO BE CONTINUED...

SUPER MANGA BOOKS!

OTHER COLLECTIONS FROM THE FIRST YEAR OF SUPER MANGA BLAST!

3x3 EYES:
FLIGHT OF THE DEMON
$15.95 U.S., $23.95 Canada
1-56971-553-X

SERAPHIC FEATHER:
CRIMSON ANGEL
$16.95 U.S., $23.95 Canada
1-56971-555-6

AVAILABLE AT YOUR LOCAL COMICS SHOP OR BOOKSTORE
To find a comics shop in your area, call
1-888-266-4226 For more information or to order direct: •On the web:
www.darkhorse.com •E-mail: mailorder@darkhorse.com •Phone: 1-800-
862-0052 or (503) 652-9701 Mon.-Sat 9 A.M. to 5 P.M. Pacific Time

超絶漫画爆弾！